IN THE SHADOW

OF THE PALMS

Art Kidwell

IN THE SHADOW
OF THE
PALMS

Across the Years in Twentynine Palms

Volume II

ART KIDWELL

The Old Adobe at the Oasis.

DESERT MOON PRESS

Twentynine Palms, California

Library of Congress Catalog Card No. 86-72903

ISBN 0-9617961-1-1

PUBLISHED BY:

DESERT MOON PRESS
Box 697
Twentynine Palms, CA 92277

TABLE OF CONTENTS

Volume II

The Plaza - 29 Palms First Shopping Center.

1931 - 1939

MILDRED STEWART DEE

Mildred Anna Stewart was born March 13, 1921 at an orange tree ranch near what is now Knott's Berry Farm. This was two miles south of what was then the little country town of Buena Park. She is the daughter of Gladys Eliza Hillebert Stewart and Melvin M. Stewart who owned and operated a service station south of Buena Park.

Because of reoccurring back problems, her father was forced to take some time off from his business. A trip to Death Valley during the summer of 1930 convinced him of the medicinal benefits of dry heat. Leaving there, he visited Twentynine Palms and decided that here he would homestead, bring his family out for a temporary stay, and hope that the climate would solve his medical problems permanently. So in January of 1931, nine year old Mildred, her brother, Howard Allen, age five, and their parents came to the desert area near Mesquite Dry Lake east of Morongo Road to homestead and to begin an eight month stay.

Today fifty-five years later, Millie Dee still returns from her home in Sunland to attend outings with the Twentynine Palms Historical Society and to visit friends and the homestead property she knew as she was growing up.

*   *   *   *   *

My father always had back problems ever since his cowpoke days when he broke wild horses. Later on when he worked such long hours at his gasoline station and didn't get enough sleep, his back wouldn't stay in alignment and became so painful he couldn't stand it. So he quit and decided to go to the desert, do no work, and try to recover. He heard about this area and decided this was the best place for his family.

He wanted a plot of land where there was plenty of good water and to heck with being close to the main road. He wanted a place where he could, if he had to, live out here permanently, and actually plow the ground and have water to grow things. That's why he picked the land that included the sand dunes. We moved out in January 1931 and left the last of August. We homesteaded the length of time that was required for veterans, which was eight months of one year.

"A month or so after we arrived in January 1931, we had friends fly in for a late desert breakfast. They found us by following the main trail in and then spotting Chocolate Drop Hill. From there they followed the two tracks north and found us kids waving wildly. Here Howard and I are getting a ride with our guests. Father hadn't had a chance to paint the house yet due to his back problems. We do have in the radio pole." Photo courtesy of Mildred Stewart Dee.

"At our homestead in the spring of 1931 with my brother, Howard. I'm wearing Mother's fancy hat and holding Bonzo, our dog. By now our windmill is installed, our house is almost painted, and the creosote bush by the front door is fast growing thanks to our dish water. Boards to keep out snakes have been installed at the underhouse areas. We kids had to walk via the rock porch to enter the house hoping sand would fall off our shoes. We had no vacuum cleaner in those days! Photo courtesy of Millie Stewart Dee.

MILDRED STEWART DEE

My first impression was the night we drove in. Apparently, we stopped at Whitewater, because in those days people always stopped there for gasoline, refreshments, and water before traveling the rest of the way. After leaving Whitewater, I was wide awake. This was the beginning of the wild desert. From here on, this was only dirt trails, no electricity, no conveniences, no "civilization." This was so different.

First, there was this long, very steep grade. Our car was an Essex about two years old. We hauled a trailer full with all our supplies, furniture, beds, cook stove, heating stove, a mature, big, wise dog to announce strangers and to protect us from snakes, and all of those wooden boxes that we used later for various reasons, especially shelving.

Father was hoping we wouldn't meet anyone on that steep grade because we had a tremendous load. Well, we did - a big truck. I remember that Father stopped; the other man stopped, and they got out to discuss the situation. They found a spot that was not only wide enough, but also long enough so we could pull in with that trailer right along the edge of the drop-off into complete blackness. It was a tight squeeze. We held our breath as the truck crept by.

When Father came out here, he couldn't do any work. He had to have all the work done by others. First, he had someone dig the well. Next, the house was built. In fact, it was during Christmas time that the house was built before we arrived.

Father came out with one load and took home the carpenter who was an older man from Orange County. Father brought him out with a trailer load of lumber and a floor plan that he had bought at the lumber company. This was typical in those days. Father left him for two weeks while the house was built, and he forgot the steps. Maybe he ran out of lumber or it wasn't on the floor plan.

Anyway, in those days when you moved, you had wooden boxes - not cardboard like now. So Father obtained the proper size boxes and turned one upside down, putting it in front of the door. That was the porch, and one along side of it adjacent to the house became the step. You really had to be athletic to climb up onto the first step and eventually walk into the house. My poor little brother! I don't think the boxes were nailed there, but eventually they became permanently as the boxes settled into the sand.

I was nine when we came out in January 1931, and I turned ten on March 13th. Because of his bad back, Father wasn't able to dig up the bushes around the house, so my mother, Howard, and I did. Father said the sand would blow, so we only dug up enough bushes so we could play around the house without danger of snakes. We did leave one greasewood in front the house where we threw all the dishwater. It grew taller than the house, beautiful, and lacy. It even gave shade to the south window located there. We left another one between the house and the windmill. There still was a lot of space around these bushes, so we could walk safely.

Then Father had to dig a wide trail out to the outhouse to the north of the house. Father had made a turn-around in front of the house by driving the car over and over the tracks, packing the ground and breaking down a bush or two. Then we cleared most of the bushes from this turn-around circle, leaving a few of the big greasewoods around the border. Mother and us kids also removed all of the bunch grass and sage. It took Father a long time before he was well enough to put in the clothes line poles.

Father had to go in and tend to the service stations at least once a month. Sometimes it was more often. This would take three days - one day traveling in, one day there, and one day coming home.

Millie and her mother, Gladys Hillebert Stewart.
Their homestead windmill is in the background.
Photo courtesy of Millie Stewart Dee.

While there, he obtained supplies, fresh vegetables, fresh meat and milk. Otherwise, it was just canned goods for us to eat, plus an occasional cottontail rabbit for meat. He always shot a jackrabbit for Bonzo, the dog.

While he was away on the first trip, Mother decided to do the washing which had been piling up. By this time we had the windmill. Mother would do the washing, but where to hang the clothes? We had no clothes line. Father had not yet been able to put in the line. Here were these beautiful greasewood bushes around the house, and on these she hung the sheets, towels and clothes.

When Father came home, Mother was crying because all of our white sheets, white towels, and clothes were badly stained by these bushes. Father laughed and laughed and laughed. "Didn't you know why they call it greasewood?" he asked. "It's because of the oil in it." Father got busy and put in the clothes line soon after that.....before the next washing.

When Mother had to wash, she had to put the big boiler on the stove to heat. She also used the wash tub and possibly another one too. All the washing was done outside, and it was rough work for her. We kids helped any way we could by hauling things - such as buckets of clothes. I remember one time there was no wind for three days and Father was gone. We were running low on water - at least clean water - so we unhooked the windmill and hooked up the handle on the pump. Then I had to pump. It was hot weather and hot work, but we loved it all.

About three sixteenths of a mile east of the house are giant sand dunes. Those giant dunes were a fun place for children to explore, to play, and to slide down the steep east slopes. In a semicircle of some of those tall dunes was where Father sunbathed that cold winter to help his back. He had found a natural warm sun pocket, even on cold days.

We had three sickly people when we came out here in 1931. Mother was not in good health, and she had lost a lot of weight. I was always having colds and was very skinny. When we left eight months later, we were all healthy. Father had gained weight, because he was eating regularly, eating good meals, and sleeping enough. Mother put on some weight. That's one reason why we loved the desert so much. It was a complete change from what we were used to before and gave us all good health.

The school out here at that time, even in '31, was very good, but limited. I was in the fourth grade. Mother knew it would be impossible for us to go to school, because whenever Father went to town or on one of his exploring trips with one of his prospector cronies, we had no car. Also the road was bad - just tracks in the sand. Even if we had a car, they couldn't afford to drive us to school every day. We were better off than a lot of people out here, but still we pinched pennies for our income was very little. Father had to hire a station manager, leaving little for us.

Before we came, the folks had decided that Mother could teach us and would do as well as the local teacher. After all her mother had taught her when they lived in the desert mining camp of Von Trigger. Mother obtained the books for my brother and me from the Buena Park school. I was in the fourth grade and my brother was in kindergarten. There was no question about schooling. Mother was going to teach us.....and she did. When Mother finished going through all of the books with us about June or so, we thought school was out. But she said, "Oh, no. I might have

"The Frank Dement's homestead had a big, nice house with celotex insulation and wall paneling. Their dairy, the second in the valley, had large acreage in alfalfa for their cows. Their place on Indian Trail was just to the east of Best's. Mesquite Springs Road is now east of their former place. They were very industrious people." Photo courtesy of Millie Stewart Dee.

"After we left in August 1931, we came out periodically on holidays and school vacations. The Strickler girls were our best friends." L to R: Joanne and Helen Strickler, Millie Stewart, Dorothy Strickler, and Howard Stewart. Photo taken about 1935 courtesy of Millie Stewart Dee.

"This photo dated December 1938 would be during Christmas vacation. Note the old Terroplane car. By this time we had developed a rock-lined driveway and walkway in the foreground." Photo courtesy of Millie Stewart Dee.

"Easter vacation, 1940. I found these daisies on the north side of Mesquite Springs lake. They were about three feet tall and a mass of color. We couldn't believe our eyes, as we had never seen anything like them before." Photo courtesy of Millie Stewart Dee.

missed something, so we are going to do it all over again." That she did till we left in late August.

Before coming out here, I wasn't doing well in any of my classes, and I was failing in math. Mother's teaching made the world of difference for us in teaching. While we were out here, she taught me math, history, geography, and geology. After this I enjoyed all of them. Later I took all of the math classes I could in high school. Then I took up architecture, studied engineering, and tutored one classmate in structural engineering.

Unfortunately, we had a problem. There was an elderly woman, a former school teacher who lived nearby. Mrs. Bullard had a meeting with my parents and all neighbors with children at her house. She said they were going to force my brother and me to go to school. Although Mother was doing such a beautiful job teaching us, they said she had not been to college and was not a qualified school teacher. Father wasn't going to give in, and they were bawling him out. They were trying to force us to start school that April, even though we knew we were leaving at the end of summer. Another lady, who knew what a good job Mother had been doing, helped smooth things over so Mrs. Bullard didn't make any more trouble for us.

We had a very good well. In the beginning it went down twenty-nine feet. Later Father decided to make it deeper, so he went down to about forty-seven feet. The water from our well was cold, even in summer. We always had good tasting water. Ironically, our water was completely different from the water the Stricklers had only a quarter mile to the northwest. Theirs had the smell and taste of soda; and it wasn't as cold. Father claimed that there had to be an underground dike between our two wells. Since we were only going to be there temporarily, Father would not allow us to plant trees.

For about fifteen months after we left in August of 1931, we came out periodically on school holidays of three days or more and even one summer. It was the mid 1940's when we stopped coming regularly. I entered college then and didn't have time to take off until summer. Then the war came and that was it for the most part.

Our homestead on the desert was the one place where I lived and learned the most during my childhood and early adult years. Thus, I have always considered it as my second home. So many good memories are associated with those days.

"After the war before 1950, Father tried an experiment. He obtained grain seed from some desert country to see if it would work here with our desert droughts and rains. He used my plow from my "Victory Garden" days and was thinking about moving back to 29 Palms. Guess what Mother had to do? The ammunition box held the seeds." Photos courtesy of Millie Stewart Dee.

272

MILDRED STEWART DEE

HILDA HOLDERMAN GRAHAM

Hilda Holderman was born in 1902 in Welch, Oklahoma which was then Indian Territory. She was one of four children born to Lena Doolen Holderman and Curtis E. Holderman who were married in 1895. Hilda married James Graham and became the mother of two children, Robert and Patricia.

Hilda suffered from lobar pneumonia and her young son, Bob, had asthma. After a visit here in 1931, her brother, Ted, and her husband, Jim, "fell in love with the place." Almost immediately, the family decided to move from Glendale to Twentynine Palms as a last resort for their health.

When they learned that the old Fox Studio was preparing to relocate, they purchased doors, flooring, and 2' x 4's. From this $20 purchase of materials, their house would be built. The family arrived in August in two vehicles towing their belongings and house materials on two trailers. The next day Jim started building, while Ted returned to his job in the city.

The family lived on $20 a month during those Depression times, supplemented by help from Hilda's family. As Hilda and Bob recovered, the family came to love the desert and chose to remain. In 1933 her mother, Lena Holderman, also moved to Twentynine Palms to live.

That same year, Hilda and a friend, Pearl Kleindinst, saw the need for a restaurant. Finding a vacant building that had been formerly an ice cream parlor, they went to work. Pooling their dishes, finances, and with help from others in town, they opened their cafe with four stools. When her partner's husband objected to Pearl working in such a public place, Hilda became the sole owner. Her continued success in this venture is her story. She was also a founding member of the Chamber of Commerce, the Parent-Teachers' Club, and active in the community.

The Grahams moved to Portland, Oregon in 1941 where her husband worked in the Kaiser Vancouver shipyard and later was owner-operator of a sporting goods store in Portland. The damp climate contributed to a relapse of Hilda's ill health, so the family returned to Twentynine Palms in 1949. Her husband, Jim, passed away in 1964 after a long illness. Her mother died in November 1978 at 102 years of age.

In 1984 Hilda Graham was selected as Grand Marshall for

Pioneer Days. In an interview then she said, "I owe a lot to the Twentynine Palms community, because it helped me and my son. I'm walking testimony of what clean and pure air can do for you." She continues to hope that future community growth will not affect its pioneer attitude towards sharing and caring for others.

*   *   *   *   *

We heard about Twentynine Palms when we were living in Glendale and Bob was about five years old. He had developed asthma, and when one of those attacks would hit, we'd rush him up to La Crescenta to my brother, Ted and Agnes'. Soon that didn't work.

On top of that I came down with lobar pneumonia. One of the doctors in Glendale said, "Why, I haven't had a case in forty years," but that was what I had. Eleven months later, I still wasn't getting any better. Finally the doctor said there was nothing to do but for us to leave that climate and get out on the desert. We didn't have any money.

About that time they were building a gravel plant in Banning, and my husband, Jim, was offered a job because he was in construction. So we came down to Banning on that job.

During that few months there, I was walking everywhere. My lungs were dry, and Bob hadn't had an asthmatic attack. We knew then that we had to live in that country. About that time they sold the plant, so Jim was out of a job.

I was down at the service station, and some people drove in, filled up their car with gas, and headed down the highway. The man who owned the station said, "There goes another one of that bunch of homesteaders out of Twentynine Palms," and my ears just picked up.

And I said, "Homesteaders? What do you mean?"

"Well," he said, "There's a bunch of veterans living out there on homesteads, and you only have to stay the seven months to get your 160 acres." That was correct...for veterans.

My brother, Ted, had come down for the weekend, and I went back to the house and told them about it. So he and Jim got in the car and came out Saturday or Sunday. The old road went down Sullivan next to the mountains and ended up where Benito's service station and store was. (The intersection of Adobe and Sullivan Roads).

The boys just fell in love with the desert. They came back and then we started figuring. How are we going to live? What are we going to do? But they knew that this was where they wanted to come. So we did.

That was 1931. We had twenty dollars a month coming in. Ted was selling washing compounds to packing houses, and he went from Pasadena to Indio. That was his route, and he made that trip once or twice a month.

Bob was not suppose to have milk, and he had to have citrus juices for his asthma. So Ted would stop and buy a crate of lemons and a crate of oranges for fifty cents apiece, and he would bring those out to us. He also brought most of our groceries. Believe me, I counted every egg and every slice of bacon and practically everything else. But you know, it was a funny thing. We all had so much false pride in those days. We wouldn't admit to anybody that we didn't have money enough to do this or that.

We went into Glendale, and we had one hundred dollars. Ted and Jim went down to the old Fox Studio which they were wrecking and moving way out. They sold us the flooring , the doors, and the two by fours and everything for the house. I think we bought the whole thing for twenty dollars.

Then the boys bought a truck and built two trailers, one to haul behind each of our cars. They hauled the lumber out, and we got out here about August the eleventh in the middle of the afternoon. Oh, was it hot! We had a car-top tent which they put up on four poles to give us a little shelter. Ted had to get back to work on the job. So the next day, Jim just started laying out boards, and we started nailing up a house. And that was it.

We got our homestead through a release. A young woman, whose name I can't remember, had filed on it. She had TB, and she had to go into a sanitarium. So we wrote to her, and she released it to us. That's the reason we got in the Desert Heights area, because at that time, there wasn't much open except way east of town.

We built our place and dug roots for fuel that winter - mostly greasewood. Sometimes we'd go up into the Monument and cut willow, but we didn't have much gasoline. We cut willow up in Rattlesnake Canyon. There used to be a lot of it growing there in the draws. It wasn't a Monument then.

The thing that really saved us was that we got mileage for bringing the children to school. I think we got five cents a mile which came to about five or six dollars a month. That hauled our water, our children, and gave us our transportation.

We lived on that twenty dollars a month, and of course, my family kept the children in clothes. We ate jackrabbits sometimes, but we didn't suffer. We had a tremendous lot of company which was just real fun. It was such a change that we used to have so many friends in town. My sister worked for the school system, and mother ran the cafeteria in Pasadena. Those people just loved to come out and sleep on the ground and go and climb in the Monument. They would come out with just loads of food. Every bit of it helped.

In those days, we didn't have any water. Everybody hauled theirs. We had a wine barrel on the rear bumper of the car, and when we brought the kids in to school, we would stop and fill the barrel at Bagley's pump. Then Jim would put that on a rack, and put the next wine barrel on. This is the way we kept our water supply going.

City Hall in the Plaza was the only place then that you could take a bath - a shower. Otherwise, you set a wash tub out in the summertime to let the sun heat the water. Then everybody climbed in and took turns. Even after we got our well out on the five acres, we still didn't have the plumbing in, so we just used the hose. We'd stand out on the front steps and take our showers because there were sand dunes all around the place.

I remember Kenny Fish had a five gallon can - like salad oil comes in - and it had a hole in it. He sat the can on the edge of the roof, and filled that full of water. Then he'd just walk out, pull the string, which would let the water out, and take his shower.

One day he was at a meeting and somebody introduced him to Mrs. Carle. The Carles were ex-missionaries, and she was a lovely person, but very prim and proper. As someone introduced Kenny to Mrs. Carle, she said, "Oh, yes. I'm very happy to meet you Mr. Fish. I feel like I know you quite well."

Kenny was a great, big fellow....over six feet tall and was in the Los Angeles Police Department. He looked at her and said, "Well, I don't believe we've met. I haven't any recollection. I'm sorry."

And she said, "Oh, I know that. But I have a pair of glasses, and I watch you take your shower every day."

Things like that were always happening. It was an unwritten rule that when you started down the road that went into anybody's house, you always honked your horn because people went practically undressed in the heat out here. So as a result, Kenny hung a curtain up around his shower. He was only out here occasionally on weekends when he was off duty.

I presume he had a homestead, because it was always known that it was just east of Louis Jacob's homestead. As far as I know, he didn't have any family or anyone. I didn't know him too well, but he wasn't married. He just built the place out there and came out.

On the homestead next to ours was another veteran, Harry Kleindinst and his wife, Pearl, who had two children. We used to switch off, taking the children to school. We organized what we called the PTC - Parent Teachers' Club - which had been meeting once a month down at the schoolhouse. Pearl, Hazel Phillips Spell, and I decided that we'd like to have a luncheon. Grace Brock was running the 29 Palms Inn then, so we went to see her.

She would serve us a luncheon for fifty cents. We thought, "We won't have very many." There were so many homesteaders out here who had never been inside the Inn because they couldn't afford fifty cents for a meal.

But Grace was very cooperative, and do you know, we had forty-five women show up for that luncheon. We didn't know that there were forty-five women living in this valley. But when the word got around that we were going to have a luncheon at the Inn and a program, why that was it. We worked hard and had a good program. We had been thinking about what a lot of fun we'd had, but what were we going to do now?

The next day Pearl and I got in our cars and we met halfway on a road that was catercorner across our homesteads. Pearl and I tumbled out of our cars to meet each other and I said, "Why don't we open up?"

And she said, "I know, I know. Mrs. Bains' ice cream parlor."

Mrs. Bains was a very, very nice person - a perfect lady. Their home was the Bill Hatch home before Bill bought it from them. She had opened an ice cream parlor which later became part of Radio Doc's workshop. It had four stools and one table. She decided after a few months that it just wasn't ladylike enough for her, and she shouldn't be waiting on people like this. She only opened up for two hours in the morning and two hours in the evening....at mail time. So the building was standing there empty.

Pearl and I talked it over. Then we went down to see Helen and Frank Bagley, and we told them what we wanted to do. Art Krushat had bought a sink out, and it was sitting in his front yard. He'd never had the time to put it in for Sarah. So we bought the sink for two dollars, and Jim put it in.

The Bagleys gave us our first month's rent, and we each put in three dollars and thirty cents. Les Earenfight delivered us a tank of propane gas; Helen put up three dollars and a half worth of groceries, and Pearl had a propane stove. We brought that in, pooled our dishes, and we opened for business.

The first month we each had two dollars and a half profit for our work. "Well," we thought, "we're just getting started and this is okay." The next month, then, we had about fifteen dollars for the month for each of us.

So we were doing very well. We were serving hamburgers and pies, but we soon found out we couldn't work two hours a day and two hours an evening. We were working all day long. There was a constant stream of miners, bachelors and everybody, who weren't going to go home and cook their meals when they could come up and have a sandwich and pie and everything right there while they were waiting for the mail. They could show up in time for breakfast and have it while the mail was coming in.

About that time, Harry began to get a little bit jealous. Pearl was very attractive, so he made her pull out.

I said, "What am I going to do? I can't do it."

Harry said, "Yes, Jim can help you."

"Jim can't even boil water," I said.

"Well, that's okay. That's okay, but Pearl's got to stay home."

Pearl cried, but Harry was adamant. And that's how I got into the business.

By the next springtime, I was egging Frank to push out the walls. I said, "We can't get people in to feed them."

So he and Jim decided they'd buy the lumber and Jim would do the work. They just doubled the size, which is the size of the building now. It was very funny. While I was serving breakfast - hot cakes, bacon, and everything - Les Earenfight was helping Jim. They were knocking out the whole side of the building, and they knocked it out while everybody was sitting in there eating. Everybody was enjoying them.

They framed it up and got the floor laid that night, and I was still cooking over in the corner. I think about fifteen people showed up for dinner! There were no chairs or anything. They put boards up, just sat there on the saw horses, and ate. They wanted to see what was going on.

Of course, the store was right next door. The big problem was that we had no refrigeration. My first great big expenditure was an icebox. But by that time, Ted, my brother, had started the ice plant. That must have been about 1933, the year after I started the restaurant.

Ted was living in town when he started the ice plant. That is, he still had his place in town, but he wanted to come out here, and he figured the ice business would be good. Frankly, the ice business was not a paying business. But because of it, he was able to get the franchise for Coca Cola, Acme beer, and a liquor distributorship. That kept the ice business going.

We built the new building in 1936, moved into it in February 1937. I sold it in 1941. I had the first legal license for wine and beer. By that time, Jay, who had run a bootleg place over by Benitos, also got a beer license. Then, about the next year, Four Corners started and the Josh went in.

I didn't handle hard liquor. We had children, and we talked about it, but we just didn't want hard liquor. We knew that was the way to the money, but the people couldn't come and bring their children. This really was the only place that kids could come and eat. We had our own children, and we didn't want them around that atmosphere.

Hilda Graham standing outside her 29 Palms
Lunch Room. This was after it had been doubled
in width to eighteen feet. Photo about 1934 courtesy of the Local History Collection, 29 Palms
Branch Library.

The Seelys sold to Currys, and Mrs. Curry had the distributorship for magazines, newspapers, and things out here. Her husband,
Al was an A-1 plasterer, and he was working out of town, and then
working around here too. She didn't want to be bothered with
food, so everybody had to come over here to eat. The miners
would come in on Saturday nights. That's the only time they got to
town.

When I first hired help, I was working pretty hard. Imogene
Aaron was just out of school, and she had come out to stay with
her father. She came walking in one day and sat down on a stool.
She was a pretty girl, and she said, "Mrs. Graham, I want to work
for you."

And I said, "Imogene, I can't afford any help. There's not enough business."

"I'll work for you, if you'll feed me. I'll come down every day, and I'll work through the dinner hour. And I'll come down in the mornings," she said.

So I said, "All right, Imogene. I'll buy your gasoline to and from."

And that's how I got my first help. I paid her fifty cents a day, and then I paid her a dollar. It was just how much money we made. Then Guy Marshall, superintendent at the Gold Crown Mine, married her.

Ted built the ice plant right next to the garage, and he really needed the garage to carry on and to help out with the ice plant. Tom Martin was getting dissatisfied and wanted to go back to Illinois where he could raise a garden. So Ted bought the garage from him - not the building - but the garage business. Frank Bagley owned the building at that time.

Sally Holland's brother had been working out at one of the mines, and they had moved into town. He went to work for Jim, who was running the garage. So Sally came out to see me, and Imogene had gone, so I put her to work. Sally moved in with my mother. I paid Sally a dollar a day, and she gave Mother a dollar a week for her room. They all ate up at the shop.

Sally was very attractive and a good waitress. This was when Lish and Bill Stubbs had homesteaded north of town. Their homestead was just two miles north of ours, and they homesteaded the same year we did. They started making adobe bricks and trying to build. So Lish fell in love with Sally and that was it.

Mrs. Campbell was good and kind. Our first year here, we didn't know anything about them. We came in August, and we'd only been here three or four months when a paving job opened up in Santa Monica. We went into town and were gone for four, five, or six weeks, while Jim picked up some extra money.

We came back out, and I came down with the flu. Of course, this always scared Jim half to death. I was really sick with the flu, and there was snow on the ground. It was cold, and we didn't have very much. We were just burning the roots in one of those little pot-bellied stoves. The big mistake that we had made when we came out was that Jim had put eight foot walls and then a high steep ceiling. So all our heat went up. If we had had a lower roof, we'd have been much better off. Then both of the kids came down with the flu, so Jim had both of them in bed with me.

When Jim went into the store one day to buy groceries, Art Krushat, who was working there then, said, "How's the family today, Jim?"

And Jim said, "Well, I've got all three of them in bed now, so

The 2nd Graham lunch room at the Plaza built in the fall of 1936. The Stubbs brothers poured the floor and walls. Walt Berg framed the roof. Jim Graham and John Walters roofed the building, while Jim finished the interior and made the Mexican style front doors. He also built the furniture with daughter, Pat Graham's help. Photo taken about 1941 courtesy of the Local History Collection, 29 Palms Branch Library.

I've got to get back in order to keep the fire going." Then he got his groceries and walked out.

Evidently after he left, Bill Campbell asked who he was. Art said he had homesteaded northeast of town, and we had these two children. In the meantime, Mrs. Bailey was working for Mrs. Campbell, and she had asked Mrs. Bailey what kind of people we were. Mrs. Bailey said I was very active at the school, that we were very nice people....and we took a bath every week.

Well, Christmas morning I was lying on the chaise lounge, and Jim had gotten breakfast, when a car drove up. Here was Burl Stonecipher with a big box of food. We were really shook. This was just something that didn't happen, and we really didn't know what to do.

There was a pound of cranberries, a chicken for roasting, and I don't remember all that was in it. The one thing that impressed me was that there was a pound of Mission Chocolates, which just happened to be my favorite chocolate. It impressed me that she could have bought much cheaper candy to put in that box, but she hadn't. She had put in Mission Chocolates. I've always been very grateful for that. She did that out of the kindness of her heart.

I thought a long, long time about the thank you note that I would write. I wanted her to know that I had enjoyed every bit of it, but I didn't want her to get the idea that we were charity. So I told her that it was our first Christmas away from our families, that I had been very ill and unable to do anything, that I had appreciated her thoughtfulness, that I had especially appreciated that Mission box of chocolates because they were my very, very favorites, and I had missed having them since we had moved out to the desert. After that she always decided I was okay.

Dr. Nicholson was one of the nicest, most kindhearted men that I have ever known. Few people really knew him, and a lot of them thought that he was stand-offish, but he really wasn't. He was a very sick man with cardiac asthma. His wife worked in town, while he was out here. He wasn't able to practice, but he was so well thought of, that in the summertime, he used to go up to Berkeley and read x-rays at one of the hospitals. Then as soon as it got a little bit cooler, he would come back.

In 1936 he had come into the restaurant and said, "Hilda, I need to talk to you and Jim."

"What's on your mind?"

"Well," he said, "I've been watching Bobby, and he hasn't grown very much this last year."

Bob was little, chunky, and about ten years old.

Then he said, "I think that we had better do something about it. You know they found a new serum to stimulate the pituitary glands to add height to young people that haven't grown. If you take him in and have x-rays made of his wrists and elbows, we'll see how far apart those joints are. If they have not grown in together, we can start those shots and get Bobby growing again."

So we did, and there was still room for him to grow. So we sent and got the stuff, started giving Bobby shots every week, and he started to grow. He's now five feet ten, so he owes a few more inches on his height to Dr. Nicholson.

Bruce Curry was the same way. Bruce was a short little thing, and all through high school, he remained short. Bruce joined the service, and when he came back, he met my brother, Ted, as we had moved to Portland by this time. Ted had been up to see us, and Bruce asked him, "I want to know something. Is Bob tall?"

Ted said, "Yes, Bob's as tall as I am or taller."

Bruce said, "You know, Dr. Nicholson wanted to give me those shots that he gave Bob, but my folks wouldn't let me take them."

Dr. Nicholson was forced by necessity to practice out here. If you had a dollar you gave it to him. Since we had the restaurant then, he'd just come in and eat. If he'd find Bob running around outside and he had a cold or something, he'd take Bob up, doctor him, come back, and say, "You owe me a dinner, Hilda." He was

HILDA HOLDERMAN GRAHAM

Pat Graham, Hilda's daughter, grew up in her
mother's cafe. Here she came after school to help
with chores. For a time she was the only girl in
the Plaza area -her playmates being the Bagley,
Martin, and Krushat boys and her brother, Bob.
After college she married James Burfield. Today
they are enjoying retirement in Oregon. Photo
taken August 1938 is courtesy of Millie Stewart
Dee.

very good.

He really went out of his way for me when I had colitis. Gerry
Guest was working for me at that time. She was an ex-Army
nurse, about five by five, and a real fine person. She always
looked like the devil. Her hair was always stringing down, and she
wore the most shapeless clothes, but she had a heart as big as could
be. If anybody got sick, she was right there.

One time I got sick and Dr. Nicholson was in Banning. When
he had bad attacks, he would go to Banning and stay at the hotel
there. Gerry came down and took care of me twenty-four hours a
day. I couldn't keep anything down, and I was getting completely
dehydrated. We had been trying to get in touch with Dr. Nicholson.

So he called up the Postes one morning to see if there were any
messages there for him. Mrs. Poste told him, "No. Only the
Grahams have been trying to get you for the last four days. Mrs.
Graham is very ill according to Gerry Guest."

Lena Doolen Holderman, was born in Chetopa, Kansas on May 26, 1876. She married Curtis Holderman in 1895 and moved to Welch in the Indian Territory, now Oklahoma where her four children were born. She came to California in 1923, moved to 29 Palms in 1933 after daughter, Hilda's arrival, and homesteaded an adjoining five acres. She was active in the Women's Guild and other community organizations, and was a charter member of the Little Church of the Desert. She passed away on November 16, 1978 at the age of 102. Photo courtesy of the Local History Collection, 29 Palms Branch Library.

Well, that poor man found somebody to drive him out, and he could just hardly walk. He was fighting for every breath, but he came down to see me. Just as soon as he sat beside me, he leaned over and put his hand on my stomach, sat there, and looked a little while. Then he said to Gerry, "She's got colitis."

And I'm still using the same medication that he prescribed then - shots of B-1, and a couple tablespoons of cola syrup about every three hours. That stops colitis and the nausea flat. He was so far ahead of his time.

So we left here in 1941 and were in Portland when in 1949 I developed tubercular glands. I had surgery but the incision did not heal. They had just brought out streptomycin and tried it on me, but they didn't know how to use it. And I was getting weaker and weaker.

So Jim said, "We're going back to Dr. Nicholson." So we wrote to him.

When he knew I was coming down, he went to one of the hospitals in Los Angeles and went through their files on every case history that had come in and had used streptomycin on. He started me on it, and I got well.

They were having a medical seminar in Los Angeles in 1950 when the flu was breaking out again. Dr. Nicholson went into town to attend and got the flu himself and died. There are a lot of people walking around in this valley who, had they not had him out here, really would not be alive. I felt that our family had just about the finest medical attention.

Hilda Holderman Graham, August 1986 at the ceremonies honoring the fiftieth anniversary of Joshua Tree National Monument. Photo by the author.

286

PHYLLIS KEYS MEIDELL

Phyllis Ann Keys was born October 3, 1931, the youngest of seven children of early Monument pioneers, Frances and William F. Keys.

With other members of her family, Phyllis participated in the activities at their Desert Queen Ranch. And being the youngest, she was the last to leave as her older brother and sisters went into military service or married and moved away. She and her mother were at the ranch while her father was incarcerated in San Quentin for the shooting of Worth Bagley. For five and a half years, they kept the ranch going during these hard times until Bill was paroled in 1948 and later pardoned.

In 1949 she met Charles Meidell, a California Division of Forestry Patrolman stationed in Morongo Valley. Two years later they married and he went into the army. After his military service was complete, he resumed his Forestry duty, and he and Phyllis became the parents of seven children. During part of his thirty-eight year career, the family moved frequently. In 1966 they moved to Hesperia, where Chuck retired in 1984.

Throughout the years, Phyllis has never lost her love for and appreciation of the desert. She is a frequent visitor to Twentynine Palms, and she has maintained close ties with relatives and family friends. Her girlhood days spent with her family at their Desert Queen Ranch are cherished memories.

*　　*　　*　　*　　*

My father, Bill Keys, decided to settle here in the High Desert after roaming the country, exploring, mining, and seeing all that he could. He chose and homesteaded the area that became the Keys' Ranch. He could see its natural resources and its natural beauty, and here he could have water, build a home, and have a family. I was the youngest of that family, and a lot of things happened before I was old enough to remember them.

My father found my lovely mother in Los Angeles where she was working in the Lankershim Hotel as a telegrapher. He took her to see his ranch, which at that time had only a few old adobe buildings. She soon married him in October 1918 and moved there where they raised goats, cattle, chickens, turkeys, a hog or two, many fruit trees, a large garden, and started a family.

We would trek to Twentynine Palms with boxes of fruit and vegetables and visit all of our friends giving them some of the produce that we had brought from our orchard and garden. Then we'd go to Smith's Ranch and eat ice cream, load up with ice, and go home. Now and again we would stay later and roller skate in their rink or watch an outdoor movie.

In the early days, my father ran several hundred head of cattle through what is now Joshua Tree National Monument. He had the the grazing rights from the Bureau of Land Management. We maintained all of the watering holes that were accessible to the cattle on the grazing land, and hired a few cowboys to help. One of those men was Hugh Tucker. He and his wife, Bessie, stayed at the ranch for a time.

A big part of my younger days was going with my dad to check out the location of the herd, clean out the water tanks, and bring new calves in to the ranch in spring that couldn't manage on their own or with the mother's care. Dad would nurse them back to health and care for the mother, then take them back to the herd. My sister, Pat and I would stay in the barn all night while Dad doctored the cows and calves. He would give us a special calf for our own, and we would lay down by it and sleep until dawn.

Every evening we would go to the valleys to milk the cows, taking large metal bins full of cut-up apples and pears out of our garden. Sometimes we would take oats and barley if we had it to give to the milking cows. Dad would put the warm milk in large cans and we would take it back home. Every four or five months he would take the beef to market at the auction in Colton.

My Dad was always very easy-going. People would come out to the ranch and want him to go in with them in the cattle business. One time a man and his two sons wanted to run cattle with my dad. They were suppose to take care of the cattle out in the field and to take the cattle to market using Dad's truck. They had their camp at the Ryan Ranch.

So time went on, and the cattle got picked up at our ranch, loaded, and taken off to auction. Later, Dad went over to the Ryan Ranch to see them and to ask where the money was. Well, the man jumped him, broke his ribs and his arm. The biggest of the brothers took a rifle and knocked my sister about twenty feet with the butt, while their father was beating my dad.

Dad told us to leave, so we ran toward the nearest neighbors who were the Haynes. They had a little cabin probably five miles away across the valley. By the time we got half-way there, my dad had managed to get away from the men. He came in his truck, picked us up, and took us home. Dad suffered because of that arm, as it never healed right. He always had trouble with it. The men packed up and left the country. As far as I know they never returned. Of course, the money went with them.

There were a few other people who ran cattle with Dad. Some of them were good people like John Paul Jones. He was kind of a gypsy cowboy, a fine man, and one of our dearest friends. Just a few years ago he went to the big roundup in the sky, but he'll always be remembered.

There were many visitors to the Ranch. Some came to look around, some came to visit, and some came to stay for awhile. There were times when we would have twenty people around our dinner table. Some we had only just met, perhaps the same day. But my folks always served a lovely dinner no matter how little they had. Dad would go to the cave and get jars of meat, vegetables, and fruit. Mother would turn it into a wonderful meal along with the eternal pot of beans.

Mother was a great cook and could make anything. She canned a lot of meat and vegetables, and we all helped her with peeling and cutting vegetables and fruit. Mother baked bread, parched corn, dried fruit, and made preserves, while Dad harvested honey from the bee hives. He was also great at making beef jerky and keeping things stored. Many times we would survive on those things, if the year was slim.

My mother kept her milk and fresh things cold in a burlap covered cooler in which water had to be put in a large pan on top. The water would soak the burlap, and the breeze would keep it very cool. If some of the milk had passed the fresh stage, my mother would let it turn to clabber. She would put brown sugar on it for us, which was a wonderful treat. Mother learned to do some of these things from my father who was a natural when it came to trying something new.

Dad would go to Banning every six months or so to buy things that we could not grow, like coffee, salt, sugar and flour. He had a stake-sided truck which he drove all of the time. He would come home a day or so later with everything that you could imagine - toys, food, feed for the animals. It was a very exciting time.

Although we were very self-sufficient, we had many lovely friends who came out from the city and brought us things that we didn't get very often - like dried fish, material, clothing, books etc.

We didn't have electricity most of the time that I lived at the ranch. Later my brother, Willis, put a generator in the shed and ran wires to the house so we could have lights and a refrigerator.

Everybody had chores to do. In the years when the garden was going, we had to weed it, and that took a lot of time. Irrigating had to be done, and the animals had to be fed. It kept us busy, and we didn't have time to get into any trouble.

PHYLLIS KEYS MEIDELL

When the older kids were gone and Dad was away at a mine, it was just Mother and I at the ranch. We used to take walks down the wash every week and look for Indian relics. We would find arrowheads and pieces of pottery, and that was always a big thrill. We'd take a sack with apples and nuts and dates, and it would be like a little picnic. That was fun. It was something that we liked to do. Dad was usually busy, but when he wasn't, he would show us where there were Indian pictographs, caves, and other interesting things.

When I was old enough, I used to go prospecting with my Dad and work with him in the mines. I would load ore in the sacks, take the burros, and lead them up the trail with the sacks of ore.

We did most of the milling at the Wall Street Mill which is on the other side of Barker Dam, or Big Horn Dam, as my Dad named it. I loved to go in there. It was the most fantastic place in the world with that big engine and those big stamps and belts going around. That mill was a wonderful place to go when I was young. I loved the tailing dumps out in back. That water was beautiful. So was the smell of the fresh soil. We had a well there from which we pumped the water up to the mill.

Basically, he did all of the work there himself. He took ore out of a lot of different mines and ran it through that mill. It was a lot of hard work. He never found a big, rich pocket of gold, but what he did find, kept us going.

I remember in the old days he used to take his gold bullion down to the assessor's office and have it weighed. Gold was only about $25 to $35 an ounce. So it wasn't worth a lot, but he loved it. That's one reason he used to do all that hard work. He was a hard rock miner, and it was in his blood. Once in a while, my mother used to go with us, but she was usually too busy raising us children.

Some of my most pleasant memories of the ranch were spent in the living room with the sun shining through the window. I would sit on the floor and play with my doll, sewing things, or making doll clothes. Mother would be sitting there in her chair mending or reading a book, which is what she did mostly when she had some free time from her chores. She would have probably just mopped the linoleum, which would be nice and clean, and I'd sit there in the sun. It was great to be able to sit there with her in the house and have that quiet time together.

We used to go skating on the lake in wintertime when it would freeze up. My dad would wrap his shoes with old newspapers and rubber inner tubes and then inch out onto the lake in every direction to see if there were any weak spots. He would take quite a bit of time to make sure it was safe for us kids. Then he would let us go out on it. There wasn't a big freeze that often so this wasn't an every winter occasion.

PHYLLIS KEYS MEIDELL

I don't remember too much about my brother, Ellsworth, except he was sweet and gentle. We climbed the rocks, explored the caves, found Indian artifacts, swam in the lake, pulled weeds in the garden, helped collect the fruit, and went to school. He was injured in a serious accident when he was eleven. He was a wonderful brother, and I'll never forget him.

I remember when that accident happened. We had two wells. One was by the house which had a pump handle on it, and you had to pour water into it to prime it. There was also the big well down behind the barn where the windmill is right now. That one had a wooden platform around it, and a big heavy iron bucket which was attached to a metal cable. The cable went around a wooden roller with a handle on it, called a windlass.

To operate it we'd roll the cable down, let the bucket into the well, and tip it so it would fill with water. We'd then turn the windlass, winding the cable around it as the bucket came up. When the bucket got up, we'd reach across, pull it over onto the platform, set it there, then lock the handle.

Well, Ellsworth was only eleven, and it was a fairly heavy bucket for him to lift. One day he was down there by himself. He got the bucket of water up, but it slipped and fell back down into the well. The handle came around and hit him on the head with a tremendous force. He staggered to the house, and I remember him coming up with blood all over his face. My parents doctored him the best they could and got him down to the doctor who stitched up the wound.

Well, it was deeper than just a scalp wound, and in the next four months he started having dizzy spells. Once we were all out in the front yard, and he staggered over and grabbed the fence. We thought he was sick, because by this time the wound had healed up.

So they tried to doctor him not knowing what was wrong, and then took him to Loma Linda Hospital and discovered he had a blood clot on his brain. The doctors told my parents that there was nothing they could do for him. They took me down there to visit him the day before he died. It was so sad. He was still conscious but very sick. His death was a shock to all of our family and friends.

I lived at the ranch most of my younger years, and I started first grade there. The County supplied our teachers, books, and materials, and my dad paid for half of their salary and supplied them with a residence and school building. He also furnished things like swings and materials for adobe buildings and things that were made in school.

In the course of time I remember four different teachers. All of these people became part of our family. Miss Starr was the first one, then Mrs. Marsh. She and her husband lived in the little cabin up by the lake. Then we had Miss Lela Carlson, who later married Chet Perkins. Then we had Howard and Della Dudley, who had been missionaries in Burma and came to the ranch to teach us. They were wonderful, knowledgeable people. They certainly helped us with our education.

Mrs. Dudley had taught the children in Burma how to make their own dolls, and she taught us how to make them out of stockings and things like that. She took us to the LOS ANGELES TIMES newspaper, to Mexico, and brought in artists to teach us painting and drawing.

There were other children who went to our school. Besides my sister, Pat, there were Marian Headington, Diane and Don McRoberts, Vernon Stephen, Sherman Randolph, and a big family who lived up by Lost Horse. The Headingtons had two nieces from Missouri who came to classes for awhile, and these kids were in school with us when I was in the first grade. The McRoberts were relatives of the Headingtons and lived in a little frame house near Quail Springs. Headingtons lived in a rock house nearby. At one time we had eighteen students at the school.

After the school closed in 1942, I came down to Twentynine Palms to go to school. I stayed with Mrs. Woodruff who used to live in the Stubbs' house. She later married a Park Service ranger named Elmer Camp. I lived with them, I believe during my eighth grade year.

Later after my sister, Virginia came home from the Navy, she married Raymond MacLeod, one of Mrs. Woodruff's sons. He had been living there at the time, and so did his brother, Bower. After he came home from the Navy, Bower married one of our local school teachers, Priscilla Timberlake, who is a relative of one of our presidents.

We were living in Alhambra when my dad had the trouble out here in 1943. My mother and brother were working in a defense plant and Virginia worked at Cannon Electric. Pat was in high school there.

The Dudleys lived in Chino when my father was going to court. They took my mother and I to court some days. I stayed with them often. Mrs. Kiler lived in Upland. She would come to be with us at the courthouse in Riverside. They were just like our family. They were very special.

After that incident happened, we came home to the ranch. Dad had been taken into custody, and the ranch had been vacant for about three weeks. By the time we got home, vandals had already gone in and stolen many things, and had destroyed some of our property. My mother was very upset over that. This was a terrible tragedy for her, because they had taken so many personal items and ruined others that they had had for years.

PHYLLIS KEYS MEIDELL

Neighboring homesteaders' children attended school at the Desert Queen Ranch. L to R: Marian Headington, Sherman Randolph, Dan McRoberts, Dianne McRoberts, and Phyllis Keys holding kittens about 1939. Photo courtesy of Phyllis Keys Meidell.

Don Carrol, Phyllis Keys, and Pat Keys in the rocks at the Desert Queen Ranch. Photo about 1942 courtesy of Phyllis Keys Meidell.

PHYLLIS KEYS MEIDELL

1942 was the last year that the Desert Queen School was in operation at the Keys' Ranch. L to R: Donald McRoberts, Phyllis Keys, Diane McRoberts, Pat Keys, Marian Headington, and Vernon Stephens. The teacher at this time was Mrs. Dudley, not shown. Photo courtesy of Phyllis Keys Meidell.

While my dad was in prison, I stayed with Mother the whole time. We were alone there at the ranch for about six years. It was sad and lonely at times for her. My mother used to write letters trying to find someone to help my dad. She spent many tedious hours at her typewriter, while I tended to the few animals which we had left......goats, and a horse or two. We didn't have any cattle then.

I remember the winters when we wouldn't have feed for the horse that we had left. I would pick grass in the desert for him. Then I would go up in the pasture above the house behind the lake, collect more feed, and drag big logs down to cut up for firewood.

One cold winter that horse was standing out in a little fenced-in place behind the lower cabin on the other side of the corral. He was so cold. I felt sorry for him, so I went over and opened the door of the cabin and took him inside. He heard the echos inside and started to get a little excited, so I took him out. I think he fared better with nature.

Uncle Aaron came up now and then to help out. At times he would stay for a couple of weeks, while my mother would go to San Francisco to see my dad. We still had a small garden, but nothing like it was when my dad had been there. We barely survived. It took all of our energy to keep the chores done and the house together. Once in a while, we would go to town and get kerosene and things like that which we needed.

There were times when no one came for weeks, but we were never afraid and managed quite well. In later years when my dad would be gone to one of the mining claims or off somewhere else, and Mother would be there alone. I hated desperately to leave her alone after a brief visit.

Even during her last illness, my dad was gone on mining assessment. I took care of her at my house for a week or so, after she had seen a doctor. She said she was feeling better and wanted to go home. She had a cat at the ranch, and she didn't want to leave it alone. She was afraid of coyotes getting it, so I took her back home. In 1963 she passed away.

When I lived at the ranch, I always found plenty of things to do to entertain myself. Just enjoying the beauty of the seasons was

Phyllis Ann Keys about 1948 at her family's Desert Queen Ranch.
Photo courtesy of Phyllis Keys Meidell.

great. Sometimes I used to sit on the gate down at the corral fence and sing western songs. I really thought it was the only life - the romance of the desert - and that someday I would be singing and a handsome stranger would drive in or walk right up.

In 1949 I met Chuck Meidell, a California Division of Forestry Patrolman in Morongo Valley. We got married in 1951, and Chuck went into the army shortly thereafter. After he came back, we moved away from this area, but the magic of this desert has lured me back time and time again. I still find it exciting and beautiful. Now new friends, old friends, and some family are here, and the desert is still my home.

On July 24th, 1956, California Governor Goodwin Knight signed a full and unconditional pardon for Bill Keys, Phyllis' father, in the shooting death of Worth Bagley. Here Bill stands with his wife Frances holding the pardon that arrived almost eight years after his parole from San Quentin. Photo courtesy of Phyllis Keys Meidell.

Phyllis' sister, Pat Keys Garry with her husband, Bob and young son, David about 1952. Photo courtesy of Phyllis Keys Meidell.

Phyllis' husband, Chuck Meidell and young son, Billy, with her at the Desert Queen Ranch in 1953. Photo courtesy of Phyllis Keys Meidell.

ADELAIDE WILSON ARNOLD

Adelaide Wilson was born in Erie, Pennsylvania on May 13, 1879. Her early education was provided by tutoring at home where she studied the classics, including Greek. Her family moved to Iowa and then to Portland, Oregon where her father, Dr. Joseph Roger Wilson, founded the Portland Academy, a college preparatory school. She attended Bryn Mawr, but ill health forced her withdraw before she graduated.

Adelaide moved with her family to Morningside Ranch near Hemet, California in 1904. Here her father became active in early citrus growing and marketing in the Hemet valley, while she became acquainted with area's Cahuilla Indians, Basques, and Spanish Californians. Visiting her family's ranch were famous writers, scholars, scientists, Indian orchard workers, prospectors, and desert wanderers. Her close association with these people provided a strong influence on her personal philosophy and the source material on which she based her writing career which started about 1909.

She first came to Twentynine Palms on a visit with her parents in 1923 when they picnicked at the Oasis on the occasion of her birthday. In the early 1920's she had married Charles Christopher Arnold, a distinguished attorney in Riverside, and about ten years later, they bought a cabin north of Amboy Road, east of Twentynine Palms. They divided their time between homes here, Hemet, and Laguna Beach. After Charles' death in January 1939, she moved here permanently.

Throughout the more than twenty years she lived here, Adelaide Arnold became a beloved member of the community. On May 5, 1949, tragedy struck this gentle lady when a fire destroyed her cabin, an unpublished manuscript, and all of her belongings, including her two beloved dogs, "Toby," and "Formy," who had been her constant companions.

During her writing career, Adelaide's stories, articles, and poetry on Indian life and nature appeared in numerous magazines and periodicals in this country and in the British Isles. Her books specialized on the Cahuilla Indians and their lore centering around the Hemet area. SON OF THE FIRST PEOPLE was published by MacMillan Company in 1940 and continued to be in demand long after it was out of print. TRAVELER'S MOON was published in 1962 by Doubleday and Company. It was also very popular and

ADELAIDE WILSON ARNOLD

based on her own experiences and those of her early Indian friends.

Her last years were spent in a convalescent home in Hesperia. She died in Hesperia on February 16, 1969, and was buried next to her husband in San Jacinto Valley cemetery.

*   *   *   *   *

"Desert Rain"

Never again in the cool north land

Shall I breathe that garden of lost delight:

But oh, the brief rain on desert sands,

And rain drenched sages in the night!

Lilacs, phlox, lilies, their tender scent

Once drew my heart home to its welcoming door;

But wet sage flooding a darkened tent

Makes the heart pilgrim forever more.

ADELAIDE WILSON ARNOLD

Adelaide Arnold with "Toby," one of her beloved
companions that perished in the 1949 fire that
destroyed her cabin home. Photo courtesy of
Lucile and Harold Weight.

ADELAIDE WILSON ARNOLD
1879 - 1969
(With her dog, General. Photo by and courtesy of Harold Weight.)

LOIS MARLOW HARZ

Lois Marlow was born in Chicago, Illinois, on August 15, 1923, to Mabel and Tom Marlow. Three years later the family moved to Santa Ana, California, where her father secured work in highway construction.

In 1933 the Marlows came to Twentynine Palms at the invitation of Les Spell to try their luck in mining at the Gypsy Queen Mine. The family slept in a tent that first winter, and later when Tom temporarily returned to his job in Orange County, he moved Lois and her mother into a two room cottage several miles northwest of Bagley's Store. Soon after her father left Santa Ana permanently and became the manager of the American Legion grounds here.

Lois attended grammar and high school in Twentynine Palms. In 1940 she was elected the town's first beauty queen to reign at the annual Orange Show in San Bernardino. During her senior year she was vice president of the student body, editor of the first high school yearbook, and senior class Salutatorian at her graduation in 1941. The following year she attended San Bernardino Junior College.

When Condor Field began operations north of the town during World War II, Lois worked at the Air Academy. Here she met Vinton Harz, a student glider pilot undergoing training there for the invasion of Normandy. They were married on January 9, 1943, in the Little Church of the Desert.

After the war, Vinton returned from the European theatre to re-establish his life with his wife and family in Twentynine Palms. Lois was busy with her two children, Michael and April. Later she would become the secretary for the Palm Vista Elementary School from which she retired after twenty years service in 1983. Two years earlier, Lois had organized and spearheaded the successful fortieth anniversary reunion of her high school class which brought many of her classmates back to town, some for the first time in many years.

Lois' unexpected death on June 15, 1986, saddened the entire community of which she had been an active, contributing member during her fifty-three years of residency.

Young Lois Marlow who arrived in the desert with
her parents in 1933.   Photo courtesy of Vinton
Harz.

From my first visit to the Gypsy Queen, I was captivated by
the desert. I was nine years old in 1932 when Oakley Spell brought
me and Mother out to visit at the mine which Dad, my uncle, Herb
Myers, and the Spell brothers, Les, Oakley, and Baird were operating.

Getting here from our home in Santa Ana was something else!
It took five or six hours and to me seemed endless. We left the
highway abruptly just past Whitewater and crept our way up a
steep, narrow, rocky track along the side of a cliff and then into
Devil's Garden. I was always terrified we'd meet a car coming the
other way,for there was no way we could have passed.

Luckily, in those days traffic was scarce, and we never had to maneuver our way back down. From that point the road was single-track dirt road full of curves and bends in some parts, and in others stretching straight as an arrow as far as the eye could see. Eventually we would arrive.

I think the first time we came out was in winter time, and we slept in a tent. The thing I can remember about it was I got up and it was dark outside. There were no street lights or anything. It was bitterly cold, but I just loved it. I remember that the men slept in a tunnel back into the mine, but they had put up a tent for us.

I was anxious to run and stretch my legs in a "yard" that had no boundaries and would be off to explore this new and enchanting land. I loved the vast open country....the panoramic view, the solitude, and the stillness. I was fascinated by the wild creatures in and around the campsite.

The men shared their quarters with a trio of these wild folk....a western fence lizard called Lizzie, Chuck the chuckawalla, and a red racer called Red. These creatures provided much entertainment for the men in the tunnel which served as home, while their new cook shack was being built. This close knit group was almost broken up once when Red grabbed Lizzie, but quick action by Dad separated the two.

I acquired a desert tortoise and was gratified when she spent the summer in the cool wet sand under our screen and burlap "ice" box which we kept drenched with water.

I spent hours collecting strange, beautiful rocks, and would accompany the men up the hill to the mine where I'd pound promising looking ore with mortar and pestle. I learned to wash this gravel in the miners' shallow pan and soon had a modest showing of gold dust collected in a little jar.

The corrugated iron and screen cook shack was the center of our leisure times. It provided the only shelter so our cots and chairs were moved around it, following the shade or seeking its leeward side during the occasional fierce winds.

The interior was sparsely furnished with a wooden table, orange crates hung on the walls for storage, and in one corner a flat-topped, four-burner wood range. Somehow food tasted better served hot from that stove. Mother says it was only the stimulation from my day's activities and the desert air that whetted my appetite. For after cooking over it in the shack, that was probably hotter than the outside temperature, she sure wasn't hungry!

Food was sometimes in short supply, as our neighborhood grocery was some twenty miles away, but somehow Mother always managed to find something to serve. Occasionally families from other mines many miles away would drop by. I can remember watching a car creep along the one track road from the other side of the valley, hoping that it would be coming our way.

Trips to Twentynine Palms were high spots. The first stop would be at the Oasis for a drink of the world's best tasting spring water. Then on to the "City Hall" at Bagley's for a shower and change of clothes before we went to the post office, did our shopping, and caught up on the news from other citizens who were gathering in front of the store. Kids played and swapped tales. Most fun was "king of the mountain" on a pile of dirt at the rear of the store.

In September 1933 Mom and I moved in to Twentynine Palms so I could begin school. Dad at this time was back at his county job in Santa Ana. We rented a well-built, two room cottage several miles northwest of Bagley's market. Our only neighbors, Frank and Mildred Dement and their four year old daughter lived one quarter mile away. Mother cooked on a two-burner kerosene stove, and we hauled water in five gallon milk cans from Bagley's well. We can't thank Frank enough for this privilege. Without his generosity, life in the desert would have been impossible.

We were fairly isolated while Dad was in Santa Ana and seldom went "uptown," as Mother was a beginner driver. Cranking up the old 1928 Whippet sedan and steering it through the sandy trails was an ordeal.

I never remember being lonely, nor did I seem to miss the "advantages" I'd known in the city. Instead of neighbor kids, I played with my black and white tomcat. He had run away from Les Cross' mine ten miles away, and two months later showed up at the Gypsy Queen, gaunt, half wild, but glad to be with humans again.

Instead of movies and radio, Mom and I spent evenings with the Ouija board, laughing at the funny messages we "received." We furnished our dream house from the Sears catalog and chose extravagant wardrobes. That we couldn't buy these luxuries didn't seem to matter. We played all kinds of games of our own invention. That is how I finally learned the states and their capitals.

People were ever helpful. Anyone driving to the market would stop by their neighbors to ask if they wanted to go along, or if they wanted some shopping done, or a can of water hauled. Bill Hockett came to our rescue the day Mother broke her wrist. It would have been difficult to have managed without this great friendliness.

I also had a dipodomy friend who visited every evening for a handout of crumbs. Once in a while Billy Barnett or Harold Hockett would walk from their homes three or four miles away and spend the day.

I remember vividly the old adobe house at the Oasis. Even then, it was surrounded by an aura of history and antiquity. We played in and around it and wondered about the early settlers it had sheltered. I am still appalled that someone allowed the

Thomas and Mabel Marlow, Lois' parents, about 1943. Photo courtesy of the Local History Collection, 29 Palms Branch Library.

destruction of this landmark.

In 1933 I entered the fifth grade in the two-room school at the corner of Two Mile Road and Utah Trail. Mother says I was the thirteenth girl enrolled. Olive Hardy, the principal, taught grades one through four in the large room, and Mary Jane La Point (later Mrs. Jack McClain) had the fifth through ninth grades. I enjoyed the heady experience of being the new girl and basked in the love of numerous boys, many of them from the primary room. I was soon supplanted by Lois Shelton, the new, new-girl, but I've never forgotten that glorious feeling of popularity!

Bill and Harry Smith built the first school bus, a big square wooden box on a truck. It had iron mesh over the windows and wooden benches......two running down each side and two down the middle. As I remember, Harry drove most of the time. When he was in kindergarten, our son Michael was given a box of candy for being the best-behaved boy on the bus.....by Harry, who was still driving!

It was during this year that I finally mastered the mysteries of math. I accomplished this in spite of hearing the ninth graders having their lessons in algebra, while I was struggling with nine times six! I'm strongly in favor of progress and am proud of our

LOIS MARLOW HARZ

Lois Marlow in the spring of 1940 when she was
the reigning Queen of Twentynine Palms. Photo
courtesy of Vinton Harz.

present schools, but don't under-estimate the country school
teacher. With very few supplies and materials, they gave us an
education!

Frank Kessler, a young first year teacher taught during my
seventh grade year. He lacked discipline, and we took advantage
of this as kids will. A few of the tough boys really made it rough
for him.

Mrs. Sarah Jessup taught in 1936, my eighth grade year. What
a great lady! She was the first to instill in many of us the real
desire to learn.

Our eighth grade graduation had twelve students on the porch
of the school house. The whole town turned out. Alan Bagley was
Valedictorian, Elizabeth Watson was Salutatorian, and Eugene
Curry and I were awarded the coveted American Legion medals.

December 1943. Vinton Harz (on left) was undergoing glider training while stationed at South Plains Air Force Base, Lubbock, Texas. He received his wings here.

The boys were in suits and the girls in their first formals.

Dad was manager of the American Legion holdings. He operated the swimming pool from May first until cold weather shut it down sometime in September. The pool was the focal point of all summer activities. The kids lived in it, and most of us were taught to swim by Sarah Krushat and Jack Cones. Fourth of July celebrations were held there with games and competitive races.

Sunday afternoon ball games were fun. Our fathers formed the backbone of the teams with younger men and a few good high school boys filling in the vacancies.

Every once in awhile, someone would arrange for a donkey ball game. All positions were played astride, and the batter had to persuade the burro to "run" the bases. Bruises and sore muscles followed.

Occasionally, a pair of barnstorming pilots would land their two-seated biplane on the ball diamond. (Site of the present football field). I'd spend my entire savings on one or two hops around the valley at fifty cents per ride. I was considered quite the daredevil. Some of the kids were too scared to go.

Lois and Vinton Harz in Lubbock, Texas during
November 1943 when he was in glider pilot train-
ing. Lois had married Vinton in 29 Palms on
January 9, 1943.

Dances were held on the tennis court adjacent to the pool. Bill
Barnett played the piano, John Bagley, the guitar, and Les Cross,
the saw. He was good too! On my twelfth birthday I invited all
the kids in the valley to come to a swim party.

Our first house on the Legion grounds was only a three room
cottage, but in it we lived in luxury. We had running water from
our own well and heated the house with a wood stove. Mom
cooked on a gas range, and we had electric lights!

The three houses, the six cabins, and the pool house were furnished electricity by a small light plant which Dad would crank
into action at dusk and shut down at ten each night. He'd flash the
lights three times, and that was the signal for late retirers to rush

LOIS MARLOW HARZ

for the kerosene lamps.

We slept on a screened porch, and those winter nights are something I'll never forget. I'd dress by the fire and hurry to bed, where Mom had placed a brick heated on the stove and wrapped in newspaper. Gradually my shivering would stop, as the warmth from the brick permeated the bed.

One aspect of the "good old days" that I do not remember fondly was the lack of indoor bathrooms! Each call of nature was an ordeal in summer or winter. In June the heat was oppressive in the little two-holer, and the fear of being attacked by the ever present black widow was constantly with us. In December the wind howled through the cracks, and the thought uppermost in our minds was to get back in by the fire.

Jack Cones, the constable, looked the other way, as we kids (at twelve or thirteen) would drive our parents' cars to visit each other. And contrary to popular belief now, we began dating early. My first was in the eighth grade when Ib Watson and I were taken to a school dance by Eugene Curry and Alan Bagley. It was only one fourth mile from my house, but we were proud our parents placed such trust in us.

Vinton Harz and his CG-4A glider near Melun, France, September 1945. Vinton carried out three missions to Holland and one to Germany. He flew another glider during the Normandy Invasion. Photo courtesy of Vinton Harz.

LOIS MARLOW HARZ

The transition from grammar school to high school was exciting, but easy. We knew all the older kids and the teaching principal, Ted Hayes and the other teacher, Helen Burr, were friendly and most important, interested. Our eighth grade class was the first to enter as freshmen (September 1937) in the new high school. The building had three classrooms. The inside accordion-like walls could be folded back converting them into one large room, one of which was a raised stage.

Ted had a small office, the walls of which were lined with shelves holding our entire library. Lockers in a short hall and rest rooms with showers completed the physical plant which by today's standards isn't much! But what went on within that confined space was what counted.

Lois Marlow Harz with her son, Michael, June 1945. Photo courtesy of Vinton Harz.

311

LOIS MARLOW HARZ

Helen Burr, a young woman of Scotch ancestry, taught Spanish, history, social arts, and girls physical education. Helen had a caustic tongue, and on more than one occasion I was the brunt of her sarcasm. But what vitality and dynamic energy she had! Anyone who was interested at all in Spanish learned to speak it, think it, and yes, even dream it. She organized and supervised a roller skating team that by anyone's standards was pretty good.

We put on dance revues (remember the "Grapevine" and the "Eagle"?) and even managed the "Truck Drivers Special" square dance. Under her sponsorship, we sold candy at noon to buy sharp looking blue and gold P.E. uniforms and participated in day long athletic competition with other schools in the district, which was the Victor Valley Unified School District then.

I think it was in 1938 that a portable building was brought onto the campus as a classroom. It housed the science and biology specimens and served as our cafeteria. You haven't lived if you haven't eaten lunch in front of human embryos, snakes, scorpions, and tape worms. In spite of the view, Maggie Deardorff's good homemade rolls pleased our teen-age palates.

Carolyn Barnes was employed this year. She taught the sciences and math. A plump, good-natured, young woman, she crammed knowledge into even those of us who weren't math inclined. In her class I learned to consider geometry a puzzle to solve and soon became fascinated by the intricacies.

I now come to a spot that I find difficult to write, because he's still very much a part of the community and seems to be turned off by sentimentality and adulteration. It will be hard to describe the impact Ted Hayes had on my life without causing him some embarrassment. He was a young teacher when he came to Twentynine Palms as its high school principal. He was unassuming and quiet, as I remember him, yet his great sense of humor and his love for teaching (typing, business methods, algebra, and English) stimulated an interest in academics in most of his students that led many of them on to very successful careers.

In retrospect, I think Ted might have been just as happy, if we could have scrapped all the non-essentials and concentrated on English, English grammar, and English literature. His classes were exciting, and he made Shakespeare, Dickens, Chaucer, and Lovelace come alive. He demanded and got respect even from those pupils who weren't students.

What good years these were! The faculty was tolerant of our failings....young love in the spring, summer, fall, and winter, our ditching school when it snowed, and the three or four who sneaked behind Caldwell's house for a cigarette. When three of the older boys wildly had a drink before a high school dance, Ted's mild comment put them in their place.

A revisit to the Gypsy Queen Mine in 1952. L to R: Lois, daughter, April, son, Michael, with mother, Mabel Marlow, and husband, Vinton. Photo courtesy of Vinton Harz.

I remember our Junior/Senior play, "Brothers of Belinda," which was lots of fun from start to finish, as was raiding the cafeteria the night of dress rehearsal at Ted's suggestion. Don Malone and I had the leading roles, but June Garvin was the star.

Ditch Day, 1941 had the approval of the faculty. It was a no chaperoned bus tour. We made our plans, invited dates, and went in student-driven cars to Pasadena. We had lunch, skated, went shopping, to the theatre, and all met at the Palladium to dance.

LOIS MARLOW HARZ

Lower classmen who went as dates of the seniors had to write one thousand word essays.

During my high school years, the town was growing. Underhills showed movies on Friday, Saturday, and Sunday nights in the high school building. I was the usherette and made seventy-five cents a night. The Congers opened a malt shop, a popular gathering place. A drug store operated by Doc White got the after-show crowds for hot chocolate.

The Little Church of the Desert was built, and the high school girls sang there and at the Catholic Church. A skating rink was built which provided hours of recreation for the kids and the young marrieds. Riding stables operated by the Healy family was another form of recreation. Moonlight rides and square dances on horseback were popular. The cost was fifty cents per hour.

"Hometowners," a club organized by the young married couples in the late thirties provided a much needed outlet for those who loved to dance. About eight couples comprised the first group. After Vinton and I were married and became members, it had become incorporated and was a pretty exclusive closed-membership organization. Their only goal was to have fun, and we did!

Our schooling in Twentynine Palms ended in 1941 with the graduation of sixteen students. Ceremonies were held at Smith's Ranch, as we were too many for the little high school building. Ib Watson was Valedictorian and I was Salutatorian. If Alan Bagley hadn't spent his senior year in Pasadena, I wouldn't have made it!

A gathering of long-time friends at Pioneer Days, 1984. L to R: Kathryn Malone, Mildred Michels, Mabel Marlow, and Sarah Krushat. Photo by the author.

LOIS MARLOW HARZ

We shared lots of good times then. Togetherness was more than a catch phrase, because that was how we did things. We were united in a common bond of camaraderie regardless of what our circumstances had been in the cities. The bond still exists after more than forty years, as attested to by the large gatherings at the annual Pioneer Days reunions, and the many old friends who still drop by for a visit and "Remember when...."

Jean Tobin Flynn visits with Vinton and Lois about 1985. Photo courtesy of Vinton Harz.

WILLIAM J. HOLMES

William J. Holmes was born in Boston, Massachusetts, one of three children born to Marie and Verne Holmes. After World War I was over, the family moved to Long Beach where Bill's father was associated with the automobile business. Here young Bill and his brother and sister went to school.

Because Bill had asthma, his parents sent him to board with Ethel and Art Strickler, former neighbors of theirs, who had moved to Twentynine Palms. Bill arrived in 1934 when he was fourteen years old, and within a month his asthma had disappeared. He remained out here for four years, living with the Strickler family for the first two years, then joining his family when they moved out in 1936.

He and his family returned to Long Beach after he graduated in from high school in 1938. Then Bill entered Long Beach Community College, graduated, served in the military during World War II, then worked with his father in the family's automobile agency. He married Betty Therkelsen on August 31, 1946, and they have two children, Scott and Cathy.

After his father's death in 1954, he took over the agency until he sold the business and retired in 1981. At that time he and his wife Betty terminated their weekend visitor status to Twentynine Palms and moved here permanently to become active members of the community. Bill is busy with the Kiwanis Club, and has served on the Board of Directors of the Historical Society.

*   *   *   *   *

When World War I was over, we came back here and settled in Long Beach. That's where I went to school. Here too, my father was associated, all his life and until his death, with the automobile business.

During my adolescence, I had asthma so bad in Long Beach that my parents moved for a year to Tujunga, which is up in the foothills of Los Angeles. I did so well in recovering that they came back to Long Beach. Six months later I was back with asthma again.

Our next door neighbors at that time were Art and Ethel Strickler. They were just out here from the East for his health, and he

WILLIAM J. HOLMES

had met Dr. Luckie. Dr. Luckie suggested that maybe he should go to the desert with his respiratory problem, so they came out to Twentynine Palms and homesteaded. I guess this was about 1932. My mother and Ethel corresponded.

Ethel said, "Why don't you ship him out here and board him with us?" That's what they did.

I was about 14 years old, and in the 9th grade. They shipped me out in '34. This happened to be the first year that the high school started. Ted Hayes was the principal. Of course, I lived on the Strickler homestead which was down at the west end of Mesquite Lake....myself and three girls. We were the farthest group of children to be picked up by the school. They were picking up kids then.

Because he suffered from asthma, fourteen year old Bill Holmes was sent to the desert by his parents to board with the Strickler family. He arrived in 1934 and after a month's stay, his asthma disappeared. He lived with the Stricklers for two years until his parents moved out in 1936. This photo taken in July 1938 of Bill when he was eighteen years old is courtesy of Bill Holmes.

WILLIAM J. HOLMES

The bus at that time was contracted by Bill Smith. What he had was a ton and a half truck, a flat-bed, from which he had just taken the sides off and thrown a canopy over the top. He also decided to separate the boys from the girls. Of course, things were a little rough in those days. So he put a partition right down the middle of the bus, and put benches on either side. As you came in the end of the bus, the boys would sit on one side and the girls would sit on the other side.

On a few occasions, the bus would come to pick us up and there would be nothing in the bus. There'd be plain old open space in fact, and all wet. Their ice would come from Banning, and of course, in the middle of the night he would go and pick up ice and come back.

The bus might be a little late, because the highway was all dirt from Whitewater to here. We came up over the little knoll from Bridgehaven (or Whitewater) instead of around the corner like the highway goes. Over the top - dirt road - and up the wash. There was no road in the wash. I mean it was just graded.

After an ice run, we'd all have to stand up, and that's about a forty-five minute run from there up to the school. We'd have to stand up because there were no benches. It had been too late for them to put the stuff in the bus. Then he'd have to run home and put the stuff in, and we'd have the benches to go home from school.

My first year the only kids in high school were from this valley right here. I don't know what the kids down in Morongo did, because Yucca wasn't developed at all. It was nothing but the Warren Wells stop. There was only myself - I'd like to name off a few of them - Dolly Benito, and Bill Krushat, a couple of guys called the Royal brothers - one of them was the bus driver - and Derald Martin. There were only seventeen in the whole high school.

The third year, I had moved up with my parents. Two years with the Stricklers and then two years with my parents who lived out here. They came out here and built the house off of Sullivan near Sherman Road.

Then the high school was tied in with the Victor Valley School District. There was no Morongo Basin School District. Busing from the west was contracted with a Mrs. Skinner who bought a Chevy Suburban. It held about eight or nine kids. She would drive in from Morongo Valley. I think there were seven of us. The two Bobo boys, myself, and her son, Harold Skinner. There were two other people that came to the high school, plus three or four kids going to grammar school.

We'd walk down to the highway from our house, and they'd pick us up. Those were the only kids that came from all of Yucca Valley and Morongo Basin, and Twentynine Palms was the only high school. That's the way it was.

The District contracted with the American Legion for the original Legion cafe to use as a school building. It was torn down about three or four years ago. It was built just off the northwest corner of today's Legion building which is on the west side of Legion Road across the street from the swimming pool. It was just one room. Behind the cafe, (the school), was a bunch of little cabins the Legion used to rent out.

The first year we were only there with Ted Hayes. He was teacher for the whole ninth, tenth, eleventh, and twelfth grades which were integrated. Of course there were only fifteen kids.

The second year the teacher that came out was a woman. Her name was Barbara Van Kirk - big, robust, good looking, well-built woman. She was about as acclimatized to the desert as a seal is. She couldn't take it. Her skin was fair. She always wore a great big hat. The heat bothered her and everything. She was good for one year.

Believe it or not, she had to teach in a little cabin in the back which we called the "chicken coop". Was it hot starting about the first of May! The last two months were terrible! No air conditioning, no cooling, no nothing.

Ted Hayes and Miss Barbara Van Kirk, the first and second high school teachers in 29 Palms. Ted's interesting career is the subject of the following chapter. Photo about 1935 courtesy of the Local History Collection, 29 Palms Branch Library.

Helen Burr came the next year. She was here for a number of years, even after I graduated. I can only remember two or three incidents in school that were interesting. Of course, Hayes did a terrific job as far as teaching four integrated classes a day. I might have been in the ninth grade and taken Spanish, and someone else in the twelfth grade would also be taking Spanish. There were no electives.

The closest thing to an elective that I can remember was chemistry. We had a little shed off the side of the store which looked like a little enclosed patio. For some reason or other the school sent out a chemical set. It was in a box, maybe about two feet square...just a bunch of chemicals. Two of the kids, Bobo and Skinner got a hold of this kit and made all kinds of concoctions....like stink bombs and things like that. Mr. Hayes didn't have - I don't think - any idea about this kind of stuff. But they played with it, because it was given to the school. I don't think they got any credits.

We had no basketball. We didn't have any kind of recreation, because there wasn't any money. We just horse-played. But we did have the swimming pool across the street that the American Legion operated in the summer time. When school started, they closed it, but they left the water in it to evaporate naturally. As long as water was in there, whether it was green with algae, or anything else (it would probably evaporate maybe a foot every month), we went over there. We would swim in that thing until probably the middle or latter part of November. By that time the water was down two or three feet, and it was getting a little bit too cold. That was our recreation.

Lots of mornings we had to wait for the bus. Sometimes the bus coming to pick us...when I was living down at Stricklers'....didn't show up, because it would break down. The second year I was there, Jack Cones got the contract by outbidding Bill Smith. He went into town and bought an old bus. It was a big thing and <u>old</u>, and it broke down all the time. He was working on that thing time and again. When the bus would break down, we'd wait and wait and wait. Finally Art Strickler would have to take the four of us (me and the three girls) to school. There was one other family that lived down that way. It was Emersons with four boys around my age.

Mrs. Emerson had the homestead in the sand dunes right next to Guy Hinshaw. His homestead, or his house, was right out in the middle of the lake....on a peninsula that ran right out in the lake. He had an adobe house. Valerie stayed with her father a good deal of the time and went to school with us. She graduated in '37. The first year of graduation.

We had a school play. I remember this was before the high

school was built, and we had to find a place to put the play on. I guess this was in 1936. Tom Martin had just built the garage down at the Plaza. And before he started his operation, someone negotiated with him to use the building to stage the school play. They built a stage at the east end of the building and brought chairs from all over the desert, and we had the play.

I remember there were five of us in my class. And over the years, I always tell people.....just for fun...that I was always the third highest in my class. I couldn't say the first or the second, because somebody else was Valedictorian and Salutatorian, so I always said third highest. The Valedictorian was Allen Bobo and Harold Skinner was the Salutatorian, and then there was myself and Wally Trigg and Edie Wiedow.

I don't know what happened to most of them, but I see Wally every once in a while. He's been out to some of the reunions. Harold is dead now. He was killed in the war, as was Troy Martin. He was a pilot and went down in the Pacific. Allen Bobo lived up until last year. He came to the last big class reunion we had down at the Elks Club two or three years ago. He has recently passed away. Eve Wiedow died a few years back. She was married to Bill Phelps.

The original homestead house of Bill Holmes and his family taken about 1938. After the Holmes family purchased this house in 1936, Art Strickler moved it on his truck to its present location off Canyon Road. The family moved back to Long Beach after Bill's graduation from high school in 1938 and about two years later sold the house. In the 1970's Bill and his brother, Verne repurchased the home and property. Photo courtesy of Bill Holmes.

WILLIAM J. HOLMES

When I was in the high school, we all had homework. I'd come home and sit down to do my homework. Of course, we didn't have electricity then. We had Aladdin lamps, and we still had the wood stove, and propane for the cook stove. We hauled our own water and had a 500 gallon water tank set up on a stilt just above the kitchen. Every time we went to school, my mother would come down and wait for the mail....I don't know....three o'clock....four o'clock. We'd bum a ride up and fill up three- five gallon tanks of water and take it home, and my brother, Verne, and I would keep it filled up all the time.

But I was a lousy student......at least for the first couple of years. I'd start studying, and I'd get tired. In a half hour I was just pooped...just ready to go to bed! That went on for a year...two years.

I think it was in my eleventh grade. One weekend, my father, who commuted from Long Beach for two years nearly every week, got tickets for a basketball game in Los Angeles between USC and Stanford. So Frank and Johnny Bagley were invited, and of course, Frank picked me up, and we drove in to L.A., and Dad met us.

We went to the game, had good seats, and I didn't say anything, but I couldn't see a thing. I could see the lights on the court. I could see movement, but I couldn't see anything. I kept saying to my Dad, "What happened?" It was then he realized my vision was lousy.

He took me right away to an eye doctor who fitted me with glasses. I came back and everything was fine. I had gone so long before we were aware of the problem, because in school we were sitting within five feet of the blackboard, and you're reading a book....so there's no need for glasses. The last year or two, with glasses, my grades picked up and everything was better.

You know I loved the old desert. I thrived on it. And when I graduated that was the end of it for a long time. I went to Long Beach, and I found that I had outgrown the asthma.

By the way, when my folks sent me out here to this desert to stay with the Stricklers, I was here for one month and the asthma disappeared. I never had another attack of asthma until I was in the service in England in the dead of winter.....rainy, and I had a cold. Then it turned into asthma. I went to the dispensary, and they gave me a couple of shots, and I got over it, and that was it. So this desert really took care of my condition.

When I graduated in 1938, I went to Long Beach and operated the business for thirty years. We all moved, but we kept the house. Then a couple of years later my father sold the house and ten acres - and kept ten acres. My mother still owns that ten acres.

I went to Long Beach Community College and graduated from there. And then, of course, I went to work for my father. He had

WILLIAM J. HOLMES

a Ford dealership in Long Beach in 1931 and was a Ford dealer until 1938 when he changed to Studebaker. He was a Studebaker dealer until 1954 when he passed away. I took over the agency then, and in 1956 I changed franchises and became a Dodge dealer. I was a Dodge dealer until 1981 when I sold the business. Then Betty and I both moved up here. We've been here ever since.

Betty and Bill Holmes, Pioneer Days, October 1986. After Bill's retirement in Long Beach in 1981, the Holmes terminated their weekend visits back to 29 Palms and made this their permanent home. Photo by the author.

MARY AND TED HAYES

Theodore J. Hayes was born in 1905 on his parents' ranch just a few miles outside of the city limits of Pasadena in an area then called Amanda Park. Here he went to grammar school and on to Pasadena High School, and to Occidental College where he graduated in 1928. He also took some summer sessions after he was a teacher at Claremont College and San Diego State.

Mary was born in Lynn, Massachusetts, and because of a mastoid infection, doctors recommended that she move to Arizona or California, which the family did. Ted met Mary while they were in high school, and they were married in Pasadena on July 21, 1931, which Ted remembers as one of the hottest days that Pasadena had had in more than a century.

A teaching job brought them to Twentynine Palms in 1934 where Ted taught algebra, Spanish, history, geometry, mechanical drawing, and athletics. At lunch time Mary would walk nearby from their small cottage on the American Legion grounds to the school located there also. Here while Ted went home to have lunch, she would teach music to his students.

Two years later additional high school grades were needed, and a new high school building was constructed on Utah Trail. Ted was named principal. When he retired in June 1969, he had served more than thirty-five years.

Today Mary and Ted pride themselves on their beautiful garden, which results from a lot of hard work, planning, fertilizer, and water. Each spring they especially enjoy visits from their many friends, former students, and others who stop by to see them and what they've grown. So outstanding is their garden, that it was featured in SUNSET MAGAZINE in 1985. During the summer, they still enjoy taking picnics into the cooler altitudes of the Joshua Tree National Monument, continuing a tradition that began almost fifty years ago by themselves and other early community residents.

*   *   *   *   *

Mary and I were in high school and college together and never had a date. After we graduated, she was earning a living, and I was working for Standard Oil and we finally decided to get married. She kept working, and I went back to school and got a teacher's credential and a master's degree. For a couple of years, I was looking for a job, but there just weren't any.

Then we heard about one in Twentynine Palms from a former girlfriend of mine who was the sister of Hilda Graham. I had been out to the desert several times by then, although Mary had not. I knew Hilda and Jim and Hilda's mother, Lena Holderman, who was out here by this time.

When this job opened up, Hilda sent word that there was a job out here in which I might be interested. This was in 1934. We had been living in El Monte for three years. As soon as I heard about it, I came out and Hilda made arrangements for me to see Walt Ketcham at her little restaurant in the Plaza.

Ted and I arrived at seven o'clock in the morning and had coffee, and they told us in the restaurant that Ketch, the clerk of the school board, would be in shortly to meet us. He lived about five miles out on the mesa. So he came in and introduced himself and was very gracious. He said, "I want you to come out to my cabin and see the dipodomys."

So at about ten-thirty or eleven o'clock in the morning, we had perfectly delicious split pea soup, leg of lamb with all of the trimmings, and we had a very gay and satisfactory dinner. When everything was over, he said, "I'm very sorry, Mr. Hayes. The position you're applying for has been taken. But we'll remember you in case.........."

Sometime later, my sister and mother and I had gone to Catalina, and Ted had stayed looking for a job up and down the coast. This being Depression time, you went everywhere.

Ted came to pick us up when we came back from Catalina, and he had a grin from ear to ear. This was very hopeful. He said, "I had a letter from Ketch, and I told him that you would not be home until the next day and would it be all right if we came a day later?"

Well, the job was going to be available to me, because the kid who was going to take it, changed his mind. His wife was pregnant,and she didn't want to come out here so far away from a doctor. So when we were informed that there still was an opening, Mary and I came out a second time and talked with Mrs. Bagley, who was on the School Board. She had talked with Ketcham, and he had told her it was her decision. She had his blessing to choose anyone she wanted.

So we went there and had a delightful time with Helen. We were nervous because this was very important. Everything Helen asked Ted if he could do, he'd say no, and I'd say yes.

Finally Helen said, "All we can possibly raise and offer you is

325

$1200. We know this is just a very low salary to offer, but this is what we have."

Mary said, "That's enough."

The third trip to Twentynine Palms was a week or so later.

We were coming up the Morongo grade pulling a homemade trailer which contained all of our worldly goods. It was a heavy load, and of course, the road was nothing but dirt. We got behind the grader and got a vapor lock. We had two little dogs, one of whom had never been in a car before. The heat of the car sort of hit her, and on the onset of the vapor lock, Saki vomited right down the front of Mary's white linen dress.

When we got here, Walter Ketchum met us and wanted to help us unload. Mary was thinking, "Oh, gee. I smell like Sinner's puke. We've got to get rid of this guy."

He was just being helpful, and wanted to help us unpack our bed, dressers, and everything we had. Anyway, we said, "No, thank you."

So we made it down to the house at the Legion. We got this place at the Legion for $20 a month. The house, which has been torn down, was right there near the swimming pool. It was later used for the office for the recreation district. It had four rooms and a front porch: two bedrooms, a kitchen, and a living room. The front porch was screened in, but it didn't have any floor in it. It was just a sandy floor. The two bedrooms were on the west side, and there was an outside outlet for each one.

We had a lot of fun there. We painted inside and decorated it up. Of course, there was no plumbing, except there was a cold water sink in the kitchen. There were lights from dark until about nine o'clock every night except on Saturdays when there was a dance, and then they would go until eleven o'clock.

We had a Coleman lantern and also an Aladdin lamp, and we would light these. If we wanted to stay up later, Tom Marlow, Lois' Dad, who ran the Legion property, blinked the lights three times, and that meant that you had about three minutes to light your lamps or else get into bed, as the case might be.

Every Thursday when they had Legion meeting, we had lights until almost midnight. Then you'd either entertain your friends, or if I wanted to, I could iron. Anything that we needed electricity for, this was the night we could do it. We had a gasoline iron also.

The Legion had a generator there. They had, over west of us, a series of little houses that they rented out like an early-day motel. Each was just a little tiny room about ten by twelve. They had about six of them. We rented one for a school room two years. Anyway, they had a bath house which we could use for a slight fee like twenty cents or two bits or something. Here was a hot bath. This was a losing proposition for the Legion, because they had to pay for a caretaker, and Tom was the caretaker.

We had an outdoor privy, and this was fine. The door opened to the north, and we could kind of sit there and watch the morning grow rosy.

So that first year, the school was just a subordinate section of the elementary school. My principal, Mrs. Hardy, was the head. If

Mary and Ted Hayes, 29 Palms first high school teacher, taken in 1934, the year of their arrival. Photo courtesy of the Local History Collection, 29 Palms Branch Library.

you got a two room school and two teachers, then one of them has to be the principal. She was older than Mary Jane LaPointe, the other teacher. Mrs. Hardy didn't give me any problems, and I don't think I gave her any.

Then came the end of the year, and we thought everything was fine, and we went on vacation. On our way home, we stopped in Pasadena at the old family residence. There we received a letter which gave us a real traumatic experience. Ketcham had written two pages typewritten. On the first page he said how pleased they had been with my work, "but," he said, "I'm sorry to have to tell you that we can't hire you for next year."

Then we got to the second page of the letter, and he said that "the reason we can't hire you is because we've annexed ourselves to the Victor Valley Union High School District, so they will be hiring you for the next year." They also raised my salary to $1600 which was a big boost from $1200.

That first year I think the highest enrollment at any time was seventeen. Our classroom was in the Legion Cafe building. It had been a cafe building and they remodeled it enough to take care of us. It was just one big classroom plus a little porch where I had some wood working tools. Because it had been a restaurant, it had two toilets so we were okay on that score.

Weather was so mild in January 1937, that 29 Palms High School students moved their desks outside and held class there. Photo by and courtesy of Derald Martin.

MARY AND TED HAYES

The first year Amo Clark engineered a trip for the kids into Beverly Hills. We took one carload which was probably six girls. We took them to Amo's, and she arranged to sleep them at various places. The girls were going to spend the night with Caroline Dickinson, who had come out and spent an Easter with us and had fallen in love with the desert.

The first night the girls all went to Dickinsons'. We had a delicious dinner, served complete by a butler, and the kids were scared to death they'd drop their silverware, or that they wouldn't know which fork to use. Later they listened to ghost stories until they were scared to death and all keyed up.

Then the next day there was a big thing at the high school in Beverly Hills where they had a fair. They gave the girls tickets so that they could buy something if they wanted to and their lunch.

In the afternoon, Bill Clark and another lad took them all on a tour where the movie stars lived. Then they took them down to Santa Monica and showed them the pier and the ocean. Sunday morning we went to Amo Clark's for breakfast. She had a fancy breakfast for us. We had cantaloupe with strawberries in the middle and this was out of season. Most of these kids' parents were on relief and weren't buying cantaloupe.

The second year, after we annexed ourselves to Victorville, we hired another teacher, Miss Barbara Van Kirk. That's when we rented one of those little cottages out back of the Legion as a second classroom.

I don't remember very much about the third year, except that Miss Van Kirk was still here, and we had a comparatively uneventful season. They started to build a new school. Obviously, what we had was pretty substandard, so they built the first wing of the high school. It is now the intermediate school, and it was completed enough so that we could have our first graduation in 1937 with five graduates.

If you really wanted excitement on Saturday nights in the summertime, when it was too hot to have dances indoors, they had them on the tennis courts. It was too hot to sleep inside, and of course, there was no air conditioning. So we brought our bed outside and set it up near some creosote bushes.

With a dance every Saturday night, sometimes you didn't want to dance as late as they'd want to dance, so Mary and I would go home and go to bed. Our driveway was about four feet from our bed, and there was a road that went around the west side of the house. So when the dance was over, they'd all start tooting, honking, yelling, and off they'd go, as we'd lie there watching placidly from our bed.

Mary went in for groceries one Saturday morning shortly after we arrived, and Mrs. Bagley asked her, "Are you coming to the

PTA dance tonight?"

Mary said, "Well, if it doesn't matter. There will be late lights tonight, and I thought I'd take advantage of that to iron or set up things."

"Well," she said, "that's all right. It is sort of a reception for you and Mr. Hayes, the new high school teacher."

"Oh, of course, Mrs. Bagley. We'll come. I didn't know," Mary replied.

Then Helen said, "Now, dear, I would just give you this little warning: If anyone asks you to dance, please dance with him - unless you have to hold him up."

Well at the dances we had Bill Barnett on the piano. Later the pianist was Ruth Nichols. We also had a little later, Les Cross on the saxophone. Whether the dance was the PTA dance, which was one week, or the American Legion dance, which was next, it went right on throughout the year - the orchestra was the same and everything was the same except that whatever contribution you made went one way or the other.

Take-off of a P.T.A. meeting. Top row: Art Krushat, Johnnie Stephens, Burl Stonecipher. Bottom Row: possibly Barney Crawford, Ed Gilpin, Les Earnfight, Heine Olson. Photo by Bill Hatch, courtesy of the 29 Palms Historical Society.

330

MARY AND TED HAYES

We had a choral group of about thirty men and women who gathered once a week at the grammar school. Ruth Nichols was our accompanist, and she could play anything - any rhythm, any type music, without music, polkas, anything. There were the Stoneciphers, Wally and Muriel Trigg, Bob Saunders, Earl Carrol, Mildred Michels, and anyone else interested in music.

Mildred Michels was a clerk at Bagleys' from 8:00 to 6:00. She would go home and get supper. Her husband, George, wasn't one to drive her anywhere. So she said, "We live near enough to the high school that I can walk. This is the most wonderful thing that ever happened to me in my life to be able to go and sing."

Mary directed them. We met once a week for two years and then she had to stop because she was going to have Sally. It was fun because we made our own music and we sang good things. We sang for the Sunrise Service at the Oasis. Cap Williamson was the minister then, and we had a little Easter pageant.

Louie Jacobs was the Justice of the Peace the first year we were here. At one PTA dance, Louie Jacobs got up and announced that Jay Beagle, who was our local bootlegger, who had the place which later became the Blue Diamond down on the corner of Sullivan and Adobe Roads, was having a birthday party, and we were all invited and nothing would be sold.

Louie, quite normal to his tradition, was dressed in carpet slippers and a shirt that should have had a collar, but didn't. He wasn't exactly neat, but he was a friendly old guy. Anyway, I remarked to my sitting companion, "Where else in the world but in Twentynine Palms would you go to a PTA meeting and have a beer bust announced?"

She hardly said anything, but the next morning it was all over town that the Hayeses were bluenoses and didn't think much of drinking.

In 1936 it looked like things were going to work out all right for us. So we shopped around looking for a place to build a house. Frank Bagley helped and he showed me out near Chocolate Drop a homestead quarter section. It had a small two bedroom frame house. It wasn't too bad and was respectable. It had to be sold because it was part of an estate. We could have gotten that one hundred sixty acres and the house for $2500, but who had $2500?

Unfortunately, it had no water. We would have had to haul water. We could have somehow managed to borrow $2500, but to haul the water, we turned it down.

In those days for land down in the flats around Jack Cones' or down around what is now the Marine Corps base, ten dollars an acre was a good price to pay. Five dollars an acre was all right. Out in the hinterland, ten or fifteen miles away, you could get it for one dollar or two dollars an acre.

331

MARY AND TED HAYES

We didn't want to put up with homesteading, so we made a deal with Frank and bought five acres from him for two hundred and fifty bucks. He put in the pipelines and furnished water free for the first year.

Gerry Charlton had finished his adobe house, and we felt it was pretty good. Adobe was cheap, and I wasn't much of a carpenter. I figured I could lay brick. We hired the Kirbys - father and son. The old man made the bricks, and the young man, Jim, laid them for us at a fee. Jim found he wasn't making wages laying brick, so he got sick.

I had to take over when the walls were about two feet high or close to it. I hired Lem Parsons from the Pipes and Bob Saunders, a friend who now lives in Montana, to help me. We finished up the first part. The next year we put on the nursery because Sally was coming, and then we skipped a year. After that we put on the living room and garage. John Bagley and Stan Krushat helped me with that.

The Twentynine Palms Picnic, Marching, and Chowder Society began in late August of 1940 and lasted until about 1970. At the time of its demise, it was the oldest social organization in town except for the American Legion. It originated in Balboa Beach where

Picnics were always a popular past-time during the early days. Everyone brought food and drink for their family or to share with others. The Monument was always a popular gathering place for such gatherings. Ted Hayes is second from the right, tending the cooking fire. Photo courtesy of Jane Krushat.

the Flickingers had taken a house for the summer or part of the summer. We along with other people visited them from time to time, and we had a poker game one night.

Well, from that time on, we met every Thursday night from 7:30 to 11:30. We were very rigid in our schedule because we were all working and didn't want to go on and on. It was a very mild game.....ten cent limit. We played all sorts of things and had a good time.

We had a lot of good guys who played with us - at least for a time. I can't remember exactly who the original bunch was, but it probably was Bill Stubbs, Lish Stubbs, Frenchie Van Mater, Frank Bagley, Ray Flickinger, and I. From year to year the membership would change a little bit. We tried to keep it at six, although it might get down to five or up to seven. We never had more than seven. Harry Roberts, Gray Stubbs, Bill Beetler, Verne Roman, Maj Huber, and Sammy Metzger were others. When the men played, the women would go to another house and play Tripoli. They could lose as much as two bits a piece during the evening. This wasn't a wild group.

Picnics were a big thing and we had lots of them. One was memorable to me. It was a big picnic. There must have been fifteen cars with the Bagleys, Schencks, and various people. We went way out where the base is now to a place we called Chilly Bean Canyon. Mary's mother was with us, and she said, "I found a little snake." It was a sidewinder and it was crawling under a bush.

There were lots of picnics and sometimes there would only be three or four of us. Other times there would be a big group. The Schencks and the Hayes used to go just anywhere. Egbert would build a little fire inside three rocks, and he would take a little can and make coffee. It was a black can with a cloth covering so his hands wouldn't get dirty, and he would build a fire with about six sticks. Or we would take fruit, cheese, and a bottle of wine. We would have lots of fun and go to places I can't even remember.

When they named the high school auditorium, the Hayes Auditorium, in 1958, Ada Hatch called up and said, "I didn't know that Ted had died."

And Mary said, "Well, he hasn't. He's very much alive."

"But," she said, "they never name anything after anybody living."

Don Malone had designed the program, and it said the "Hayes Memorial Auditorium" on the program.

Mary and Ted Hayes, Pioneer Days, 1980. Photo by the author.

MAJOR HUBER

Major Huber was born in a suburb of Cincinnati, Ohio on January 19, 1914. Two years following the death of his father in 1927, the Huber family moved west to the Silverlake District in Los Angeles.

On his twenty-first birthday in 1935, Major ventured to Twentynine Palms to accept employment - such as it was. Never once did he realize that this quaint desert settlement would become his permanent home. His initial employment was found to be at a small rickety building known only as "Jay's Place." It was the settlement's only bar, and the second of only two small structures serving food.

Approximately eight months later, an opportunity presented itself for him to learn the plumbing trade at the town's first plumbing shop. The owner was Z.V. Pegram from Beaumont. The eventual opening of a new, presentable bar and restaurant by owners, Harry Burgner and Don Lawrence, soon led to Major's move to this establishment and an end to his plumbing career.

He met Helen Watson, a visitor from Altadena, who was staying at the Adobe Hotel from time to time. They were married in April 1938 in Yuma, Arizona. Major was then twenty-four and Helen was twenty-one. They soon purchased the Joshua Tree Inn, and before long changed the name to "The Joshua Tree." Through public usage, it eventually became known as the "Josh." Following the outbreak of war, they sold the Josh in June 1943, moved to Westwood, but returned in 1945.

With building construction now on a definite upswing in this area, Major's next venture was the construction of a sand and gravel screening plant east of town. Heavy truck crane excavations and rigging were later added.

During these years, in Major's opinion, Helen's accomplishments were, by far, the most rewarding in raising three fine children: a son, Bradley, and twin daughters, Nicole and Stephani.

Major retired in 1965, and Helen died in February 1981. Today Maj lives quietly in the same house that he and Helen had built in 1938 when they were first married. Since his relatively early retirement, the subsequent twenty-one years have been almost completely absorbed in specific scientific research. The resultant data is intended for publication in the near future.

*   *   *   *   *

Through the information of a friend, it was learned that a job opening was available in Twentynine Palms, California. With an apparent distaste for life in the big city of Los Angeles, the vision of open country separated by at least one hundred and fifty miles was most becoming. In addition, the offer of free room and board along with a fifty cent per hour wages was the deciding "carrot-on-a-stick."

Two days later on January 19, 1935, my twenty-first birthday, found this naive individual launched upon a new, unpredictable future. Each added mile, left behind, induced an increased sense of freedom. Not until the turn-off east of Whitewater did a feeling of elation further enhance my already contented frame of mind. The long, winding stretch of unpaved road ahead did, somehow, represent a symbol of untethered nature. Unfortunately, such euphoria soon gave way to one of rattling confusion. "Washboard" roads up to now, were a new experience.

In retrospect, I may never had made it to my destination had not the good fortune of a seasoned traveler in an old pick-up truck passed me at a good sixty miles per hour with apparent full control of his car. It all made sense. With ample speed one only rides over the high convexes with no time factor to allow dropping into the low concaves. My first lesson. Incidentally, the then ten miles of paved road between the main highway and Twentynine Palms was, thereafter, a thing of beauty.

It was evident that the town of Twentynine Palms was not far ahead when on my left stood what was then Donnell's Hotel and beyond that a structure high on a ridge, later found to be Clark's "Stardune." However, dropping over Donnell's Hill produced a panorama of quasi-desolation. Twentynine Palms, California? Near what is now the Four Corners there existed to my right, a new but empty rectangular building (late a part of the "Josh"). On my left stood a lone water tank tower. At the intersection, signs were posted. Pointing to the right were two signs indicating the existence of Benito's Groceries and gas and "Jay's Place." To the left were directions to Bagley's store and Smith's Ranch. In neither direction were signs of life. All was beautiful in its simplicity.

In pulling up to the front of Jay's Place in my dust-covered '29 DeSoto roadster, any existing signs of desolation were dissolved. Even before opening the door, I was greeted not only by my prospective boss, but also by the four customers there at the time.

Jay's Place was a rectangular building with a flat roof. The in-

336

terior consisted of two separate, partially divided rooms. The entrance side provided about twelve stools for the convenience of those at the lunch counter/bar. The other room sported lunch tables and chairs of conglomerate design and vintage. The back bar was designed of three saw horses supporting two - one inch by twelve inch pine boards. For cosmetic purposes, the pine boards were covered with clean white dish towels.

To the best of my recollection, a one and a half ounce shot of Old Quaker bourbon (aged four months) sold for fifteen cents. Wine and/or beer was likewise available for those preferring something less expensive.

Major Huber serving his wife, Helen, at their Josh Cafe about 1940. Photo by Ruth Schneider from the author's collection.

Serving food in such isolated areas posed a challenge, considering the fact that no electricity was available for efficient refrigeration. Fortunately, Ted Holderman's ice plant on the north end of town (now the Plaza) proved a blessing in allowing the use of ice boxes for food storage. In addition, a freezing section of the plant made possible the storage of additional stocked meat supplies. Jay did, however, in addition to an ice box, possess a kerosene operated refrigerator for limited storage of perishables. In all truth, Jay was an experienced fry cook - nothing fancy, but good. Although his homemade chili topped the list in popularity, other limited meat entrees were often available.

Jay Beagle, a man in his forties at that time, was a forceful individual, but I think trying to describe his personality would be rather like attempting to describe a kaleidoscope. He could be most jovial and friendly - but then again, most unpredictable with changing moods. Some people liked him, others didn't. He ran a "tight ship." When he spoke, those around him would sit up and listen.

Jay was lanky and walked with a slight stoop. In my opinion he was never in the military service as such was not mentioned in his conversations. For an unexplainable reason, a constant sense of cautious respect, on my part, discouraged any close familiarity between us. Nevertheless, he treated me well and that was all I asked.

His living quarters, a simple but nice appearing structure, stood a respectable distance behind his place of business. Whether he had ever married was never mentioned, but not too sparsely separated periods of visits by the fairer sex from out of town places was testimony to his doubtless inclinations in that department.

The clientele at Jay's consisted mainly of World War I veterans and their families, homesteaders, and gold prospectors. Here was a meeting place to see old friends and to swap stories, hackneyed and otherwise, in an aura of soft gaslight. The total absence of such a monstrosity as a propane operated juke box guaranteed an atmosphere of serene tranquillity.

Among the many interesting prospectors with their unscheduled visits to Jay's were names such as Jack Meek, Hughie Leonard, Dan Leahy, Mickey Thornton, Karl Schapel, Frank Sabathe, Phil Sullivan, and on more rare occasions, old Sam Joiner. He, I was told, operated the old bar at the Virginia Dale district, continuing to do so until visited by a Fed informing him of the long past passing of the Eighteenth Amendment. It may not be authentic.

Each prospector sported a unique personality. Most memorable to me, was old Hughie Leonard. He reminded me of the familiar caricature of an old Irishman in a high hat carrying a shillelagh. He wore a constant broad, sparsely, toothed smile, which of course,

338

affected his ability to close his lips. This in turn rendered it near impossible to understand the thick Irish dialect. Hughie was always accompanied by Dan Leahy, who according to the town's flourishing grapevine, was a nephew of Hughie's. Together, they apparently pinned their dreams on their mining claim rumored to be identified as "the Topnest."

There were very few prospectors who mined and sold their gold ore. Completing their necessary annual assessment work, stockpiling their best ore samples as show pieces for potential investors, and somehow managing to interest such investors to grubstake additional work. Such was their primary aim.

I yet recall Mickey Thornton's response to a curious tourist's inquiry as to why he chose the lonely life of a prospector. "Well Ma'am," he drawled, "it's the fascination of being either one foot from a million dollars, or a million feet from a dollar." Such, in general, was their perspective.

Not until a year or two later when Roosevelt doubled the gold values, did the real monied investors and their miners move into the area. The welfare of a few prospectors then improved - not, however, the majority.

When eventually summed up, though, I believe my personal choice would have been to accept the money put into the ground of the Virginia Dale area, rather than settling for that amount in gold removed.

In a small, distant town with poor radio reception and no television, rumors were the ultimate form of entertainment. Jay's Place received its share of merits as a source of such. In later years, interestingly enough, such related stories coming my way were from individuals who had never set foot in his establishment. To put things more in perspective, there were no abnormal problems at this, Jay's original location. I can't recall one incident of a brawl, and at my young age, such would have remained indelibly in my mind.

To augment this rumor factor, it is very possible that some stories could very well have originated following his move to its new location on the corner of South Adobe Road and Sullivan Road (previously Benito's grocery store). Having never entered this relocated bar, I can neither confirm or dispute that which occurred there. This corner location was later operated by a new owner and renamed "The Blue Diamond." No doubt Jay was credited, as well, for some savory tales from this source.

Twentynine's first plumbing shop opened in the building later operated as a restaurant known as "This Way Jose." My advancement to the second rung on the ladder of success presented itself here as a plumber's helper. The starting wage was fifty cents per hour plus living quarters. This meant forgoing the included free meal ticket offered by prior employment, but the promise of learning a relatively more constructive trade compensated for the sacrifice. Mr. Pegram, with a like business in Beaumont, California, furnished an experienced plumber at a much better wage. I was his work horse.

By this time in late 1935, development in town was on the rise due to active promotion of Ole Hansen's tract southeast of town. Adding to this was ongoing promotion of the Four Corners area by the Southwest Subdividers. Construction became quite active, including of course, the plumbing business.

With the passing of time, Mr. Pegram's experienced plumber's appearances dwindled and Z.V. was presenting me with the blue prints for new contracts. Being now chief plumber did raise my personal status, but somehow the weekly pay check reflected no such advancement. Adding salt to this wound, he saw no reason to furnish me with a helper, even though he now had the need for me to work from dawn to dusk.

Remaining a naive, trusting kid, I hopefully looked forward to an eventual raise in pay to no avail. Approximately one year of such blind trust terminated as employer and sucker. This dissolution precipitated when he at last handed me the now insulting paycheck with the bonus of an undeserved complaint. Without a word, I shredded the check, stuffed it down the front of his shirt, walked next door, and went to work at the Joshua Tree Inn." The spent year was not wasted nevertheless, having learned a trade and an unforgettable lesson in employer-employee relationships.

The original structure, later housing the Joshua Tree Inn, was built just prior to my arrival in the town. Carl Jensen, a resident builder, did the work. Its outstanding feature was two large back-to-back fireplaces, each serving one of the two adjoining rooms. Carl's beautiful rockwork can be seen to this day in the Hansen Tract, as his own small house was completely built in the same manner.

The Joshua Tree building was enlarged in preparation for its opening as the "Joshua Tree Inn." The owners were partners, namely Donald Lawrence and Harry Burgner. Both were from Bell, California where Mr. Lawrence already owned a bar and restaurant. Later, a fair-sized enclosed dance hall was adjoined to the south side of the existing structure. This dance hall was truly designed for desert climate, as its two elongated sides were constructed to open widely during the summer months and closed with the coming of winter. That this recreation room and banquet hall soon became widely known as "The Barn" was no misnomer.

Another building was built by Harry Burgner on the west side of the Joshua Tree serving dual purposes. One half of the building facing the highway served as living quarters for the Burgner

Helen Huber at a reception in the 1940's. Photo
by Bill Hatch, courtesy of Ada Hatch.

family: Harry, Louise, and their daughter, Patty. The other one
half of the structure became "Louise's Beauty Salon."

My period of employment at the Joshua Tree Inn
(approximately one and a half years), was relatively pleasant, although not uneventful. It was well managed by principally Harry
Burgner as Mr. Lawrence's business out of town allowed only in-
frequent visits.

By early 1938 both Don and Harry began considering selling
the bar and restaurant business. Following Helen's and my marriage in June 1938, a deal was made with Harry and Don, whereas
we became the new owners.

Soon following acquisition of the Joshua Tree Inn, the name
was reregistered as the "Joshua Tree." This discouraged prior long
distance calls for "Inn" room reservations. Other alterations in the
interior decor were made to eliminate prior plainness and thereby
enhancing an atmosphere paralleling that expected of a small business in a small desert town.

MAJOR HUBER

By mid-1938 real estate agents were transporting a good number of prospective buyers to town. Tourist travel had also increased due to the then completed paving of Twentynine Palms Highway.

Claude Creasy, a super chef, brought out by Don and Harry, remained in our employment. Customers from out of town would compliment him on his menu. He had been recommended by their friends who had been diners there at an earlier date. For a few years we served prepared lunches and dinners, including homemade soup, salad, and homemade pie for dessert. The Chamber of Commerce and Lion's Club also enjoyed their banquets and meetings in the "Barn." We had long collapsible tables and folding chairs for such occasions.

Dancing, with "local musical talent," was a Saturday night event. The walls were lined with regular tables in individual "stalls." From these walls also hung old pack saddles, horse collars, and other mining or desert paraphernalia easily found abandoned in those days. The 29 Palms Women's Club annual dance was a gala event, bringing in local residents rarely seen at other times.

In the bar business one becomes a good listener with a short memory. I was twenty-four when we bought the Josh. That's a little young to operate such a business, albeit there was no serious trouble from the miners. They were the nicest bunch of guys in the world - except once in a while, but such is normal. They were good people, and they were polite. Should one get out of line, all I had to do was open my mouth and that brought an apology. None of them wanted to estrange themselves with one of the few places they could go in town.

There were four slot machines at the Josh. They paid a lot of the overhead. After Condor Field was established, the "slots" went out. We were too busy to watch them. There were customers lined up three deep from the time I opened until closing time. Good help was at a premium which finally forced me to open at three P.M. By this time my chef, Claude, had moved on. With no time to be bothered with the kitchen, I gave it to a family to run providing they maintained my expected quality of food.

After the war broke out, we sold the Josh to Mr. Paylor who also had the PX at Condor Field. Business was booming, but we had to leave. There was no doctor in town, and one of our twins was not fairing too well. Added to the demise was the possibility that I might be drafted, really leaving Helen in a dilemma.

The Josh was sold in March '43, at which time we moved to Westwood, making it possible for me to commute to Firestone Rubber Company where employment was waiting. Two years in the city, and we were homesick for the old homestead. Firestone would not release me until after the surrender of Germany. Unable to predict the future, Helen with her mother and family moved back here before my release. I rejoined the family several months later in 1945.

The original Joshua Tree Inn on the corner of Twentynine Palms Highway and Cholla Avenue changed hands several times subsequent to Mr. Paylor acquiring the business. To the best of my wavering recollection, other owners of the property were a Mr. Groggins, Phil and Eunice Phillips, and finally Bill Watkins. The Watkins eventually moved the business to the Smoke Tree area, carrying with them the "Josh" name by renaming their new Smoke Tree location the "Josh Lounge."

The infamous Thornton/Burton incident occurred in the Smoke Tree area while Helen and I yet owned the old "Josh." This final bit of information related to the "Josh" has here been injected for a good reason. It sets straight another example of misleading rumors indigenous to any small settlement.

On my return I had decided that five years working at the Josh and two years of office work at Firestone meant time for outside work and the exercise that went with it. This brought about the construction of a sand and gravel screening plant east of town on a ten acre tract of land. From this developed an accumulation of excavation equipment which operated in the town and outlying districts consuming the next seventeen years.

By this time, long past involvement in a specific research in the field of science, reached time demanding proportions requiring abandonment of all other business ventures.

Any inaccuracies herein, based on recall, are truly regrettable. No apologies will be forthcoming, however, for diverse and sundry items judged best deleted.

MARGARET KENNEDY

Margaret Kennedy came to Twentynine Palms in February 1936 expecting to spend a few months vacation. For several years, she had been legal secretary to David R. Faries, a Los Angeles attorney, who was a member of the Twentynine Palms Corporation. This had been formed in 1929 with the purchase of 480 acres of land including the Twentynine Palms Inn and Oasis.

When plans were made to subdivide part of the property, Margaret Kennedy began working on a subdivision map. She also acted as Chamber of Commerce secretary until July 1937 when she returned to Los Angeles and worked (until 1941) for a law firm specializing in motion pictures. In the intervening years she made return visits here.

During World War II she worked in the photographic section of a defense plant, and then was in the WAC's from November 1943 to August 1945. Later she served as secretary to the recording director for MGM from April 1946 to October 1952. In 1950 she returned to Twentynine Palms for weekend visits and began building a home here.

After the Marine Corps Base opened, she served as supervisor of civilian personnel from 1954 to 1961 when she took office as Postmaster of Twentynine Palms on September 29, 1961. She served until December 30, 1965, when she retired. The present post office building was planned during her administration.

Margaret Kennedy, who now lives in retirement in Riverside, has returned to Twentynine Palms on several occasions to visit her many friends here.

*   *   *   *   *

Originally when they moved the Gold Park Hotel down here, they had a bath house that was approximately south of the main buildings with one side for men and one for women. I believe the foundation is still where there is a shuffleboard court or something.

Of the old wooden frame buildings, only about three remain. All the wooden buildings were around a swampy area where there was quick sand. Everything else is adobe....adobe blocks which the Stubbs brothers made right here. The Stubbs came out from Chicago, stopped in Santa Fe, New Mexico enroute, and became fascinated with adobe construction. So when they came out, they got the idea that it would do well in Twentynine Palms.

When David Faries and Harry Johansing bought this Oasis property from Roberts in 1929, he paid him fifty thousand dollars for it, and I believe it was four hundred and eighty acres. There were forty acres on Amboy Road, and then, in addition, there is what we now call Shadow Mountain up here. There were forty or eighty acres in there, but it was two long pieces.

Then I think the market broke. A man named Kingston had put a little money into it, and Fitzgerald was the engineer. He had no money to put in, but he engineered the whole thing. So he got stock for the work he did. There was another man whose name I don't remember.

I first came here in 1936 for a visit. When I first went into the real estate business, I found we were not entitled to sell the property, for there was no subdivision. So I went into Los Angeles and worked with Mr. Fitzgerald all summer until we drew up the subdivision. Then in the fall I came back to sell.

Johansing built a house right on the north side of Cottonwood, which is still there. He wanted to have everything insect proof. He couldn't stand things that crawled. Rogers bought the lot across on Cottonwood, but as I recall, he did not build. In the first place, all of this area was kind of swampy.

Johansing was unwilling to put any more money in, so he and Faries split the property. Mr. Faries took the real estate, and Mr. Johansing took the Inn property. And it was Mr. Johansing who gave the Oasis property to the National Monument.

Miss Brock was given a lease on the Inn. She never paid anything for it. She kept any money she got, because there wasn't much money in those days. You paid six dollars for a room and board a day or seventy-five dollars a month. Mr. Faries and Mr. Johansing wanted someone living in the Inn, to talk to people, and to try and sell them property, because this was the way it was done in those days. Miss Brock would have no part of this. She was going to run the Inn the way she wanted it run.

So I came down here in 1936....maybe around the first of January and stayed until July 1937. When I lived at the Inn, I paid $75 a month for my room and board. That was three meals a day.

Miss Brock was a pretty good cook. At least she had to be prepared to cook, but we had some nice little old lady who would do the cooking. It was good country cooking. For breakfast there would be bacon and eggs. They'd say, "Today we're having hot-cakes...or today we're having bacon and eggs, or today we're having ham or waffles." All were served family style.

Bill Hatch took care of the Delco lighting system and got his meals for this. We might be sitting or eating dinner, and the lights would go out. Everybody would run and get lamps. We'd just get them on the tables, light them, and the electricity would come on again. This might happen a couple of times during dinner.

I gave Bill Hatch a picture of me with our dog who looked like a Labrador retriever. This dog just worshiped Bill, and when Miss Brock finally left the Inn, she gave the dog to Bill.

During the Depression Charles E. "Chuck" Kilbourne came out here because he could get room and board, and I think, maybe about fifty dollars a month is what Miss Brock paid him. The young men made the beds, swept out the places, and mopped them. They came in and lighted our heaters in the morning on cold days. Then you could get up to a warm room. We did have wash basins, but no toilets....and just cold water. The only inside plumbing was the first two buildings.

At first there was only one phone here. There was a phone booth in the Inn lobby. People would come in at night to phone, and we took telegrams and other messages on it. Sometimes the conversations were terrific, as the booth had no top. We were all there with our knitting or whatever, but actually having the time of our lives while people carried on confidential conversations.

Once we got a call asking how much to send a message out to the Gold Crown Mine. "Five dollars," Miss Brock told them, and we waited around for the message to come through. Miss Brock told whoever was there to take the call, to take it out to the mine, and they could keep the money. After three or four days, it still had not come, so I guess they used the mails rather than pay five dollars. If Miss Brock couldn't deliver telegram messages, then anyone who answered the phone would take it and ask for the delivery fee.

We had picnics all the time, and sometimes Sunday morning cookout breakfasts. We would go up Utah Trail, mostly to the first draw to the west where you could drive by auto or ride horseback. It's the big draw back of Imogene Aaron's. (On the west side of Utah Trail - now part of Joshua Tree National Monument.) This would be in winter, but it was a nice warm place. Sometimes we would go all the way to Split Rock.

For these picnics Miss Brock did something I had never seen done before. She had a great big gallon jar into which she would break eggs and slide them. In a great big frying pan she'd fry a lot of bacon, then just dump this jar of eggs into the pan, and they would all separate. She would make biscuits ahead of time and put them in a pot. After the fire was built, the pot would be put down beside the fire, and those biscuits would be piping hot when we were ready to eat.

The 29 Palms Inn where Margaret Kennedy first stayed when she came to 29 Palms in 1936. Photo by Bill Hatch, courtesy of the 29 Palms Historical Society.

Other times we would take a whole big pot of stew up to Bill McHaney's property. We would sit near his little cabin out of the wind, make a fire, and have hot stew and biscuits.

Among noted people who came to the Inn was a world famous ornithologist, Laidlaw Williams of Carmel. One morning we were sitting there eating breakfast and he was facing the Oasis. He had just ordered bacon and eggs or something, and it was being put on the table, when he jumped up and went out. He had seen a blue grosbeak and had never seen one before in this area. He never came back for his breakfast.

It was in the middle of the winter when Bill McHaney died (January 1937). On Bagley's bulletin board where we got our news in those days, we found "Funeral will be at two o'clock tomorrow afternoon." So I talked with Lee Watson whose station wagon was parked at Bagley's. They were bringing the coffin down from Keys Ranch in Dick Rutherford's laundry van.

I was dressed in black with hat and gloves for a proper appearance. There was Burl Stonecipher, who was a preacher, and some woman. They were arguing as to who was going to conduct the services. It wasn't determined that day, because word came through they couldn't get down because of the snow, and the funeral would be the next day.

So the next day I put on my riding clothes and a couple of sweaters and coat...anything I had around. I'd told Lee I'd meet him out at the cemetery. When we went out, Burl had won out, and we nearly froze to death waiting. Finally they brought the body down.

I have never seen more beautiful sheaves made out of palm fronds and perhaps pine cones. Here was poor old McHaney who had never been in church in his life, I guess, and they were going to see that he had a Christian burial.

They had the Bible, and it was a terribly windy day. Oh, it was bitter cold! And poor old Stonecipher would be reading, and the page would flip over, and he'd have to go back. It was just terrible. Lee and I had all we could do to keep from laughing or to keep a straight face.

Margaret Kennedy and early homesteader, Alma Steeg, at the Underhill's "Old-Timers' Get-Together," Pioneer Days, October 1977. Photo by the author.

ADA WATKINS HATCH

Ada Elizabeth Watkins was born in Los Angeles, California in 1909 to Walter and Hortense Pattee Watkins. After her parents' divorce, she and her mother moved to Claremont where she attended high school. When Scripps College was formed in 1928, applications were solicited, to be followed by personal interviews. Ada was the first person accepted and was part of the first graduating class of fifty in 1931.

While she was at Scripps, a classmate, Eunice Hatch, introduced her to her brother, Bill. Five years later after having completed a Master's Degree in Child Development and Parent Education at Columbia University, Ada returned to Scripps for her class' fifth reunion. She once again saw Bill Hatch. The following year on January 27th, 1936, they were married at her mother's home in Glen Ridge, New Jersey.

She and Bill returned to his home in Twentynine Palms and together they became an integral part of the growing young community, active in numerous community projects and organizations until his death in 1975.

Ada's continuing interest in education resulted in her helping to establish the Little School of the Desert preschool, and to become a co-founder of the Friends of Copper Mountain College, which culminated in the establishment of a junior college campus in our area. Her continuing interest and generosity to this community in all her endeavors have endeared her forever to a multitude of friends.

*   *   *   *   *

Bill Hatch's first trip to the desert was in 1930. He had just graduated from Cal Tech and had a job with Fairchild for aerial photography. But of course, that was canceled with the Depression. Since he didn't have anything special to do, he drove out here in his Model A Ford and went to the Twentynine Palms Inn.

Miss Brock was the hostess for the Inn at that time. Others living there were Les Earenfight and Nona, whom he later married, Gerry Charleton, Tom Hopkins, and the Stubbs brothers: Bill,

349

Gray, and Lish.

The first night there was no electricity because the light plant had gone off. So Grace Brock asked if Bill could fix it. He said he would and drove into Banning the next day to get parts. When he returned, he fixed it, and Grace offered Bill a job if he wanted to stay on and run the pump.

About the third day an old Model T Ford bounced up over the road and came to the Inn. The driver said he had heard by the grapevine that a surveyor was there and was that true?

So they called Bill, and the man explained that one of the first citizens had just died, and someone had given sixty acres for a cemetery. If Bill could find it, they could bury him. It was Hassell Donnell who had died.

So Bill went out and found the cemetery. He had his surveying instruments, and that was his first survey job. From then on, people would come and ask him to survey their homesteads which were one hundred and sixty acres.

It was amazing how many people had homesteaded, and yet built on someone else's land, especially in Morongo Valley. Jeff Overbay had Bill survey his homestead, and then discovered that he and his neighbor had both built on each other's land; yet they each had one hundred and sixty acres apiece. They settled the dispute by deeding each other their houses.

Young Bill Hatch came to the desert in 1930 after his graduation from Cal Tech in Pasadena. He came looking for a place to improve his health and lived at the 29 Palms Inn. In November 1932 he completed his homestead house and made this his permanent home for the remainder of his life. Photo from the author's collection.

Then Bill decided to come out here and live. He was going to homestead near Les Earenfight's homestead, but then he found a hundred and sixty acre parcel that was right next to Johnny Stephens on Two Mile Road east of Adobe. Someone else had filed on it but had not claimed up.

Well, Bill waited until midnight the night the claim went off that land, and then drove all the way in to the land office in Glendale to file his claim.

When the office opened at eight in the morning, he was there, and he filed on that hundred and sixty acres. As he came out of the door of the land office, he met Gordon Bains who had come in to file on the same piece of land.

In order to homestead, Bill had to have a cabin on his property. He bought one of the Olympic cabins left over from the World Olympic games held in Los Angeles in 1932. The cabins were sold off for desert and mountain use, and folded up for transport. They consisted of two rooms with a bathroom in between.

There is a picture in some magazine we have of that Olympic Village being taken down, and it shows Cliff Blake loading Bill's cabin onto his truck to bring it out here. They drove it all the way out and put it up on the hill. Bill lived there to homestead. That was in November of 1932.

Bill also acquired some property later to be known as the "30th Palm." It was owned by Gordon Bains who had bought it from the Michels I believe, and he had built the house, the well, and some sheds. Suddenly Bains decided to go back to New Zealand, so he wanted to sell his property, which was five acres.

Anyway Bains sold the well, the house, and the light plant, which in those days was very important, for one thousand dollars. And Bill bought it. Mother and Father Hatch came out and stayed there. While they were there, he had Walt Berg come and start building the fireplace out of natural rock. Walt was living right next door at that time.

I first visited Twentynine Palms in 1936. That summer I had come from the East to attend my fifth reunion at Scripps College in Claremont. I came with a friend, Marian Broderson from Glen Ridge, New Jersey, and we had taken a house at Balboa for the month of July. Bill's sister, Eunice, was one of my great friends at Scripps, and it was through her that I had met Bill.

Bill asked if Brodie (Marian Broderson) and I would like to come out to see his desert cabin. Brodie and I said, "Yes, we'd love to," and we went out and bought pith helmets. We must have looked awful, but we just thought it was marvelous, as the temperature got higher and higher. It was 112 degrees at Whitewater. Oh, that was great!

He didn't tell us about the road, and we had come across the

Whitewater bridge and then straight up that mountain. It was just two ruts and dirt, of course.....no pavement all the way to Twentynine Palms.

Brodie and I stayed at the 30th Palm, and Bill stayed at his homestead. Someone said Grace Brock had her binoculars trained on the homestead to see whether or not his car was there. Bill Hatch had two women coming out to see him, and the whole town was talking.

Then we went and ate at Graham's Cafe which was at the Plaza. I can remember that Hilda came over and sat down with us and said, "Guess what? Sally has just eloped with Lish Stubbs." Sally had been her waitress and oh.....everybody was buzzing about that.

At that time Bagley's store was in the old Radio Doc building, and they had just finished building Tom Martin's garage. Bagley had plans for his store which he built the next year, I believe.

Brodie and I decided to give a party for all the people whom we had met. We got these big slabs of mud left over from a flash flood, like stepping stones, and we wrote our invitations on these slabs. It was quite a poem. It started out:

"The two Jersey mavericks invite you to dine,
But don't think it's fancy with caviar and wine...."

It went on. We delivered these to all the different houses, very carefully so they wouldn't break. And then we had our party.

We had no liquor or anything, because we couldn't afford it. All I knew about cooking was to have hot things hot and cold things cold. This was our first party at the 30th Palm. We had a wonderful soup....all from scratch, of course.

Before the party I had planned every fifteen minutes. For instance....from 4:30 to 4:45 I was going to take my shower and get dressed. Brodie would bathe and get dressed after that.

Well at 3 o'clock the first guests arrived to take their showers. We had the only bathtub in town and were known as "the bathtub set." As the guests arrived, they waited their turn to take a bath, and I never did get mine! Ted and Mary Hayes were the only couple that could bathe together, because one could take a bath while the other took a shower! It was really something else.

Brodie and I stayed here in Twentynine Palms about a week on that first visit. We had a lot of fun. When we left, I hung my safari hat on a peg and that was the first hint Mary Hayes had that I might return. As it turned out, I became engaged to Bill Hatch that week and did definitely plan to return and make my home in Twentynine Palms.

Then Bill drove Brodie, me, and Ted and Mary Hayes up to San Francisco. We were heading back home to Glen Ridge, New Jersey. We sailed from San Francisco to Vancouver, then took the train east.

ADA WATKINS HATCH

When I became engaged, I wired Mother and Dad to tell them the news. They were staying in Maine that summer. The telegram I sent arrived early in the morning, waking them up. I said in the telegram that I had become engaged to Bill Hatch and went on to say, "Will live in the desert. Hatches think it fine." This referred to Mother and Father Hatch whom my parents knew quite well.

When the telegram arrived, it read, "Will live in desert hatches. Think it fine."

Dad said, "Well, of course she thinks it's fine, but what in heck are desert hatches?"

As was the custom, I sent out little formal announcements with our two names on them, the way it was done in the East. But I guess it really threw Bill Underhill. He came to Bill and said, "What's this....your name and some woman's on a card?"

Bill explained what it was, so in the DESERT TRAIL it said, "Neat white envelopes, postmarked Glen Ridge, New Jersey, appeared among friends this week announcing the engagement of local surveyor, Bill Hatch to a Miss Ada Watkins." Then it said, "Bill Hatch admits succumbing to Cupid's darts."

When I became engaged here in the desert, it had been 118 degrees, so I returned to New Jersey and immediately had a trousseau of sun suits made. We were married in Glen Ridge in January 1937, and for our honeymoon, we sailed south through the Panama Canal to Los Angeles.

It was the coldest winter California had, and when we arrived in Twentynine Palms, it was 8 degrees above zero! As you can imagine, I wore all my trousseau in one day and wired home to request my ski suit.

Upon our arrival at my new home, the 30th Palm, we discovered that the light plant was cracked, and therefore we had to use kerosene lamps. Of course, I had never in my life used a lamp before, and I had to write to my grandmother, "How do you clean a lamp?" It was bitter cold that winter, and all the water pipes froze.

At that time "Pa", Alan Batch, was living up in the tower room of our tank house at the 30th Palm. He was an architect and was designing buildings. He was building a house for Johnny and Virginia Stephens. That year he also built the Casa do los Tejidos (the House of Weaving) on part of Stephens' homestead, which later became Bill's office.

About a week after we arrived, Bill came home and said, "We've been invited out for dinner tonight."

I said, "Oh....fun..where?"

"Well, I don't remember."

"What do you mean, you don't remember? You've got to remember these things."

"Oh, don't worry about it. I'll see you later. I'm going off on a survey."

So he tore off, and I said, "What time is it to be?"

"Well, I don't know....sometime around six."

Time meant nothing to anyone out here, and that was one of my greatest adjustments to Bill Hatch, because I had been brought up to be not only on time, but ahead of time. Bill could care less. If you didn't get to a party, it was because something had happened to your car. You didn't bother to let people know. You couldn't.

By the time Bill came home from his survey, I was fuming. He said, "Just sit down and relax. Sit out on the front porch."

"How can you just sit out on the front porch when this party is probably for us, and we've got to at least know where it is?"

"Well," he said, "just sit down a minute."

So we sat down, and pretty soon we saw a cloud of dust, and the Schencks came down off their hill. Then Bill said, "Now if you'll just follow their car....where the clouds of dust stop, that's where the party is."

Sure enough, the dust stopped up at Virginia and Johnny Stephens', and that's where the party was. Bill had to start remembering things better when they paved the roads.

The first dance out here was held at Norm and Kay Bremer's. Theirs was a beautiful hand-built adobe house. They worked long and hard on it, and it was the biggest place in town. So we had a dance there - a spring dance.

Heavy summer rains were more of a problem in the old days before the construction of the flood control channel through town. In 1938 Ada Hatch knew a lot about the dangers of desert storms just two years after her marriage to Bill Hatch. Here she checks driving conditions on 29 Palms Highway in the Smoketree area near the present K-B Mart in Smoketree. Photo by Bill Hatch, courtesy of Ada Hatch.

ADA WATKINS HATCH

I remember going and dancing with this man. I had met him before but didn't get his name. I asked him if he lived out here, and if he had any children. He said he had five children. After the dance, I went over and sat next to this beautiful dark-haired girl, and I asked her if she had any children. "Yes," she said. She had five.

Meanwhile someone had greeted me in Bagley's store and said, "I saw five storks flying over your house, Ada!"

I thought, "Well, we'll go out and shoot a couple of them."

Anyway, it turned out that the two at the dance were Ray and Bess Flickinger, and they had come out to visit Ray's cousin, Amo Clark, who was building Stardune at that time. Then later, they came out to live here with their five children.

The Bremers had finished their home at that time. After the Bremers, the Schutses bought it and lived there. They subdivided that 160 acres which is now Harmony Acres.

Bill did a lot of the early road work out here. I helped him survey Lear Road. In those days it was hard to get a crew, so he taught me how to run the gun or transit. I couldn't read it, but I could find him in it and wave whether he was on line or not. Usually Ketch would help us or Les Earenfight.

But this was a case of just finding corners, so Bill and I went out to Lear Road which was just dirt. He left me with the gun and said that in about five minutes to give him the signal, as to whether or not he was on line. So two hours went by and nothing. I couldn't find him at all. He'd taught me all the signals except, "I can't find you!"

It turned out later that he had had a flat tire on his Model A and had stopped to change it. Well, finally he swam into range, and I was able to signal to him. He had set the transit on line, and all I had to do was give him signals for right, left, and ok.

Later we surveyed for Frank Rogers who had a whole section down in Yucca Valley. My brother, Wad Watkins, was here with us that summer; so he helped us. Both of Frank's legs, I believe, were off, and he had two wooden legs. I know the first time I met him, we were out some place, and there was a snake, a rattler.

"I'm not afraid of rattlers," he said, and put his foot down and the darn snake bit him all over the leg. Well, he just laughed. I was just horrified. Of course, it was a wooden leg and made no difference.

The military base in Twentynine Palms was first a glider school, and Bill was the engineer for the base during the war. He suggested to the military that they not build on the dry lake (where the Marine Corps Base is presently located), because you could see how the wind blew all the sand right up against the mountains. He recommended that they build the main buildings in the area now called "Ocotillo Heights", but they paid no attention to his suggestion and went right ahead and built on the dry lake.

Most of Bill's surveys were done while Howard Way was the County Surveyor. He was a dear friend and used to make many trips out here with other members of the Board of Supervisors.

In those days our children helped paint the wooden marker stakes, and then I often helped Bill put them in on the different corners. In one subdivision he named the streets Bagley Drive and Howard Way, after the County Surveyor.

Since then, of course, you can't name any streets after anyone who is still living. But when people would do subdivisions, they'd have different names that they wanted for their streets. Up in the Hansen tract, they had Morning Star, Evening Star, Sunrise, Sunset, Twilight, Araby, etc. Bill would often try to suggest different names for people, but a lot of them liked to use names in their families.

In one subdivision near Chocolate Drop, they asked Bill if he would name the streets for them, so he started by naming them alphabetically from east to west and using flower names from the desert: Abronia, Baileya, Chia, Daisy, and Encelia. I guess that's as far as the subdivision went. But he had hoped that all the names could be desert ones.

My mother and father's first trip out here was by train, and they got off at Amboy. They were coming out when Ada was about to be born - their first grandchild. In those days Amboy was a flag stop. Mother was in her furs, hat, and gloves coming from New Jersey, and Father was in his spats, derby, and cane.

The train stopped in Amboy and, of course, there was nothing there.....absolutely nothing. They had to catch Mother as she came off the back end of the car because there was no platform. Egbert and Sara Schenck had gone over to meet them because I couldn't ride. They drove their open yellow Ford.

Well, here were Mother and Father out in the middle of nowhere, and they got into this yellow car and started back to Twentynine Palms. It was all dirt road, of course.

About the middle of Bristol Dry Lake, Sara said, "How about a picnic?"

Mother said, "A picnic?"

Her idea of a picnic was on the way to Princeton by a stream with lovely fall colors and egg baskets with chicken wrapped individually and potato salad and all that sort of thing. So she asked again, "What do you mean, a picnic?"

"Well, sure.....let's eat right here."

The Schencks had gone all out that day. They'd taken a cloth to put down on the ground on the solid dry lake. They had a loaf of bread, avocado, and a raw onion. You quickly took the bread out and put everything on it, and that was a picnic....Schenck style! She made a tiny little fire with the old coffee pot on it. I'll never forget that Schenck coffee pot. It had its own carrying case.

So Father and Mother finally came and got to the house. That day I had caught one of these tremendous beetles, and Mother took one look at that, and when I went in the next morning, their shoes were still on the dresser.

Father went completely western. He bought a ten gallon hat with a horsehair band, a cowboy shirt, and boots, and he used to sit on Bagley's store front porch. That was the meeting place. He just loved it, and everybody that came up to Bagley's was greeted with, "Howdy, stranger. My name's Thompson. I'm Ada Hatch's father."

More people knew my dad than ever knew me. He greeted everyone. He loved it out here. He and Mother would come out to visit us several times a year. Then they moved to Claremont, California, from New Jersey, so we saw more of them.

Mother wrote after I'd been here two years, "You realize you have been in your new house two years, and it's time to change your wallpaper and drapes."

Well, I had no drapes at all, and nobody ever heard of wallpaper. But she finally got used to the idea of my living out here.

For me, life in the desert was lots of fun, but I had to learn a lot too. I learned how to spit nails and hit them before they fell down. I learned that from when I did the roof on the garage.

Jack Cones was the Constable and had his little airplane down at his airport. One day he came to Bill's office and said, "Guess what? There was a road stolen last night."

Bill said, "What do you mean?"

Well, it seems that in those days, the desert mix came out from the county. There was a whole row of it down near our place to be used for paving the road, and when the county workmen came out Monday morning, it had disappeared. Somebody had stolen it.

So Jack got in his plane and went zooming up flying low over the desert. Out near the dry lake, he saw this little guy making a nice smooth asphalt road. So he landed his plane and arrested him for stealing a road. Jack couldn't take it back, but the guy had to pay the County.

In 1941, the year of the War, Ada was born. Sunday was the attack on Pearl Harbor. Monday night they declared a blackout, and the Lion's Club was meeting down at the Josh Lounge.

Leonard Wikoff, when he heard about the blackout, just pulled the main switch on his generator, and the town went black. The Lion's Club didn't know about this, so they all went out and turned on the lights from their cars, so they could continue with their

ADA WATKINS HATCH

Ada Hatch with her daughter, Ada, and mother-in-law, Eunice Morton Hatch, in 1942 in Altadena. Photo by Bill Hatch, courtesy of Ada Hatch.

magic show. If there had been any bombing, it would have been a perfect target. We all had black windows and everything.

Then we had the watchers. In fact, Bill's homestead was used for civilian watching for enemy airplanes. I had the four to six watch in the morning. All during the war, we had to watch for planes, and Sara Schenck, of course, had silhouettes of all the different makes. You had to report, if you saw a plane go over whether it was a P-38 - that's the only one I remember. But I always hated that watch, because I could never tell one plane from another.

Finally Ray Flickinger said, "Look, don't worry. If a plane comes over with a blazing sun saying 'Japan' underneath, then for heaven's sake, call, but don't worry about anything else."

There were twenty-four hour watches up by Jumbo Rocks. In fact, one of the professors at Scripps was head of all this watching business, and they made a trial run with a plane, flying low over the Monument. By George, it got by. They immediately had people start watching lower.

Bill Hatch diverting flood waters away from the family's 30th Palm home on Utah Trail, early 1940's. Photo by Ada Hatch, from the author's collection.

The Hatch family about 1946: Young Ada, Liz, Ada Sr., and Bill.

Just before the war, Bill did a survey for two Japanese men who came out, and they always wanted to buy a mine. It was Phil Sullivan's mine. He was always selling that mine. Bill did the survey and said, "Now, what names shall I put on them?"

Well, they didn't want their names put on them, and it turned out that they were editors of a Japanese newspaper in Los Angeles. They paid Bill in cash. I can remember that. They didn't want any transaction tracing of it at all.

Then the day of Pearl Harbor, Jack Cones went out and picked them up out there. It was thought they were going to make a small landing field for the planes to refuel, because they later found planes in submarines in the Gulf of California.

Bill and I also went out to Giant Rock once when Critzer was there. We watched him making roads which was very interesting. He had roads going in there from all over, and he made them all himself. He made them by dragging pipes behind his car through the brush and all.

We once had a picnic at his place with the Schencks, I believe. Later he was being investigated. I think he had his place wired and blew himself up. There was a big fuss about him being a German spy, but I doubted that.

At one time there was a great deal of animosity between Four Corners merchants and Plaza merchants especially when they were trying to put the main highway through. Oh, people were just really fighting over that situation.

Bill did a survey for Mr. Perkins of the Dolores Motel, and when Bill wrote up his description of the survey he said, "This is located in a wash, and I would not recommend it be built on."

Perkins said, "That's typical of Hatch, because he's Plaza and against any progress at Four Corners."

And yet Perkins was the one who was screaming so when he had the flash flood all through his place. The river cut right through, and that's why Bill didn't want Perkins to come back and say, "Why didn't you tell me there was a flood channel there?" That's why he brought it up.

Then there was the big feud to either pave Amboy Road or the road to Rice. That was ridiculous. Everyone thought the road to Rice was just stupid, because it was terrible terrain to go through, and what was at Rice? Nothing. So we were always fighting for the road to Amboy, because that was the main highway - Route 66 in those days.

Betty Campbell had decided one day to have the Women's Club come to her house for a meeting, because one of her friends, who was head of the Audubon Society in New York was coming out to visit her. She thought this was a cultural deal, and we all should benefit from it. So she invited the Women's Club, and we hunted for hats, gloves, and everything.

To go to Betty Campbell's was really something, because she was "the queen." As you went in the gate, you had to show your membership card in the Women's Club. On the table outside were "No Smoking" signs on every table. Across the stairway was a chain with "No Trespassing" on it.

So we went in and all sat down. The head of the Audubon was really a great guy and played all these different bird songs. One of them he said, "I want you to guess this one, and I want just Mrs. Campbell to guess it." And he played the cuckoo, which we all thought was great.

In the midst of this the phone rang. Well, Betty had one of the few phones in town, and the phone was up on the mezzanine. So Betty, who was quite deaf, went tromping out, and you could hear her step over the "No Trespassing" sign, and up she goes to the phone.

"Hello....," and everyone stopped listening to the birds to hear what the bees were saying. "Is that right? Oh, I'll get Mr. Ketchum immediately."

So she came down the stairs and over the sign and dashed in. Ketch was sitting there. He was known as the Lone Ranger for a time.

Betty said, "Ketch, you're wanted on the phone."

So he dashed to the phone, then a few minutes later came down grabbing his hat. He said, "Worth Bagley's been shot and killed, and I'm on my way up to Keys' Ranch."

Well, of course, you can imagine how listening to birds interested us. We couldn't wait to get out of there and go find out what had happened. Later Keys came down and gave himself up to Judge Poste.

In 1944 I was about to have another baby, and there were no doctors out here at all. When my mother wrote and seemed quite concerned, Bill wrote back and said to her, "Mother, don't worry about Ada, because there's a well driller out here who's delivered all his own children, and so in case anything happens, he's around." Needless to say, that did not comfort my poor mother.

Because of the war, we were limited to how much gasoline we could get. I was able to get enough gas rationing tickets to go to Pasadena to have my first daughter, Ada in 1941, and also later in 1944 when Liz was born.

People would say, "How come you get to go to town so often and get all that gas?"

So I said, "Well, it's easy. Just get pregnant." A lot of them didn't want that much gas!

I remember one trip when we were asked to go with Bill and Betty Campbell to do a survey. They had found evidence of early man on different lake levels up at Owens Dry Lake. So we went up and stayed at Olancha, a tiny town, and there was a little motel there where we stayed.

We had our station wagon and the stadia rod, which is used to determine differences in elevation. Betty would go along and pick up these beautiful points. She would never let me touch one of them, because she had every one labeled according to the different beach levels where they were found.

There was a tiny restaurant near the motel where we stayed, and we went in one morning and had our breakfast. The second morning when we went in, Betty said to the waitress, "I don't care for your orange juice. Here are our oranges. Will you please squeeze them?" So they squeezed them.

Then the third morning, she said, "I don't care for your bread. I have brought my own. Will you please toast it?"

The fourth morning, she told us about how she had "roughed it" out here in the early days. She drank water out of wells with dead coyotes in them, etc. etc. And with that she'd say to the waitress, "I said CRISP bacon. Please take that back and make it CRISP!"

At that time I wondered why the waitresses were so nice, gentle, and friendly. Then I saw the tip that Bill Campbell left them every day.

Then one day, we were surveying and a horrible wind came up. There was sand everywhere, and I wondered how we could go on. I asked if we could stop.

Betty said, "No, we're going to have lunch right here. So, Bill, dig a hole in the sand, and we'll make a fire and have some hot cocoa."

So we dug a hole, made a little fire, with sand just blowing everywhere. Well, she made her cocoa and handed each of us a glass. Of course, it was scum and sand the minute you got it. You had to lift up a little layer of sand and then drink it real fast! We were their employees for ten days. And ten days was all I could take of saying, "yes!"

Bill Campbell was a great Legionnaire, of course. I think he liked getting away to meetings. All Pasadena Legionnaires had a big meeting out here once, and Bill had invited them all over for breakfast. Betty stood at the gate and smelled each one, as they came in. And if they'd been drinking, they didn't get in for breakfast.

Later on, she told about how she had some medicinal whiskey in case of a snakebite, but she had buried it by one of the posts when they put her wall in. Allie Wrubel, who later owned her house, dug through every one of them and hadn't found it.

The Campbell's house was beautifully built. They had tongue and groove floors. It's just like their house in Pennsylvania. She duplicated it every place she went. In fact, she took kegs of nails with her everywhere she went, and after she died, I think they finally sold those kegs. She never did use them.

Betty was a large woman. She had lost several children, and was a very maternal type. She should have had a large family. There was no one more compassionate or thoughtful than Betty if she wanted to be.

In the early days the Baskervilles had the best place in town to eat. Lida Donnell ran the Desert Hotel. We used to eat there, too. She later worked at the library.

I remember once someone wanted to get a book...one of the early ones on sex - The Kinsey Report. Judy, Lida's sister, who also worked in the library, wouldn't let her check out the book. She said, "Why do you, a married woman, want to read a thing like that?"

Liz and her sister, Ada T. Hatch with miner, Jack Meek, on porch of Bagley's store in the Plaza about 1947. The girls are wearing the gold nugget necklaces that Jack made for them. Photo by Bill Hatch, courtesy of Ada Hatch.

Helen Bagley had the first library out here. That was in 1928 when they first came. When it was moved out of Helen's shop, Mabel Marlow took it over, and the Woman's Club paid the rent for awhile.

Bill liked to square dance. He was a good square dancer. That was the only kind of dancing he liked. Some of the ones who used to dance were: Lillian Skaglioni, who was a very good dancer, the Earenfights, Virgie Lashett and his first wife, and the Crittendens. We usually had four or five squares. The children would have their own little square at one end of the building.

I remember one day we had been riding in the car with Ketch, who was a lousy driver. We had the transit with us, and I was sitting in the back seat. Bill and Ketch were in the front. As usual, Ketch went through an intersection without looking either right or left, and sure enough, a huge car was coming down the highway.

I heard the guy hit his brakes, but it was too late....wham into the side of our car! Ketch wasn't hurt a bit, but I seemed to be pretty sore on my side.

We went on home, and Bill asked if I still wanted to go to the dance that night. He said, "It'll do you good."

Impromptu picnics were popular in the early days. This one in 1949 included left to right: Sherm Clark, Sidney Wilson (Amo Clark's father), Anna Wilson, Amo Clark, Ruth Pattee (Ada's aunt), Sarah Schenck, John Atkinson, Egbert Schenck, Howard Pattee, June Clark Atkinson. Photo about 1949 by Bill Hatch, courtesy of Ada Hatch.

Season's Greetings 1953
from the Hatches of 29 Palms

The Hatch family Christmas card, 1953 with left to right: Ada, Liz, and Martha Hatch.

So we went down to the old school house, and of course, at the first dance Jess Hayward wanted to dance with me. I didn't know it, but I had several broken ribs at the time. So he grabbed me right there and started dancing. And I started screaming.

Everyone said, "Isn't she having fun? Mrs. Hatch is just a riot. She's just having more fun."

And I was in such pain, I couldn't see straight. Of course, I had to go home, and later went to old Doc Nicholson.

Doc Nicholson was a great guy. He was kind. For example, Nona Earenfight had terrible asthma. She often would call him up, and he'd say, "I've got asthma too. If you're worse that I am, I'll come to you, but if I'm worse than you are, you come to me." And that's the way he did mostly.

The first dentist out here was Glen Barry. His wife, Bernice, was Thelma Smith's sister. He had a foot pedal thing to grind your teeth. His office was at Smith's Ranch in one of those little buildings. I remember his wife had special curtains made so the kids wouldn't peek in and watch people. It was quite a lot of fun to go and watch people get their teeth fixed.

365

He told about one woman who arrived in town, who apparently had all her teeth pulled before she left the East, and they hadn't taken any of the roots. Well, they were abscessed all the way through. He really had to work on her, and all the kids in the neighborhood came and watched. How she screamed!

The Sherman girls always loved to go to dances. They were a very musical family. Dodie and Harry Sherman had four girls, and they all played some kind of musical instrument. One played the accordion/marimba, one played the piano, one played the drums and violin, and one played the accordion. Harry played too. They would entertain us Saturday nights.

Hal Paradis, President of the Friends of Copper Mountain College, bestowing Ada Hatch with the title of Honorary Life Director in December 1985 for her extraordinary service and commitment to help raise the necessary funds which resulted in the college campus near Joshua Tree. Photo courtesy of Copper Mountain College.

ADA WATKINS HATCH

Ada Hatch was responsible for the 29 Palms Historical Society's revival of the Weed Show, a long-time tradition, which was ceased to be held about 1981. Working with other former Weed Show participants, she planned and organized the program which made the November 1986 revival show a success. Her daughters (L to R) joined her at the show: Liz Meyer, Martha Reich, and Ada Hatch Merrill. Photo by the author.

Bill Underhill ran the newspaper, and he used to go around with a little pad of paper in his pocket. He'd see you and say, "Well, what's new?" And then he would write it down and put it back into his pocket. Every Thursday night he would sit down at the linotype, pull these little pieces of paper out, and type them off.

My husband had one of the early Boy Scout troops out here. We have a picture of him with the Bagley boys, Bill Hockett and others. He and Jack Cones used to take the troop on hikes into the Monument. That was early in the 1930's, because I remember once there was a big Scout Jamboree, and Bill wanted me to put his merit badges on his sash. In going over them, I found he had every badge except surveying and photography! And of course, surveying turned out to be his means of livelihood, and photography was always his hobby.

Fifty years have passed since I first came to this land of little rain. We were blessed with three daughters: Ada, Elizabeth, and Martha who went all through school here.

So many changes we have seen. The school was a quonset hut then, and now there are three elementary schools, an intermediate school, a high school, and now the College of the Desert. From the one Little Church of the Desert, we now have eleven churches.

The original two ruts in a dirt road have become a state highway through to Amboy and Parker. From one local market, Bagley's Store, we now have numerous stores with unlimited supplies.

From the original light plant at the Inn, which provided power for a few individual lights, to a panorama of sparkling lights which I view from my home in Sherman Highlands west of town.

I feel blessed to have been a part of Twentynine Palms for half a century. I see this community as an example of how America has progressed from the homestead days to modern times. I hope all future residents enjoy and appreciate this lovely desert and its inhabitants as I have.

Ada with her family, Thanksgiving, 1986. Front: Jennifer Reich, Liz Hatch Meyer, Ada Sr., Angela Meyer. Standing: Dave Meyer, Cary Reich, Katie Reich, Martha Hatch Reich, Jim Merrill, Ada Hatch Merrill, and Jeff Meyer. Photo by the author.

SARA AND LEONARD WIKOFF

Leonard P. Wikoff was born in Chicago, Illinois, on July 7, 1892, and after graduation from high school, completed three years of mechanical engineering studies at Bradley Polytechnic Institute. Initial practical experience came between 1912 and 1916 when he was involved with several companies in Illinois working on field surveys and industrial building design.

He came to California in 1916 to work at the Long Beach Electric and Machine Works. Here he was involved in the design and installation of electrical and mechanical equipment for office buildings, industrial plants, and oil fields.

During World War I, Leonard served in the U.S. Army Signal Corps, after which he worked in Los Angeles and Long Beach doing structural, electrical, and mechanical designs for office and apartment buildings and eventually for Associated Telephone where he was involved with the rebuilding of existing pole lines and telephone systems. During this time he met and married Sara Brown.

Sara Louise Brown was born in North Carolina on October 13, 1902, to Sterling Price Brown and his wife, Annie Leona Keener Brown. After her marriage to Leonard, Sara traveled extensively with him as his job assignments took him all over the U.S. and into Mexico. When bad health started to plague him, Leonard terminated his employment in May 1936 and came to Twentynine Palms to regain his health as well as look for an economic venture with which to apply his skills.

On the way, Sara and Leonard stayed overnight at Whitewater on the evening of May 9th and met developer, Ole Hanson. Hanson's enthusiasm for the future of Twentynine Palms so fired the Wikoffs that after looking over the then small community, they made plans to establish their own power company, then utilizing the know-how that Leonard had developed through his many previous engineering positions.

Unable to find backers for such a venture in his former city of San Francisco, Leonard and Sara returned to the desert where he worked as a surveyor for various subdividers and at several mines east of town. After building up their capital, they were able to lease the following summer, an old 25 horsepower Fairbanks-Morse engine and install it at Four Corners. Electrical service for Twentynine Palms started on September 4, 1937, with fourteen consumers. The Leonard P. Wikoff Electric and Power Company was born with Sara's brother, John C. Brown, and the Wikoffs operating the generating plant on a twenty-four hour basis.

As local demand for power increased in the growing community, so did the number of the Wikoff's engines, power lines, transformers, and other equipment. Finally in October 1943, Leonard built a second plant at Condor Field. He and Sara continued to man the equipment on a twenty-four hour basis, prepared the rate schedules, did all of the company records and accounts, as well as constantly maintained and repaired their equipment. Working with them were Milt Nowak, Bob Scriven, Ralph Owen, Ray Owen, and Neil Carr. Another familiar face around the Wikoff plant was Bill, their 140 pound Great Dane.

During World War II the demands for power from Condor Field, as well as the continually growing community, began to take their toll on the Wikoffs. They finally decided that the time had come for a larger utility company to take over their operation, and on March 31, 1944, they sold their company to California Electric Power. At the time of the sale, they had over fifty miles of pole lines, more than 700 poles, 75 transformers, 370 meters, and about 600 customers.

After selling the business, Leonard continued to be active working both as a utilities consultant and as an engineer in the planning of several subdivisions in Twentynine Palms. In 1952 he was approached by the County Board of Supervisors to complete the term of office as County Engineer which was left vacant by the death of Howard Way. He was a practicing engineer from 1930 until his final retirement in 1968 in San Bernardino, and held California State Certificates in Civil, Electrical, and Mechanical Engineering.

Sara and Leonard's last visit together to Twentynine Palms was in October 1977 when they attended the Pioneer Days reunion at Prudie and Bill Underhill's. Leonard's ill health prevented further visits, and he passed away in San Bernardino on July 6, 1980. Sara died there on May 13, 1983.

*   *   *   *   *

Well, Leonard put in a terrible winter in San Francisco. He was with a big firm which had lots of engineers. I had him in the hospital with a terrible throat condition.

We'd heard about a little telephone company that was for sale in Arizona. So we took a trip and stayed overnight at Whitewater.

SARA AND LEONARD WIKOFF

And we were sitting there eating breakfast when Ole Hanson, one of the original subdividers of Twentynine Palms, came and sat down beside us. Leonard told him that he was an electrical engineer and that electric power was his specialty.

Hanson said, "Leonard, you're just the guy we need out there."

So we did. We went out there on May 10th, 1936. Leonard had a great imagination. He could see that the plant was already built as far as he was concerned, but we had an awful time making it, because we were on a tight budget. It was going to require $100,000, and that was quite a lot of money out in Twentynine Palms. It was more money than we had. That's a cinch.

My friends in New York with the Public Utilities Commission tried to talk me out of it. They thought I was crazy. I had three good job offers I could have gone to, but I wanted to get into business for myself. So when Ole Hanson came along...why I thought we'll go along and take a look at what's the deal.

It took a little while to get under way. We started on September the 7th, 1937. I constructed a building and installed a small 25 horsepower Fairbanks-Morse Diesel electric generating set, generating 120-208 volt, 3 phase, 60 cycle current, and distributed at this voltage in close proximity to the power plant. Ray Owen, Ralph Owen, and Sara's brother, John, worked with us when we first started.

New diesel generator being unloaded outside of the Wikoff's power plant near Four Corners in 29 Palms. Photo by Leonard Wikoff, author's collection.

SARA AND LEONARD WIKOFF

The same year I installed a duplicate plant. We ran them all at once, and handled them by ourselves. Each one of the Fairbanks weighed about three or four tons, and at first we had to lease them. The following year I constructed my first 2400 volt distribution line, and also installed a 50 horsepower Diesel generating unit.

Then we decided to buy a new Caterpillar because those old engines were worn out. They were nothing but trouble all the time. They'd run during the day, and then I'd stay up all night tearing them down to get them running in the morning.

At first we tried to borrow some money from the bank in Beaumont. We wanted to borrow $1500, but we didn't get it. But we were at the point where I had to get one of those big engines for $20,000. So we went into the Banning Bank and asked for it.

Leonard and Sara Wikoff with their dog, Bill, late 1930's. Photo by Ruth Schneider from author's collection.

They asked us, "What are you going to do with it?"

"I'm going to buy an engine with it," I said. "We had the customers already there. We had a demand for going into business. We don't have something we have to sell. They'll come after it." So he loaned us $20,000.

The Caterpillar was the first one that we bought. I mean it was our own. We had the other old thing that was leased, and I was always having problems. That was the one that Leonard got so mad at that he started pounding it with a hammer. That took a lot out of us.

That's how I got the first big engine. And every time after that when we'd get short of power, I'd go in there with Sara with me and say, "I need more power."

"How much do you need?" he'd say, and I'd show him my financial statements, and I'd get what I'd needed.

So in 1939 I installed a 120 horsepower 75 KVA caterpillar generating unit. During the time that these various generating units were being installed, I was continually adding to my outside distribution plant.

Then we built a new modern plant, and we bought one of the big Fairbanks 180 horsepower complete. That came from the All American Canal when they had it down there. And then we bought another one....an exact duplicate from an ice plant in Coleville. And then we still had to have more, and we always had bills. So we went to the President of the Citizens National Bank in Redlands. If it hadn't't been for him, we wouldn't have been here.

Anyway, we had to buy another.....a 150 KVA Van Severin unit from a branch over in Phoenix and put it in. I installed it in 1943 down by the base. This was used as an auxiliary unit and was located adjacent to the air field. During the latter part of 1943 and 1944 I was making studies and completing plans and designs for a new power plant which I intended to install.

I don't think this story would be complete if we didn't include the two men who were so faithful and such wonderful working people. One was our lineman, Bob Scriven, who was highly trained here and helped to build Boulder Dam. And then we had Milt who was Alma Steeg's brother. He learned everything from Leonard and just followed him around. Every time anybody was doing anything, here he was. He'd learn so fast.

During the war you couldn't get a night man. So I put a cot in there by the switchboard, because we had to monitor there about every fifteen to twenty minutes unfortunately. I set the alarm for fifteen minutes ahead and would lie down on that cot to sleep, then get up, check everything, and then go back to sleep again.

When we built down at the base, we were going to share joint poles with the telephone company, and they sent their heavy gang out to set their poles in. They started at the base and built toward town, and we started the other way. They had four men and a truck driver and all this heavy equipment. We had a little half ton Dodge pickup truck, and we set five poles to their three.....because they were union men. They couldn't do so much.

We'd put a pole up on a rack and trench the hole. Then we'd put the pole down in the hole and start backing up a bit. It would fall right in the hole, and that's the way we set thirty-five, forty, forty-five foot poles. In the end we had fifty miles of lines. We built the whole fifty miles ourselves....myself and two men.

The Los Angeles Water Department had built a construction line from Banning to Parker. So after the dam was built, they were ready to abandon that line. I made a deal with them to buy the poles and the wire. I bought $20 poles for $3 and a half. I had to take them down myself, of course. And I bought the copper for about fifteen cents on the dollar.

Then the Edison Company salvaged in Los Angeles. They would call me up and say, "Leonard, I got something I think you'll be interested in." And I'd go in there, and that's the way I built my switchboard. I wrote the specifications for it and built it for about six thousand dollars. I put everything on it that the Edison Company had except it was much smaller of course.

We had three steady ones working with us.....four including a woman that often helped Sara. There were three men to man the day shift and one on the night shift. Sara did the billing and all the accounting and worked a regular shift of eight hours. Sometimes she worked all night long.

Bob Scriven was the lineman. He read the meters. Our minimum was a dollar and a half. We had one customer who cheated us every month. He had a pin on it so it slowed the wheel down. When it was time to read the meter, he'd take that off, and we couldn't catch him.

One day we had kind of an accident down there. We had been changing some transformer hook-up with the substation at the plant down at the base, and that night came a slow drizzly rain. Bob Scriven, when he tried to jump together from the big transformer, had used a broomstick to hold them apart until he had got them formed.

Well, I was walking in the drugstore that night and the lights went up, then down again. What had happened was that 12,000 volt lamp had arced over on the broomstick. It lit up that whole end of town. Milt was scared to death after that. Distribution voltage around town was 2400, while transmission down at the base was 12,000 volts. So that was a pretty hot line.

We had a lightning strike and a burnout right down town and

I had help in the office, and I could go lie down and nap a little bit. Well, she came running in and said, "There's something awful going on in one of the engine rooms."

So I jumped up and ran out there and oh boy, the whole alternator was on fire. Leonard was down at the other plant, and the man who was working in there was a diesel man. He didn't know anything about electricity. And although he had been warned, he lost his head and was going to put a hose on it. If he had, he wouldn't have been there either.

Well, I grabbed a wrench and started for him and said, "If you go any further, this is it. I mean it." I still don't remember getting down over there and shutting down those engines. I never could remember it, but I did.

One time our lineman was working on this line, and something happened. He was very careful and almost never had an accident. But this time he did and burned a hole in the palm of his hand. Milt was there with him. So he ran in and asked Mrs. Campbell to use the telephone.

And she said, "Well, it's upstairs." But as soon as he started, she said, "You're not going up there."

Then he said, "That's what you think. I'm not going to let him die out there."

So she had to let him go.

I never really figured out how I built that place down there with no money. It took ourselves for one thing, and we darn near starved to death. There were two big mines operating east of Twentynine Palms and also a big chemical company. Both were tickled to have electricians in the area, so I had sort of a retainer with them, and we were living on that. It was probably two or three hundred dollars a month that they were paying. I had to get up in the middle of the night and go over there and take care of their problems too.

I remember the dedication of Joshua Tree National Monument. They gave me ten pounds of beans to cook. We had this little kitchen which was about as big as this here chair. It had a two burner stove. So I was soaking the beans and got up the next morning. They were all over the kitchen and everything else.

So I said, "Leonard, you go down to Grace Brock's and ask her if she can loan me some bigger pots and pans." So he did. I cooked the beans all right.

Doctor Leonard was a good doctor. He was there during the war. He and his wife were personal friends of ours. They used to come and visit us at night. Very few people ever came to the plant at night, because we were always so busy and that sort of thing. People who didn't have any reason to be here could not get the gasoline to come out here. So he finally had to leave town because

Sara and Leonard Wikoff (foreground) on their last trip together to 29 Palms to attend 1977 Pioneer Days' Get-Together hosted by the Underhills. Ill health prevented Leonard's return, but Sara came back for Pioneer Days, 1979. Bill Underhill is in the background on the left. Photo by the author.

he didn't have enough civilians to treat. Everyone was being treated at the base.

From the beginning, I provided 24 hour service to the community. In 1941 the California Electric Power Company approached me regarding possible purchase of my properties. I was not interested in a sale, but they continued to contact me every six months or so, hoping that we might negotiate a contract for purchase. As Sara and I were sole owners of the business, we tentatively set a figure at which we might sell the properties.

Mr. Albert Cage, who at that time was vice president of the California Electric Power Company, personally approached us in the fall of 1943 regarding purchase of our business. As his offer was somewhat in excess of the figure we had fixed for sales consideration, we started negotiations with him for the sale. A contract agreement was entered into, and on July 1, 1944 they took over ownership and operation.

Exhaustion prompted us to finally sell the business and leave. Leonard was ill, and I was so tired and uptight. When we sold out to California Electric Power, they ran their own line in eventually, but they used our power plant for about a year. And they had more trouble than we ever did, and they were down more than they were up.

While our operations were small in comparison with modern day electric power systems, they covered considerable territory, and we had all the problems, except on a smaller scale, which beset larger companies. No matter what problem might present itself - financial, public utility commission, generating, distribution, or public relations - Sara and I were the ones who had to make the decisions as to how it would be handled and what ultimate disposal was made of them.

From a physical operating standpoint, all problems were actually exaggerated in this area, due to the fact that we were one hundred fifty miles from Los Angeles where all material, equipment, and parts had to be purchased and transported to Twentynine Palms. We were operating an isolated plant and system and were entirely on our own.

It so happened that in earlier years I had worked as a lineman; had served a great deal of time in machine shops, foundries, and power plants. I was a good practical mechanic, as well as engineer and administrator and was, therefore, able to handle and dispose of the many and varied problems that arose in operating an electric power system in an isolated area. It was natural that my operations during the first few years were a losing proposition. However, the last several years were very profitable, as was the sale.

RUTH HONN SCHNEIDER

Ruth Honn was one of nine children born to missionary parents assigned to China. At the age of three she and her family returned to Los Angeles where Ruth grew up and attended public schools.

On April 19, 1937, she married local Twentynine Palms realtor, Ralph Schneider, in Prescott, Arizona. They and another prominent town couple, Donald Lawrence and Ethel Jean, quietly slipped out of town on the pretext of visiting Palm Springs, and then from there the foursome proceeded to Prescott.

Ralph Schneider came to Twentynine Palms in 1927 and was a real estate subdivider who was briefly involved with the Pinto Basin Land Development Company. This land later became part of Joshua Tree National Monument. In 1935 he was the original sub-divider of 30 acres of land at Four Corners, and at the time of his marriage to Ruth Honn, he was personnel manager for the Hamilton Sales corporation in the sale of the Twentynine Palms village.

During their marriage, the Schneiders had homes in Twentynine Palms, Palms Springs, and Hollywood where Ralph also had offices. The couple commuted back and forth as business dictated, but after January 1940 spent more time visiting Twentynine Palms than living here. While he was here, Ralph subdivided twelve other subdivisions, the last one on Two Mile Road in the vicinity of Chocolate Drop Hill.

Previously they had both been active in the community. Ruth was a member of the 29 Palms Women's Club, and a performer in the Lions Club Mystery Minstrel when she played Aunt Susan in the May 30-31, 1938 presentations, and served as secretary to the Chamber of Commerce. Ralph had been president of the 29 Palms Real Estate Board until his resignation on January 17, 1940. By then the couple was living almost exclusively in Los Angeles.

Ill health forced his early retirement and the couple's permanent move to San Bernardino in 1952. He died in his sleep at his home on November 30, 1955, at age 58.

After her husband's death, Ruth passed the examination to get her brokerage license in order to manage their investments. She remained in San Bernardino helping take care of long-time friends, Sara and Leonard Wikoff, until their deaths. After which, she moved to the Sacramento area in 1980 and later to Santa Ana, California.

RUTH HONN SCHNEIDER

*   *   *   *   *

The first trip that I ever made down there to Twentynine Palms was in 1929. I had known Ralph at that time, and this group of people were going down there. He said, "You can have a life if you get to Twentynine Palms." So we formed this group and went down.

At that time there were no real roads in there. It was just a track, but the miners and the people here used it. From Whitewater you went right up the side of the hill instead of the way we go now.

At Twentynine there was the Mission Inn, but we didn't stay there. We stopped for a minute, then we went on over to the oasis where they had those little cabins. So we gals had a cabin, and the men had a cabin. They also had a restaurant, and that's all they had there. It was during Prohibition, and we heard all of these wild tales about not going into the desert without anybody knowing you're coming or you'd get shot or something. Well, we had a pleasant trip, and then I forgot all about it.

Years later, Ralph called me and then it all began. We went together for quite awhile. At that time he was going to Twentynine Palms every weekend to begin subdividing. They were selling on weekends out of a tent which was located on the northeast corner of Four Corners. When the wind blew, we had to stand outside and hold the tent together. We really did. Sometimes it was just jammed packed with people, even though there was just a plain dirt road out there.

When we first went down there, we had a lot of fun. It was a very interesting place. We went up into the Monument, but there was no Monument at that time. But that's where we went. We had a Ford, and we traveled all over the desert and took trips.

On one trip we just ploughed across the desert heading for Parker. There was no road or anything, but we finally made it. It took us all day, and we stayed with Joe and Nellie Bush who were the pioneers of Parker, Arizona. She used to run the ferry across, and they owned the light plant there.

We got married on April 19, 1937. There was another couple that ran the Josh Cafe, and they were going to get married too. So we all hopped into the car and went to Prescott. Don Lawrence and Ethel Jean were their names.

Ralph had his office in Hollywood, and his mother lived there too. I wish I had a nickel for every time I've driven to and from Twentynine Palms two or three times a week. We never did really move and stay there even after his mother died in World War II.

At that time there wasn't anything you could do in the desert. The transportation was bad. He didn't do anything except make sure it was still there. Ralph was instrumental in getting people started out there. The building we had was later Dean's Cafe, and we built a house up on Wilshire Boulevard. It was the only house in that subdivision at the time.

Chet Bunker and Ralph were in partnership for a while, and he had a group of cottages up on the hill off Utah Trail. So he was having some phones put in.

One morning he woke up and heard this funny noise. He looked and here was Mrs.Tucker with a saw. She was sawing the poles down. He called the telephone company, and they said, "She can't do that."

And he said, "What do you think that funny noise is? The poles are going down."

They had to come up from Palm Springs so there was no way they could get there in time. But Chet got her to hold up. He said he finally persuaded her to stop. She wasn't going to have those poles there on her property. They hadn't asked her. She was a character.

Well, when I was waiting for Ralph to come back or do something, I would go over to the Josh Cafe and sit there, especially in the winter when it had a nice fire. So I'd sit there and knit. Major Huber was one of our closest friends in Twentynine Palms. He was just a barrel of laughs.

Ruth Schneider and friends at the Josh, late 1930's. Photo from author's collection.

We had a flat tire up in the Monument. It was getting dark and Maj Huber said, "Well, we're just stuck here." Fortunately, we were on the main road, but we had been all over the place. You never left without telling someone where you were going whether the Monument, Pinto Basin or wherever.

So he said, "Well, all we can do is sit here and wait for somebody to come and get us."

Well, we were really getting cold. About that time here came about four automobiles with coffee, sandwiches.....the whole works. The rescue party came looking for us.

Ralph seldom got to go on these trips because he was busy working and keeping the office going. But I'd just take off with friends, see things, come back, and tell him about it.

We also used to do square dancing on horseback. Twentynine Palms wasn't much then, and they were having the Riverside County Fair at Indio. So we got our horses, and we taught them to square dance... that is to do certain ones. We went over to the fair and square danced every day. We stayed at the hotel, and while we were there, we had quite an earthquake.

We had an offer to go back to Madison Square Garden, but we didn't have the money. The town didn't have the money, so there wasn't anyway we could do it.

We were really busy. We were in business to make money and didn't have time to attend many social functions. So we didn't get mixed up in town the way many of the people did. Living there we had a few friends like Major Huber, and Virginia and Johnny Stephens. They owned the property where Adobe Acres is....where the Little Church of the Desert is. They gave lovely parties and had a lovely home there.

Well, we bought their land when they left. We had bought down to where the bowling alley is. That was part of it. We subdivided it and donated part of the land to the church. We subdivided all down over the hill. We called it Adobe Heights. One hundred foot lots sold for $985.

We didn't really sell so much to people that came out there. We had Sam Stevens there, and he would sit in the office. If anybody came in and wanted to see something, he'd say, "Well here's a map. You go out and look at it, and if you like it, come back and buy it." And they'd come back and buy it. But we didn't do as much there, as we did in Los Angeles. People would come out by appointment later.

Anyway, Ralph and I were in and out of Twentynine Palms and weren't as closely tied in as the rest of the people. With his advertising in the L.A. papers, he had other things that he was doing. But he subdivided several areas in town. Smoketree Mesa was one, and also up there where Wilshire Boulevard is.

Ralph Schneider, early real estate developer and subdivider of 29 Palms. Photo from the author's collection.

I'll never forget that one, because we came in to Twentynine and stopped to see the engineer who was a journalist. "What are you going to name those streets, Schneider?" he said.

"Oh, I don't know."

"Well, they've got to have a name to put on this map."

So Ralph said, "Let's take all the big cities in the United States. We'll start out with Wilshire Boulevard, and then something for Chicago." And he started naming of the names of these streets.

I said, "That's kind of silly."

And Ralph said, "What difference does it make? Nobody's ever going to live there anyway."

Years before he had subdivided Pinto Basin. I knew him then, but I wasn't interested in what he was doing. But they didn't pay

Ruth Schneider at her home in San Bernardino in summer 1980. Photo by author.

much for Pinto Basin. $100 a lot, but that was a lot of money in those days.

Ralph eventually gave up the office, but we never really felt that we lived in Twentynine Palms, because we were always going someplace else. If we weren't going to L.A., we were going fishing. If we weren't going fishing, we were heading back East or something.

His release from tension was to go down to Ensenada and go fishing. He always carried a fishing rod in the back of the car, and I had a suitcase full of clothes and his old clothes, and that's the way we lived. I just had a very lovely, interesting life.

Even when we were in San Bernardino, we went out to the desert. because Ralph hadn't been well. He went out to the desert and stayed about two months when he was ill, because he enjoyed Bill Ince so much. I had my job in L.A. and would come out on the weekends.

Then he came back home and didn't live very long after that. We had several subdivisions when Ralph died in 1955. He was only fifty-eight. That's why I got in the business.

The Division of Real Estate wrote me and said they felt that in the last twenty years I had been associated with Ralph Schneider who they respected very highly. They asked me if I would like to have a brokerage license. I'd never even had a salesman's license. Ralph didn't believe that a husband and wife should be working at the same thing at the same time.

Anyway, we had all those subdivisions going when he died and so I said, "Sure." I went in, took my test, and passed it. I needed that. I needed to continue, because I had to pick up and continue with the selling of these properties and take care of the trust. It was good for me, because I was grieving so much.

JOHN C. HASTIE

John C. Hastie was born in 1906 in the Province of Ontario, Canada. He left his farm home with $35 in the fall of 1927 "to go West to see about the other half of the country and to make some money helping to bring in their harvest." His money got him train fare as far as Swift Current in Saskatchewan where he found farm work which lasted several weeks.

From there he headed down through British Columbia to Seattle and on to California where he found work with a company that sold packing house and irrigation equipment. His salesman's job took him through Arizona, California, Nevada, and as far north as Washington. He was successful, but found his job lacking. He wanted to be involved in a business venture where he could work for himself.

On a chance trip to Palm Springs in 1937, he learned of the new community of Twentynine Palms which was beginning to grow. After analyzing the potential business needs of the town, he discovered what was most needed was a dependable transportation system.

Realizing its potential, he returned to Riverside and resigned from his job. Johnnie then moved to Twentynine Palms to begin his new career - owner and operator of the 29 Palms Stage - a dependable service and one that would consume his time and energy for seven days a week for the next thirty-six years. When he retired in 1973, he had driven over seven million miles without a traffic citation or an accident. That same year, Johnnie Hastie was chosen as Grand Marshall of the annual Pioneer Days celebration.

*   *   *   *   *

As I drove through the main drag, I recall it was just gravel. Four Corners was all real estate offices....one on every corner. Everybody came out to the middle of the road to see what I wanted. And I said to them, "What does this town need worst of all?"

Someone said, "We need transportation." I knew I couldn't make it on transportation alone. I could haul for these people. I could haul express or light freight or things of that kind. So that's what really made the bus line.....hauling.

To get started, I had to build the bus. It was a 1928, twelve-passenger, ton and a half, four cylinder, overhead Chevrolet motor. It was one of the first ones built with overhead valves. It had a Ruxel rear end which helped me coming up the hills. It only had single wheels on the back. It didn't have duals.

I had to carry about three spares because there were stones on the road. If you hit a rock with one of these old tires at that time, you'd bust the tire. When I started, San Bernardino County probably didn't think it would ever be a town here, so they didn't pay attention to the road unless there was a big wash or something like that.

I'd take two or three tires along and fix them on the ground. Then I'd have to take a flat board and lay it down and change the tube on the road. We didn't go to a garage. We had to do it ourselves. I had a thing that was made with a ratchet and gear that spread the tire when it was taken off, and it would pull it together when getting it back on. They didn't make tires that would stand up.

I also had a stove in the middle of the bus for when it was cold. Wood had to be gathered at both ends. The passengers did this mostly. They brought their own wood most of the time and kept the fire going. I only had to drive. If they couldn't get wood, they used to cut brush.

At the end of the first year in business, I went to the Chamber of Commerce for a meeting and offered to give them the bus line back. I had just been offered $250 a month at the mines, and it was more than I was making with the bus.

So they decided to give a benefit dance for the bus line. I think the tickets cost a dollar and a half for the dance. We sold tickets in advance that were good for a year on the bus to Banning. It was spring time and the ladies picked flowers and made bouquets to sell at the door. So I got $450 right off the bat from the dance, the bouquets, and the tickets that we sold in advance.

So I said I was still not interested. I wanted to be able to make money. Then I said, "I'm going to make a deal. I will haul anything you want from Banning out here for ten cents. It can be thread. It can be simplicities. It can be clothes or automobile supplies. Whatever it is, it cost ten cents."

Well, they couldn't get over that because they couldn't drive down to Banning for that. At this end, I'd go around and pick up orders on horseback early in the morning. It was faster, and I wouldn't have to go in. I'd just go to the windows and they holler out their orders.

At Joshua Tree I had a tree, and I put a hoop around it and the people pinned their orders to the hoop. They wouldn't have to wait for the bus there. I also did that at Yucca at Warren's Well. People didn't want to wait so I just had a pin cushion there where they'd pin their stuff on and then they left and they'd meet me at night when I came back.

It worked out pretty well, and they were just like depots. They all had the little things they wanted. I'd go to Penney's in Banning for dresses. I had to tell them if it was for a big woman or a little woman. If it was for a big woman, the material was little dots. If it was for a little woman, it was big dots. They watched out for me at Penney's every day, and the only thing I had to do was to keep the names straight, because these people came to the bus if they lived out quite a ways. I didn't have an office.

There were some funny incidents. One windy morning in the fall, I went to get the order from Dean's Cafe. He started rattling off the stuff he wanted me to buy and said that he wanted a "Kitchen Bouquet." I heard him say it, so I wrote it down on my flower list.

I went to Banning and told the florist that I didn't know what he wanted, but it was a kitchen bouquet for a restaurant. I got nasturtiums.

Johnnie Hastie and his Twentynine Palms Stage. From 1937 until his retirement in 1973, Johnnie had driven over seven million miles without a traffic citation or an accident. Photo from author's collection.

It was dark when I got back and at Dean's Cafe there were a bunch of people eating there. I carried the flowers in and said, "Here's your bouquet," and started out.

He said, "Wait till I get your money." So he got the money. It was forty cents I think plus the flowers. So on my way out I heard him say, "If you want a kitchen bouquet from Banning, order with Johnny and he'll bring you flowers."

I didn't know about Kitchen Bouquet seasoning, but that gave me more advertising than any of the papers could.

I also had to haul live fowl, and this particular time it was ducks. I couldn't keep them in the bus because it was full. I had pastry in there, a whole tray of pies, and other things so I had to put the fowl on top. It was very windy, and these ducks were only a few weeks old. There were about twelve of them, and they were in a crate which the wind could blow through.

Well on the way here, it blew all the feathers off of the ducks. So when I got here, this woman wouldn't take them. So I got stuck with them. I kept them and then I eventually had to sell them because I didn't want them.

Once in a while people didn't come to pick up something or wouldn't pay me. I had some pigs once that came on Christmas Day and nobody came for the pigs. I got them out of the Railroad Express, and they wanted them to be delivered on Christmas. I didn't know where these people lived, so they had to wait for the mail to come to tell them where the pigs were.

Then there was banking. There was no bank here for years and years. So I said it would be ten cents to take transactions in and ten cents to bring them back. Nobody would stand behind me at the banks. They knew I would take a long time.

I didn't carry a gun. I never once had any trouble. But Frank Bagley, Ted Holderman, and Ed Kenney got their own insurance on me separately. That's how they protect themselves. I made ten cents taking the money in until Ed Kenney came and said, "Hastie, if this is not worth a quarter, it's not worth anything." So I got a raise out of him. He helped me a lot.

One of the old-timers I knew was Frank Sabathe who lived on the Morongo Hill. He had a contract before the regular buses came in and hauled freight for people out here. He drove a freight wagon with horses and had to change horses at Warren's Well and at places along the line especially when they were climbing those hills.

He had two wagons and would leave one wagon at the bottom of the hill and go back and get the other. The horses didn't like that. He did that about once a week. It was kind of hard going especially with horses.

I dealt with Mrs. Campbell who would send for things with me and do a lot of shipping of pictures and things. She was very exact with everything she wanted to have done.

I did a lot of work for John Hilton. I hauled his pictures and sent them off by express. I also dealt with Lida Donnell at the Mission Inn. That was an easy delivery....right on the road. I brought in food mostly and would sometimes bring people there to the Mission Inn.

The towns had different names then. Yucca Valley was Warren's Well, and Joshua Tree was Coyote Hole. Morongo was Covington's, and then there was Mission Creek where the Indians got on.

We didn't have an ambulance in the early days, and I used the bus as one. If I got an emergency call to go to Banning, I would take the call and start over again. We used a cot, and we'd put it over the top of the seats in the bus, and that was the ambulance. Once I got a call in Yucca Valley and turned around and came back to make the ambulance run, and then went back to start the bus trip to Banning.

I also had a taxi service. It was a four cylinder Dodge Brothers car with wooden spoked wheels and had a running board. It was five cents a ride...any place in town. Of course, gas was cheaper then. If a person lived very far from town, then I let them take the taxi home and bring it back the next day.

Then in 1938 this fellow from Los Angeles came and said to me, "We want you to haul newspapers and be our agent for the Herald-Examiner in Twentynine Palms."

So I started with seventy papers in 1938, and I got it up to twelve hundred. Then I quit and sold the dealership because it took so much time to keep track of the papers....whether they were sold by the month or the year. The Sunday paper would come in, and I'd have to go down to the highway at Whitewater where they dumped the papers off and get them all delivered. Then I had to get back and ready to go to Banning by nine o'clock.

I got things for Mr. Bagley in the early days, but as he got bigger he drove his own truck. I would haul for the restaurants more than I did for the stores. I hauled drugs for White's Drug Store, and I hauled the flowers, the laundry, and the cleaning. I also hauled the bread from Weber's, and I hauled bales of hay on top of the bus for fifty cents a bale.

Meat was never cut up and put in packages. It was in whole chunks like a quarter. A quarter would be one leg and any part that hooked up either the front end or the back end. I'd put that at the back of the bus and let the feet stick out.

There wasn't too much at Yucca.....just the cattle raisers were there. They ran cattle in the Monument and people from San Bernardino would lease the land to run the cattle and their cowboys would be through there. That was Barker and Shay. I dealt with some of the cowboys. They wanted things like taking their watches in for repair. I'd take it in for ten cents and bring it back for ten cents. They couldn't go themselves for that. They had gold watches too with chains. And I'd get their tobacco.....all kinds of tobacco.

It was the same with the miners. They got two and a half dollars a day, and they had money. They would meet me at the Blue Diamond. That was at the end of Adobe Road and Sullivan. That was also called Jay's Place. They had some wild times there.

My route went to Banning and back until the base came in, and then I got an extension to the base from Four Corners. When the base opened with fliers, that's when I actually started to make money. The Army came in, then the Navy, and then the Marines. With each I did a little better, and there was no problem. When I finished, I had seven buses. They weren't like the ones they have now. I bought school buses and fixed them up. They called them "The Blue Bullet."

Driving the bus every day, I got friendly with the people on the highway, and they would run out when they wanted something. There was this fellow in Morongo Valley whose name was Hicks who lived alone. One day he said, "I want to go away at Christmas time, and I'll be gone for two weeks. I want you to do my chores." I said, "Ok."

So he made a list of things that I had to do. He had two cows, two horses, chickens, ducks, and a dog. And I had to feed them twice a day.

I'd go down in the morning and feed them and come back in the afternoon. The people I was hauling had to wait in the bus till I did this work. I parked the bus so they couldn't see from the bus what I was doing in the barn. I had to get the hay down, and the cow had to be milked every morning and every night....twice a day, and then I had to feed them.

Then all of these animals started meeting the bus. It went on for two weeks, and they got used to me. No one on the bus bawled me out like they would today. It didn't seem to matter so much. It was a little unusual, but they didn't say too much. Time didn't matter.

I worked seven days a week. I never had a day off. On Sunday, I still had the papers and then the films for the show. I brought the films in three times a week, and I'd have to take them back too. That was important to get them back, because they had quite a fee on them if one was lost or late.

There was inevitably a wash-out at Christmas time when I had a load of turkeys on. The water would just wash out the road so bad that I had to wait till it dried and then could go over it with the bus. The wet weather was time consuming, but that was a crooked road through Morongo then. I never got stopped as long as overnight. I always got through even though I might be two or three hours late. That's all.

I sold the bus line in 1973. In seven million miles of driving from 1938 to 1973 I never had a moving violation or accident.

"Johnnie's Tree" in the middle of the highway in Joshua Tree where people left messages of things they wanted him to pick up in town on his way through. They'd meet the stage coming back, pick up their freight, and pay Johnnie. Photo about 1940 looking west, courtesy of the Local History Collection, 29 Palms Branch Library.

Bill Hatch Surveys Condor Field.

1940 - 1965

Margaret and Ed Kenney

MARGARET FLYNN KENNEY

Margaret Flynn was one of five children born to James and Mary Flynn in Omaha, Nebraska. She met Edward J. Kenney when he was attending Creighton University, College of Pharmacy, and they were married in Omaha on July 17, 1934.

Soon after, they moved to Santa Fe, then to Phoenix and finally to Globe looking for a place to settle and to establish their own pharmacy. A friend who was affiliated with a wholesale drug company in Los Angeles told them about a drug store that was for sale in Twentynine Palms. They arrived here in January 1940 and decided that they "would give it a try." They purchased the business and Kenney's Drug Store was born.

Margaret and Ed worked hard not only establishing their business, but were also instrumental in assisting others to get started. They were also active in the Chamber of Commerce, Holy Name Society, and provided some of the major funding for the construction of the Blessed Sacrament Church. Margaret was also involved with the Women's Club.

Ed was also on the Board of Directors of the 29 Palms Foundation, which acquired and donated land for the civic center and library buildings, and was active in Lions Club, and Knights of Columbus. He was also a long-time member of the Joshua Tree Natural History Association Board of Directors, and was instrumental in the establishment of the High Desert Medical Center in Joshua Tree. Throughout his entire life here, Ed was always modest about his civic achievements and the many contributions that he made.

Edward J. Kenney passed away on November 17, 1981, deeply mourned by the community. His wife and partner, Margaret, continues to live at their home in Twentynine Palms and is also overly modest about their involvement with the development of our community.

*   *   *   *   *

Twentynine Palms was very much like Globe, so that's the reason we stayed. We came in January 1940 to look over the town and the drug store. A friend of ours told us about it being available. He said, "The road to Phoenix was going right by the door."

Les Spell, miner Jack Meek, and Ed Kenney. Photo taken in the 1940's, courtesy of the 29 Palms Historical Society.

Kenney's drugstore during summer flash flood conditions. Ed Kenney standing behind sandbags in the doorway. Photo taken in August 1941. Photo courtesy of Elise Poste.

We really liked the people that we met when we first came out. The drug store was across from where we are now, and we purchased it from a lady who had backed the Kurtz's drug store. The building was in fairly good shape. Of course, during floods we sandbagged the entrance like crazy. A lot of people in town thought it was very thrilling that our end of town was getting the flood down in what they called "Whiskey Gulch."

Bill Hatch and others would come down and take pictures. Some of us used to float on inner tubes during these times. It was fun, but really kind of dumb with all of the debris that was also floating by...including snakes and glass. We ended up with a couple of palm trees that came from Fortynine Palms Canyon. The seeds had washed down during the flood, and after we planted them, the trees grew and grew.

When we first opened the drugstore, we were concerned that it was getting close to this country's eventual involvement in the war. Ed's number was the first or one of the first to be called for men to go into the service. Since he was the only pharmacist in a radius of sixty miles and there was no doctor out here, many in the community requested that he not be drafted. And eventually he wasn't.

Ours was like any other business. We worked hard to start with. Ed bought most of the lots on the back sides of the street and eventually sold them for just what we paid for them so to get people to develop them and to start their own businesses. We built

A meeting at the Joshua Monument National Bank in late 1940's. Margaret and Ed Kenney are second and third from the right. Second from the left is Esther Williams, who was made mayor of 29 Palms in March 1948. Photo from author's collection.

The Hometowners' Club was a popular social group during the late 40's and early 50's. This gathering took place around the pool at the 29 Palms Inn. Photo from author's collection.

the bank building first, and then the medical building. All of this kept us busy too. Later Ed worked hard along with Jean Crowl and Marie Sharp to get the High Desert Medical Center going.

We were also involved with the Hometowner's group which got started for its own enjoyment. There were a certain number of couples, and then others were voted in. It finally got to be fairly good size. We met once a month and these gatherings were held at different places. One of them was the DAV Hall which the group had contributed money to fix up. It was in very good shape as a result.

Ed was working so hard because pharmacists were scarce. A friend of Al Beller's was going to come out and work for us, but something happened, and he couldn't come. So he wanted to know if it was all right to send Al. So that's how Al got here and eventually he became Ed's partner in 1958.

Ken Carter, Bob's dad, was really involved with the Chamber of Commerce. He worked hard, had the cleaners, and was also a member of the Hometowner's Club. He was a nice guy who was really good for the town.

I've been here for forty-six years, and I think that Twentynine Palms is a nice lush place. The people are what I like the best! I still have contact with glider people who were here during the war.

GUINEVERE FERRY KEYS

"Gwyn" Keys was born September 19, 1915 in Waterloo, Iowa and attended schools in Nogales, Arizona and in Fresno, California. At the age of sixteen she was "on the road", as a professional dancer and toured the United States and Canada with a Fanchon and Marco unit. Later with a partner, she worked nightclubs in the Los Angeles area and the Follies and Burbank burlesque theatres there.

While living in Joshua Tree, she was the founder of the Joshua Tree Gem and Mineral Society. Her husband, Willie Keys, was the club's charter president.

After moving to central California, Gwyn was the editor of the NORTH FORK JOURNAL for fourteen months, then resigned to work as a service station attendant in her husband's garage. She also organized and "Friendly Ventured" a Ritual of Jewels chapter of Beta Sigma Phi International Sorority for her community and founded the Squirrel Cage Theatre there. Gwyn is presently working as a sales associate for Century 21.

*   *   *   *   *

When World War II was declared in 1941, my husband, Clarke Ferry, and I left San Bernardino to live in Joshua Tree. Clarke went right to work at Condor Field in Twentynine Palms as a dispatcher, while I kept house in a tiny cabin that we had rented from Julia and Jeff Overbay.

As the Twentynine Palms Air Academy grew, Clarke advanced to the status of a glider flight instructor. We built our own one-room cabin to live in on his folks' property in Joshua Tree. When Clarke learned that employees were needed at the Canteen, he introduced me to Helen Parsons, the PX-Canteen manager, and I was hired.

Some of the waitresses that I remember were: Jerry Lane, who was small, blonde, and sharp, and Mrs. Parson's assistant; Flo, from Nova Scotia, with red hair and beautiful violet eyes; Tillie W., a good looking brunette; and two sisters, Edith and Betty Gallup and Kay Jones. All three were nice looking.

Later there was Sara, a brown-eyed southerner, vivacious, and a student pilot's wife, and Belle. Belle was very tiny and had the largest blue-green eyes I have ever seen! Rosalie "Pinkie" Garlock

399

was the cashier. Pinkie was tall, strawberry blonde, nice profile and endowed with a terrific sense of humor. We were to become dearest friends. Katherine Willis, a natural blonde and friendly, was hired later as a cashier.

I thought that all of us in the Canteen looked rather nice until one day a fellow walked in, took a glance around at all of us and said, "This place looks more like a zoo every day!"

Several well-known persons visited or were stationed at the Air Academy in the early 1940's. Among them were Jimmy Stewart, movie star and AAF Captain; Eduardo Cansino, Rita Hayworth's brother; and the one I remember best - Jackie Coogan, former child movie star.

S/Sgt Coogan was stationed at Condor Field as a glider pilot instructor about the same time that I had joined PX/Canteen personnel as a waitress. The Canteen normally opened in the dark morning hours so that the glider pilots could breakfast or have that extra cup of coffee before assembling on the flight line at dawn. Usually a driver with a station wagon would bus the Canteen waitresses from Twentynine Palms to the field around 3:30 to 4 A.M.

One morning after waiting twenty minutes past the time I should have been picked up, I decided that something must have happened to the stationwagon. So I hurriedly drove my own car the eight miles to the base.

There was no one at the Canteen when I arrived. Strange, I thought. But after turning on all of the lights and unlocking the front door, I put on my apron and measured out coffee for four pots and got them started. I was cutting oranges in half for juice when the rising murmur of male voices and the sound of eager footsteps barely proceeded a rush of student pilots through the door.

There were twenty-nine stools at the counter, and they filled in five seconds flat with another eight or ten fellows standing in-between those seated. Someone called out to me that Herman hadn't opened the Mess Hall yet, and they were all hungry and in a hurry. The expression on my face must have registered dismay for the group suddenly became quiet.

Sgt. Coogan was in the crowd and sizing up the situation. He jumped behind the counter and went right to work. He grabbed cups and saucers and started doling them out, while I accelerated my pace with the orange juice. I set the toaster on high speed, while he poured the coffee and passed out the creamers. That morning the gp's all had o.j., dry toast, coffee, and a few left-over doughnuts.

The Canteen at Condor Field about 1943. Photo by and courtesy of Harley Porter.

There was no time to make out slips, so I hastened to the cash register to take the cadets' word for what they owed. Some I'm sure plunked down more than was necessary and dashed out leaving their monies on the counter.

About 6 A.M. the rest of the crew arrived, and I learned that the manager had decided to open the Canteen that day at a later than usual hour. I was the only one who hadn't been notified! I fondly remember Jackie Coogan, who saved the day for me!

Another event for me was being elected the "Queen of Condor Field." It was the first and only annual picnic ever held to celebrate this honor, and it coincided with the worst storm that many old timers had ever experienced up until that time.

The four attendants: Natalie Cody, Army; Barbara Swift, Personnel; Consuelo Moreno, Hangar No. 1; Jeannette Rodgers, Hangar No. 2, and I were ensconced on our "thrones" on the temporary stage held at the Oasis before the oldest adobe structure in the area. Then a few dark clouds appeared.

About the time the "King" Dick Pettinger, chief dispatcher, and the visiting firemen were being introduced, the clouds opened up and the downpour began in earnest.

Bill Underhill shouted, "Head for the skating rink!" and everybody did. After, of course, first grabbing the food and the liquid refreshment.

Everyone got soaked running for their cars. Several cars had to be abandoned, as they were flooded and filled with mud. One such vehicle belonged to Frank Kennison, the chef, whose car was washed two hundred feet off of the road. He narrowly escaped drowning along with Frank Woodward who was with him.

The storm didn't dampen the spirits though of those who made it to the skating rink. Pinkie was right when she said that all that was salvaged from the cloudburst and picnic was the beer. But later at Smith Ranch, we did enjoy hot beans, potato salad, and other things gathered in the stress of the moment by the Paylor Commissaries, the Condor Field Mess Hall.

The "picnic," the pie-eating contest, and dancing were enjoyed. I was presented with a $25 Victory Bond, $5 in cash, and a dozen fine photos from Harlow Jones. The attendants were also presented with a beautiful perfume set and $5 cash each.

Helen Parsons was in charge of gifts and decorations and Horace Gillett did the Honors and much of the hard work which is a concomitant of all of these large affairs. THE FLYING CONDOR, the base monthly newspaper, entitled their story on the event..."The Annual Picnic was a Washout!"

I do remember a few of the student glider pilots: Mel Brockman, who was responsible for starting the first Classbook, 43-2, at the Academy; "Buzz" Raymond, who was from the Fresno area where I went to school; Bill Berlin, Edward "Babe" Hillyard, Jim F. Cox, John Hancock, Tommy Clarke, who would play the piano in the PX, and Albert Geyer.

Al Geyer was tall, heavy set, and uninhibited. He would sail into the Canteen with both arms outstretched like a glider, and as he waltzed around the counter, he would sing..."Praise the Lord and pass the ammunition." We enjoyed the entertainment!

After he left Condor Field, we learned that at his next assignment, he had crashed and had broken nearly every bone in his body. He was rushed to Walter Reed Hospital. While he was there, Pinkie and I (I was a cashier by this time) had everyone that came into the Canteen write a note to Al in one long continuous letter. He answered and said that he would come back to see us all some day. We're still expecting you, Al!

"Buzz" Raymond presented me with a Chimayo blanket purse as he was about to leave the base. He said it was from "all of the guys in his Class" (43-2). As there was no Post Office on the base, some of the fellows entrusted me with their money to purchase War Bonds, money-orders or whatever they needed from town. At one time I carried $1200 with me to the Post Office for the g.p.'s (glider pilots). The purse was a gesture of appreciation which I have not forgotten....and I still have the purse!

In 1943, one of the cadets - his name may have been Nehring or Neufeld - came to the Canteen with an album of pictures which he said belonged to his brother. The black and white snapshots seem to be circa World War I and are mostly of military personnel based on an island. The album cover features an island scene in color. The cadet asked that I keep it for him. When I asked him for an address so that I might mail it for him, he answered, "No. Someday I will come back and get it." I still have the album.

The Canteen attracted some of the personnel from the Dispensary too. I remember Cecil Pomeroy, Robert Clark, and Wayne Judy. I always wanted to write a story entitled, "A Boy Named Judy."

Some of the civilian flight instructors at Condor Field were: John Robinson, Phil Livingston, Don Downie, Bill Helling, Bill Was, Ed Reeder, Jim Gilliam, Wally Neugent, Bill Atwood, Bill Putnam, Frank Wolcott, Jim Grainger, Kimball, Heideman, Rush, Couts, Ballard, Hannaford, Pettit, Edgar, Sangster, Larry Creighton, Ray Park, and so many more whose names are hard to recall after forty plus years.

Guinevere Ferry Keys about two years after her Condor Field days during World War II. Photo courtesy of Gwyn Keys

Tow pilots I remember were: Henry "Hank" Moore, Howard Sevdy, Chet Knee, Wayne Yunke, Pfaender, Geise, Zarth, Wolfe, Haansen, Czukor, and others whose faces are clear but my memory fades at this point.

During Condor Fields heyday, several parties were held in Twentynine Palms. One, hosted by Wally Neugent, included (I think) Helling, Was, Andy Houghton, Frances and Hank Moore, Clarke and myself, Donna and George Scurlock, and others. Donna worked in Bud King's office and George was a dispatcher. We danced to music from the record player and enjoyed a buffet. Toward the end of the evening, the host played back a secret tape he had made of the party by hiding the recorder somewhere between the bedroom and the bathroom. There were some red faces!

Red-haired Andy Houghton stands out in my memory of Neugent's party, as most everyone agreed that he was the best dancer there. He was very good at doing the tango. Several months later, we learned that Andy had been killed while flying "the Hump."

Another party, which stands out in my fond memories, was held - I think - at Clint Worthington's. Harry Commer was there and some of the people who attended the Neugent party: Edie (I can't recall her last name), Phyllis Orbison, Dick Pettinger, Donna Scurlock, and me.

Clint had spent some time in the islands and was prevailed upon to do an island dance. Since he needed a partner and Donna knew that I had been a professional dancer before I married Clarke, she pushed me out on the floor. I kicked off my shoes and followed Clint's lead as he danced and chanted our accompaniment. It was fun! Clint had several of the single girls begging for dancing lessons after that demonstration!

Clarke went to Quartzite, Arizona about this time for a refresher course in powered planes. He was away for two months. When he returned, he checked out as a primary student flight instructor.

As Pinkie has mentioned in her chapter, we civilians were invited to ride in a glider, as the program was being phased out in March 1943. My pilot was lst Lieutenant John S. Bowers. I will never forget that ride. It was great! He put the TG6 through two loops, an Immelman, and a spin before coming in for a perfect landing!

One of the prettiest girls who worked at Condor Field was Frances Moore, wife of Hank. Frances was a control tower operator. Her call letters were "2PJ", and that's what everyone affectionately called her. Ruth Downie, wife of Don, also worked in the tower. When Ruth turned in her notice, Frances suggested that I take her place. So I did! I missed the congeniality of the Canteen, but I did enjoy the tower -- and it was good experience.

The last time that I saw Troy Martin was while I was on duty in the tower. Troy had secured permission from the CO to..."visit my nice guys that everybody loved." I was flattered! Troy was one of these truly nice guys that everybody loved. His death in June of 1944 while on duty in the South Pacific grieved all of Twentynine Palms. The American Legion Post there was named in his honor.

Clarke controlled our finances. He would pay all of the bills and buy our food. This arrangement was all right with me, as I had learned early in our marriage that he could be terribly unhappy without money in his pocket.

I remember that Clarke failed to pay the Wikoff Electric bill in Twentynine Palms, and after several notices, they cut off our power. We had a gas range, a gas water heater, used a sad iron when necessary, and dined by kerosene lamp or candlelight -- for months. The situation probably bothered the Wikoffs more than it did Clarke or me. Still, it was something I would rather have resolved in another way.

Saturday nights would usually find us at Jimmy Williams' Smoke Tree Broiler where Clarke would play his cornet in the little dance band. Bill Barnet played the piano. Sometimes George Scurlock would sit in with his saxophone and clarinet. At the close of Condor Field's primary flight training program, both Clarke and George asked for active duty and were sent to Fort MacArthur.

Pinkie and I went to live at the El Adobe at the request of F.R. Whyers. Sam Bailey was the general manager and Bill Ingram and I were, more-or-less, caretakers. Pinkie landed a good job at the Post Office. We weren't paid for services at the El Adobe, but we did have a nice place to live in spite of the fact that the place was in receivership.

Pinkie's job at the Post Office was full of surprises for some of us. One day I opened my mailbox, and there reposed a dusty old bird's nest! Another time I opened the box and out fell a dozen marbles!

My many memories of Pinkie include the poem - a declaration - that she and I wrote for Onie Overbay and Harlow Jones when they announced their engagement. It was about...."the party of the first part - and the party of the second part....etc." Pinkie wound it up with, "Hell, fellas, let's ALL have a party!"

It wasn't long before Condor Field was host to the Sea Bees who prepared the entire field for USN occupation. Lt. William L. Calhoun, USNR, was the Officer in Charge. With the arrival of the Navy pilots, the El Adobe took on new life as an Officers Club.

When special parties were held, I was encouraged to ask some of the local girls to fill in with the Navy wives. The nicest girls I knew were Lois Marlow and the Strickler sisters, Helen and

Dorothy. They were always invited. Alma and Sam Bailey and Pinkie and I were on hand too.

While I was at the El Adobe, a tourist asked me to recommend a realtor, so I sent him to "Watty" Watkins. Watty sold him a nice parcel. In appreciation, Watty gave me an elegant box of stationery with my name imprinted!

Do you remember the movie actor, Charles Drake? He appeared at the El Adobe one morning asking for a place in which...."to rest and to hide-a-way" for a few days. All of El Adobe's rooms were taken, so I let him use Bill Ingram's room, as Bill was out of town at the time.

Clarke and I were divorced in 1944, and I left the desert to work for the Civil Aeronautics Administration as a control tower operator, first at the Madeira Airport and then at the Santa Barbara Airport in Goleta.

Gwyn and Willis Keys appeared in the 1976 film, "Challenge of the Desert," which detailed the early life of Willis' family at their Desert Queen Ranch. Both were considered "naturals" by all the film crew as they spoke of ranch life before the camera. Photo by the author.

GUINEVERE FERRY KEYS

I had purchased property in Joshua Tree and would camp out there occasionally visiting with the Overbays and Norman and Frank "Bud" Pauley. In 1953, on one of these visits, I met Willie Keys, of the Keys Ranch family in the Joshua Tree National Monument. We were married in 1956, and I returned to live and to work in Joshua Tree. The Gholsons, Leona and Burt, were my bosses for eight years at the DESERT JOURNAL newspaper which they owned and published.

In the early 1960's, Willie and I adopted a beautiful, ten year old Joshua Tree girl named Suzanne Marie. Suzanne grew up, as girls will do, and presented us with a beautiful granddaughter, named Amy.

We visit the desert regularly. With so many memories dear to our hearts, we shall always live in the shadow of the palms.

Former glider pilot student, Ed Hillyard, with Gwyn and Willis Keys who joined other Condor Field Alumni at the October 1986 Condor Field Reunion hosted by the 29 Palms Historical Society. Photo by the author.

PRUDENCE UNDERHILL

Prudence Mason was born June 4, 1915, in Pasadena, California, the daughter of Lemuel and Matilda Mason. "Prudie", who never reached five feet tall, attended early grades in the once historic "old wooden school house" at Raymond Avenue and Dakota Street. Shortly after graduation from John Muir High School in 1933, she started newspaper work. While employed by a Pasadena area publication, "learning to be a cub reporter, keeping books and the subscription list up to date," she met Bill Underhill who frequently came from Twentynine Palms to visit her boss. Later she became his bride, as well as associate editor-publisher of the newspaper he founded in 1935 - THE DESERT TRAIL.

William John Underhill was born June 12, 1899, on the family homestead in South Wayne, Wisconsin. He was the first of four sons of James Kimball Underhill and Anna Marie Strub Underhill. A few years later the family moved to Mindoro, Wisconsin where they owned and operated a general store.

At the age of seventeen, Bill had the urge to migrate west to fulfill a dream to homestead. World War I erupted, and on August 10, 1917, he was among the first army enlistees at Cody, Wyoming. Sent to France in December, he saw action at Chateau Thierry during the "big push" the following July. He was honorably discharged as a corporal upon his return to the United States on March 10, 1919. Though injured in the line of duty, he was ready to start life over again.

Unable to afford college, he took a variety of jobs until 1923, when he began to get on-the-job training at a newspaper in Dawson, Minnesota. Here Bill Underhill learned the printing trade; operating a linotype and presses fascinated him. He had found his career and became proficient. A fine letter of recommendation from his publisher helped him secure jobs in various city newspapers, one special one being in Pasadena.

In 1928, while a linotype operator in the Crown City, he learned that World War I veterans would be given preference for 160 acre homesteads in Twentynine Palms. He had been denied the homesteading privilege in Montana, as he was too young then. Here was his chance to continue a family tradition begun by his grandfather in Wisconsin in 1846. He selected his "160" four miles south of Four Corners and named it "Broadview".

In April 1935 Bill started THE DESERT TRAIL newspaper. Its early editions read like a history book for the developing community of Twentynine Palms and this desert area. He was reporter, editor, manager, typesetter, pressman, and bookkeeper in the beginning.

In 1937 he rented a school room and began showing the first motion pictures in Morongo Valley. He soon leased property at Smith's Ranch and constructed an indoor theatre and roller skating rink which opened in 1940. November of 1945 saw the Underhills constructing a modern "hardtop" theatre at the intersection of Two Mile and Adobe Roads, and in 1952 they built the Starlite Drive-In Theatre and outdoor rink on Gorgonio Drive east of Adobe Road.

Bill and Prudie were married May 11, 1941, and in the following years they worked together as a team in all their ventures. Prudie helped him produce THE DESERT TRAIL and operate their entertainment enterprises. Even when their two children, Ann and Bill, were young, they became part of the family team.

Bill's death on January 22, 1984 brought to a close nearly fifty-six years in our community that he watched grow and to which he had contributed so much during his life here. Prudie continues to live in the family home on Underhill Lane. Their daughter, Ann Marie, is an architect and lives with her family in Washington, D.C., while the original family homestead is occupied by son Bill, busy in construction work.

*　　*　　*　　*　　*

One day in 1928, while pawing the keys of a PASADENA STAR NEWS linotype, an Associated Press telegraph release read "Homesteading Opening in Twentynine Palms -- 160-acre plots for war veterans."

As he frequently said, "I was twenty-nine years old and the thought was renewed --- since Grandpa was a '49er, why couldn't another Bill Underhill be a '29er and go homesteading?"

On March 5, 1928, the bachelor took a couple of days off work and piled high his 1925 Dodge convertible, sans top, with anticipated needs of a tent, water barrels, camp stove, cooking utensils, and a supply of canned and dehydrated foods. And yes, a shovel plus a canvas bag full of water hanging on the radiator cap on the hood.

Shovel and water bag -- two essentials of those who journeyed to the desert and which forty-eight years later Bill had memorialized in a bronze sculpture by Michael Hill and which stands now in front of the Adobe Road Civic Building. He had it dedicated to World War I veterans who settled Twentynine Palms and to its hardy homesteaders.

Devil's Garden, the area that once was profuse with cactus just north of now Interstate 10, was a seldom-traveled, winding one-track path of stones and chuck-holes. But this was the only route to Twentynine Palms from the west. "It had no respect for my 'lingerie' tires," the homesteader often remarked, "and there was hardly a place along the fifty mile trek I didn't have to stop and patch a rubber tube in a tire that blew out." The "road" didn't improve as he continued, so his patching kit was another necessity.

Experience on the rough, dusty ride was the first of many on this homesteading adventure and a mild initiation to the trials and tribulations to follow during his years of pioneering. He liked this "roughing it." Little did he realize then, he'd comment, when some called him "plain crazy," how rewarding this episode in his life would be in years to come.

Bill was one of the scores of early-comers who sought out the Old Adobe at the Oasis for a night of sleep, and here he spent his first night. Jackrabbits and quail were there by the hundreds, as they feasted on the foliage, mesquite beans, and relished in the artesian water that profusely flowed.

Chugging up Gold Park Road, another rocky, narrow dirt lane (now known as Utah Trail), he surveyed the barren country and selected his hillside "160" slightly east and almost on the border of what is now known as the famed Joshua Tree National Monument, proclaimed as such in 1936 by President Franklin D. Roosevelt. He chose that location because he was entranced with the view of the valley below, as his land was several hundred feet higher than the Oasis of Mara. He liked the slant of the land, as he foresaw no danger of flooding should the desert get some rain!

"I named my homestead 'Broadview'," he explained, "because that was the name of a place in Montana that I thought was so peaceful and beautiful and where I hoped to homestead in 1917. I worked there on a cattle ranch awhile as I was making my way across the country upon leaving Wisconsin.

"That was a fine, healthy life -- it taught a man self-reliance," he said philosophically. "In short -- the virtues that ought to come from life in the open country. I enjoyed that life to the full, and I felt some day, for sure, I'd find it again." All this he told me one night in the fall of 1941, as we were swinging in the wood-slat swing on the porch at Broadview Twentynine Palms.

"I have almost all I want now -- you and this, but we'll have some kids running around here some day and that'll make our lives complete," he lovingly told me.

While he "camped out" in his tent the first few weeks of 1928 and between stints at the newspaper in San Bernardino, he dug an oblong hole of about 14' x 20' for his cellar. He walled it up with large stones he had hauled from a few miles south. It wasn't until

Bill Underhill and the then, Prudie Mason, in
their courting days in April 1940. Photo courtesy
of Prudie Underhill.

eight years later that acreage became a preservation and from then
on not one pebble or weed or anything could be removed from this
Monument. He had some mining claims there, though none paid
off.

He couldn't afford a cement floor, but he folded up his tent
and moved into the cellar. The basic flooring for his house then
provided a roof for the basement, and he lived down there "high
and dry" until he hauled out cement, framing material, three inch
siding, and cedar shingles on the sides of his roadster from Banning
sixty miles west. He described how the heavy load shifted as his
"Studie" slowly bumped along, and he had to unload and reload
several times on the numerous journeys.

Once Bill remarked that all the early day homesteaders should at least have a BA degree! The "BA," he explained, stood for "Before Anything - before electricity, telephones, mail delivery, paved roads, cooking gas, newspaper, water service, cooling, fire protection, entertainment, and television!" But, without all those modern facilities and despite what would seem like hardships, Bill felt those early years proved to be enjoyable and carefree times. "Secluded on this faraway desert, we soon found it easy to forget worries of the outside world," he would say.

He would fry quail and rabbit in his big, old frying pan over a mesquite wood fire out of doors. For showers, after working all day building, he explained how he rigged up a frame outside on which he hung a five gallon can filled with water and a spigot he could turn on.

While he stayed weekends in his tent and later the cellar, he would return to the city to work on newspapers throughout the week for his livelihood. Framing of the two-bedroom house and wiring was followed by wood siding and a cedar shingle peaked roof. Here it is fifty-eight years later, and the homestead house proudly stands up on the hill with the same siding and shingles that are kept oiled and painted by our son, Bill, thirty-four, to whom his father gave the homestead to "keep it in the family." A large, beautiful native rock fireplace gives the living room, with his hardwood floors, a true "homey" atmosphere. This is one of a few homestead houses still standing.

Bill put claim to having the first bath tub and indoor flush toilet of this area with water flowing by gravity from his twelve hundred gallon cement underground water tank that he built one hundred yards south of the house. He hauled his own water from the village in a homemade tank trailer "get-up" to Broadview. There was the mirrored medicine cabinet with many girlie pictures pasted inside when I first saw it, but these were all cleared out when we arrived back from our honeymoon in 1941.

His ambition was to be as modern as possible in this pioneer's land, and this prompted him to buy a generator that he placed in a cute little house one hundred feet east of the home. Only the generator to produce electricity and two fifty-gallon drums of white gas were in it. Electric wiring was strung from the light plant to provide night brightness in each room - two bedrooms, living room, kitchen, bathroom, and back porch. There must be lights in the cellar and all around the front porch which measured the width of the house and had a lattice-work top to let in the sunshine. Planning not to be without lights at anytime, he installed three wall gas fixtures fueled with propane from a tank set up several feet south outside. I was told that when ironing to keep at least one bulb illuminated so the generator wouldn't be overburdened with "going off and on."

PRUDIE UNDERHILL

This early settler often commented that from his porch in 1928 he would look down over the wide expanse of Twentynine Palms and see but one light, and that was a candle in the window of Donnell's Desert Hotel.

Bill knew his pride and joy, Broadview, would be seen for miles, as there were few houses, just those on 160-acre plots, and these were the nearest neighbors. Subdivisions, such as the Hanson Tract to the north, were to come later. He painted his cedar shingles green and the house a pretty yellow, trimmed in green, one of the neatest bachelor houses around. The big rock fireplace on the east outside was a masterpiece and made the place look sound.

Building his house wasn't but a part of what Bill Underhill did in those late twenties. Few are left here who know of his donation of labor in aiding development of Twentynine Palms, working on roads, and helping other veterans build the first public swimming pool. Those who could not work might donate a little money to other willing laborers out of a job. All donation labor was a labor of love. He and other homesteaders frequently helped each other in constructing their homes or cabins.

"There was a variety of people when I came and everybody knew everyone and just about knew most difficulties or problems that arose for them," he used to say, adding "Many were World War I buddies who came to seek improvement in their health, but many like myself just came to pioneer, and we able-bodied men did whatever we could to make life more comfortable for the ailing neighbors and friends. You couldn't be here without being a friend."

As time passed, Bill became more and more thankful that he had "taken the road less traveled" for it "paid off" in numerous ways - a happy family of four, a "team" that had fun working together for many years in our businesses - and it all culminated in success in our view. Many times we both expressed our love for this ever-beautiful desert to which we felt we owed a heavy debt of gratitude.

It was seven years after bachelor Bill Underhill planted his heels in this dusty, sparsely-settled desert that he conceived the idea of founding THE DESERT TRAIL newspaper. He foresaw future possibilities of this high desert, mostly as a health-giving resort because of its fine climate. This, combined with the need for creating a job for himself, was incentive to assume the mantle of spokesman for the community in effecting the weekly tabloid.

As he was gifted as a linotype operator and printer and knew the shop work was the most expensive part of publishing a paper, he - with his magnificent self-confidence - decided to launch into producing THE DESERT TRAIL April 18, 1935. Editor-publisher Underhill dedicated the newspaper and himself to serving Twentynine Palms and the surrounding area in helping the community and valley grow, prosper, and perpetuate harmony. The pioneer adopted in his first edition the slogan, "Watch Twentynine Palms Grow" and used it as a "filler line" throughout the columns. He not only watched, but helped in many ways.

THE DESERT TRAIL was the first newspaper of the entire Morongo Valley. It was not a "house organ", but was the first printed publication with its type set on a linotype and produced on a printing press. It was the first legal newspaper of general circulation here and affiliated with the California Newspaper Publishers' Association.

Naming of his publication was the first order of business for the thirty-five year old. He vividly recollected the rugged, forty mile rocky and narrow dirt road he had traversed hundreds of times since his 1928 homesteading days. This would be his inspiration. Thus, THE DESERT TRAIL.

The next important decision related to the need of a distinctive masthead for his paper. In conjunction with a San Bernardino artist it was created to include the natural, beautiful, desert growth of palm trees, cactus, and Joshua trees forming a background for the title in script style.

"Dedicated to the mining and resort industry" was first printed under the tabloid's name, along with the prevailing price of gold in six point type as $34.79 per ounce and silver at $.7307 cents per ounce. And forever extolling the virtues of our desert, Bill included another pertinent line: "A dry spot comfortably inhabited all year; 29 Palms average rainfall 2 inches." Of course, today we all know gold's value is in the neighborhood of $340 per ounce and silver $6 per ounce.

Although Bill's trails had previously led to working on many newspapers, and he was fully aware that all publications were geared to meet a deadline, never did he realize or appreciate the task involved when all phases of such a production fell on one person. Here he found he was not only to do the mechanical work of production, set the type, run the presses and fold for distribution, but also he was reporter, editor, manager, bookkeeper. He wrote the entire paper, except for a contributed column now and then.

He always admitted his journalism experience was limited and recalled the chiding he took from those more learned for his mistakes of phraseology and typographical errors. But upon reaching his eightieth birthday he said, "I revel in the fact that a very few newspapers of this country have survived continuous publication for so many decades, and my newspaper had a very humble beginning. Credit must be given to succeeding publishers of THE DESERT TRAIL who have made continuous production and dedication possible." He added to this always: "My successors have carried on our aims and purposes and consistently grown with this desert which is very gratifying to me."

In 1935 Bill didn't have the capital for a printing plant, so for two years he rented equipment in already established plants in San Bernardino, Colton, and Beaumont, traversing there each week to set the type, print the paper, and fold it by hand. Back to Twentynine Palms he'd drive, usually breaking the speed limit, he'd recall, with the five hundred copies of the four-page tabloid. In Whitewater, at the once popular Bridgehaven Cafe stop for desert travelers, he'd proudly begin handing out his paper freely, continuing throughout Morongo Valley, Yucca Valley, and Twentynine Palms, lastly, "to get people reading about our desert." He was what one might have called a "one-man Chamber of Commerce."

News was mighty scarce at the birth of THE TRAIL, and it was necessary for Bill to reach out and print anything (and almost) everything that happened up and down the eighty mile "strip" from Morongo Valley, that boasted only one lodge and a few homesteaders, through Yucca Valley on the unpaved road with only a little post office, a small store, and a service station, through Twentynine Palms to Old Dale mining district, up to Amboy. Joshua Tree did not exist. Bill was a congenial, friendly man, and he didn't pass up anyone for a "hi" and a friendly visit. Each contact meant a news item, usually.

When a "local yokel" drove to Banning to buy a pair a shoes, when friends or relatives visited, if a kid broke his arm, or if a family bought a new or used car - anything that would make a line-o'-type or two - went into Bill's columns. One time he was challenged quite severely when he printed a three-line "personal" about a couple (who had lived together here for months) going to San Bernardino for the night. He was angrily corrected that they were "now married and had been for a few days" but didn't tell anyone - especially the editor. So the item should have read "Mr. and Mrs." instead of "Dick and Wilma!"

Columns had to be filled with anything worth reading, for as yet no land developments were taking place, few businesses existed, and no signs then of any big expansions. But extolling virtues of this desert was a "must".

"Advertising was a painstaking job of solicitation, for anyone venturesome enough to establish a business in those early days had no competition," Editor Bill once said, adding "so therefore they felt they had no apparent need to advertise! And if they did run a little ad, say for fifty cents or a dollar, it was tendered only as a goodwill gesture and to show appreciation for some news item that had been printed about them."

Some eating places, and yes, even a furniture store in San Bernardino agreed to run an ad if Bill would "trade it out" in meals and furniture. "Just sign the slip" is what the restaurant owner would say after a meal, and then when Bill brought in his advertising statement at the end of the month, they'd balance off. His living room set at the homestead was a "trade-out" at Fooshee's in the city that became our county seat.

The country publisher's display advertising price was fifty cents per column inch if the customer didn't buy anymore than that. But if a merchant chose more space, the price was thirty-five cents per column inch.

Of course prices of store items were comparable over fifty years ago, such as a 4-piece mahogany bedroom suite with its poster bed, dressing table, bench and chest was $39.50, and a Simmon's inner spring mattress was $19.95. A deluxe Chevrolet coupe was $335. In the grocery store ads prime rib or lamb roast, 19 cents per pound; asparagus, 5 cents a pound; sugar ten pounds for 51 cents in a cloth bag. Eggs sold for 23 cents a dozen; flour 70 cents for a 24 and a half pound bag; thread 3 cents per spool; men's socks 9 cents a pair; Stetson hats, $5; Florsheim shoes, $8.95. Beauty shops charged $2.50 for a permanent wave and 65 cents for a shampoo and fingerwave. You could buy a cup of coffee for 5 cents and a can of beer for 15 cents. Yes, and land now known as Harmony Acres was selling for $25 per acre. Believe it!

In the April 18, 1935 edition there were actually eighteen Twentynine Palms advertisers, some one column by one inch (50 cents) and some two columns by two inches ($1.40). The few oldtimers remaining in Twentynine Palms will remember them: Bagley's Store, Ted Holderman's Ice and Cold Storage Co., Elise Dumas Beauty Salon, The Adobe Hotel, Joe Brady's Garage, Graham's Lunch Room, Benito Grocery and Garage, Builder Walter M. Berg, Legion Laundry, 29 Palms Inn, Casa de los Tejidos, Walter Godwin Liquefied Gas, 29 Palms Produce, Legion Grounds Sleeping Cabins, Donnell's Desert Hotel, Jay's Lunch, Twentynine Palms Lumber Co., and William and E.G. Stubbs Contractors. A two column five-inch ad drew attention with "29 Palms Has A Future - We Are Investing Here" paid by Southwest Subdividers of Los Angeles, and they turned out to be among the top developers.

However, among the first to start land development, too, was Ole Hanson, once mayor of Seattle, who successfully started San Clemente, California, and who had a vision of the local Hanson Tract, south of Twentynine Palms Highway and east of Utah Trail, becoming the attractive area of white stucco homes topped with red Mexican-tiled roofs, to stand out like San Clemente properties which Hanson previously developed. But many varieties of homes have been constructed in that area.

Like other developers who followed, Ole Hanson each week

purchased hundreds of copies of THE DESERT TRAIL that he mailed throughout these United States to potential land buyers. Sale of these editions at two and a half cents each was a small subsidy for the country editor. It at least helped to pay for the paper stock!

Underhill related that in the beginning THE DESERT TRAIL didn't have a "home", at least not a business building, for he first quietly headquartered at his homestead house to write. After two years of trekking westward sixty or more miles each week to produce the newspaper on rented equipment, Bill explained that in 1937 he became sufficiently established to warrant a bank loan to build his first newspaper building and equip it with presses and a linotype.

He had opened a checking account and savings with the Bank of Beaumont in 1928, in its original location and had set up a credit rating. The officers had faith in his abilities and ambition and loaned him five thousand dollars which was a lot of money in those days. There was no bank here until the forties. Thus, the first newspaper plant of this high desert was constructed, and the building still stands on the west side of Adobe Road between Desert Trail and Two Mile Road.

This was the first business building in the then new Adobe Acres subdivision - but there was no electricity to the property. The only solution to that was to invest in a kerosene-powered generator, and later a single cylinder diesel engine to create power to run the printing plant. That's how Bill immediately met head-on handicaps of producing the publication in its new beautiful headquarters. As he often philosophized to our daughter Ann and son Bill, "the difficult can be done instantly, but the impossible takes a little longer."

Designed and built by the late Allen Balch, it is of frame-stucco construction and all local workmen were hired to use all materials purchased of local businesses. So thankful for the Bank of Beaumont loan and its confidence in his future success, Publisher Bill retained a bank account and conducted other business with them from 1928, following through with their successors ever since. We recently were recognized at their anniversary as their oldest customers.

September 11, 1937, marked the "open house" of the new DESERT TRAIL plant and three hundred visitors showed their spirit of friendliness, much to the gratification of the publisher. They all wrote their names on the newly-poured concrete walk between the flagstones. In his follow-up editorial, Underhill not only thanked everyone, but stated "it is such neighborliness and community spirit that will continue to be the policy of THE TRAIL which will make not only it a successful enterprise, but also make

Twentynine Palms a thriving and progressive place to live."

The newspaper press, a turn of the century vintage, Bill purchased from a Banning plant that was updating its equipment. And the linotype, he bought from a Los Angeles daily. He guessed the reason the big city establishments replaced their older equipment was so small country publishers like himself could get as economical a start as possible in area like this pioneering community where all business investments were limited because of the depression and lack of capital.

THE TRAIL got printed in its own home even if it was sometimes late, and despite a few possible grammatical errors, the citizenry always stood by the front door waiting to read the weekly. Lateness could have been that "old" Clem, the town's welder, had to be summoned during the night's pressrun - a part broke off. There might have been so much electricity in this desert air that the newsprint couldn't be hand fed through the platens. Plain Christmas tree tinsel probably had to be strung around and over the flat-bed press to absorb the static.

Though lack of telephones posed a problem for soliciting news and ads, there was always "mail time" at the post office where Editor Bill would be obvious with his pad and pencil taking down notes. Most of the time, contrary to the usual newspaper reporter's procedure of writing out news items on a typewriter, Bill would save time and energy by sitting down to his linotype keyboard, take notes out of his shirt pocket, and set the type ready for the galley and a hand proof. Not all linotype operators could or liked to do this, but Bill would set a line of the hot metal, read it backward, and if there were mistakes, he'd throw the "slug" in the "hell box" for discarded type, later melted for re-use, and set it again. Visitors interested in how a newspaper was printed liked to stand by the linotype and watch this fascinating, most complicated typesetting machine operate, for they knew a little later they'd see it all in black and white on newsprint.

In November of 1936 THE DESERT TRAIL banner line on the front page read in striking bold, inch type: "Light and Power for 29 Palms." The "scoop" bore the news that Leonard P. Wikoff of San Bernardino and Los Angeles had received the certificate of convenience and necessity from the California Railroad Commission which then gave Wikoff and his associates the right to exercise the franchise to provide electricity to Twentynine Palms.

Wikoff had labored on this privilege for many months. In fact, San Bernardino County Board of Supervisors had in the summer of 1936 granted Wikoff the right to operate and maintain a telephone system as well as the light and power system. However, as California Water and Telephone Company was already operating in an adjacent territory, the railroad commission gave that company a certificate to operate in the Twentynine Palms area.

The Wikoff generators were soon set up in a new building at the northwest corner of Adobe Road and Twentynine Palms Highway, now situated immediately north of the service station and mini-mart. Later owners have made considerable addition for various small businesses and the complex is referred to as Adobe Courts.

In 1940 Leonard Wikoff and his wife Sara had plans to increase output of the generating plant and extended electric lines up North Adobe Road. But not until Underhill advanced several hundred dollars for the expense of the extension, since THE DESERT TRAIL was one of the very few potential users on that route. The editor was grateful for this new service.

Preparing for their annual "Old-Timers' Reunion" during Pioneer Days 1960. The Underhills hosted this get-together in their home for more than twenty-five years until Bill's ill-health prevented it. In 1983 the 29 Palms Historical Society took over hosting this annual event. Photo courtesy of Prudie Underhill.

For many years the town flourished, Bill recalled, and early settlers reaped rewards by selling parts of their large homesteads and investing small amounts in business ventures. Many kept coming to what once was a sleepy, quiet place to live in hopes of "getting in on the ground floor" of what showed promise of being a boom town!

"The boom dropped, however, and this desert and its inhabitants had to meet slowing down of progress and unemployment, paralleling the entire nation's problems of the times - an admitted depression in 1929 and the early '30s," Underhill once wrote.

Although development was slow, it proved to be steady and substantial before long. By the early '40s this once vast span of barren desert was now well plotted with subdivisions, networks of roads and paved streets, businesses springing up in remote sections, each believing his to be the nucleus for a permanent town site.

April of 1936 found telephone company officials here for the first time to survey Twentynine Palms relative to establishing phone service locally. They were the division managers of California Water and Telephone Company, which was operating in Palm Springs, and their franchise was to absorb this section of the desert.

"Here our newspaper played a key role in editorializing for a modern system of communication when it was learned the utility company was planning to install a magnet hand-ring type of instruments discarded from the neighboring resort of Palm Springs," Editor Bill said. They listened to us. "So, the first phones they gave us were the type that signaled a central switchboard when a receiver was lifted, which proved a great innovation to subscribers here. The first panel totaled less than a dozen," Underhill recalled.

"Twentynine Palms had one of the most unusual telephone contracts in the annals of a town," he remarked in referring to Dave and Anna Poste, awarded the "hello" job by the phone company. At their small home west of the Plaza on Homestead Road, the Postes had a switchboard, the operator's bunk bed, and their dining table all in a 10' x 12' room. It proved to be almost an answering service for the few subscribers. For upon returning home from an absence of an hour or day, "we lifted up the receiver and asked Dave or Anna if there had been any calls." Sometimes the caller could solicit a "tip" of any new happenings of the day.

Being a telephone operator wasn't enough for Dave, so he filed for Justice of the Peace, and after a little campaigning, got himself elected "JP." Court was sometimes held in his dining room so his "number please" job wasn't neglected, should Anna have to go shopping.

Come May 1936, TRAIL readers and homesteaders were elated over a page one five column headline that said, "More Oiled Roads for 29 Palms!" That month bids were opened by the State Highway Department for oiling a twenty-foot width of Devil's Garden road, the 11.5 miles from Highway 99 (now Interstate 10) to connect with the county road beginning at Morongo Valley. This was exceptionally good news as Devil's Garden had the roughest and most hazardous section of a trip to Twentynine Palms. This same period saw county equipment dragging roads in many parts of the community, such as Two-Mile Road.

Indicative of the early community spirit that prevailed in 1936, a group of civic-minded citizens of the north side pledged two thousand dollars for purchase of oil for three miles of Adobe Road leading from Two-Mile Road to Smith's Ranch. The county road superintendent explained the county would in "all probability" transport and spread the oil without cost. Hauling of gravel preparatory to oiling would have to be done by local gratis labor, he said.

Twentynine Palms might have been referred to in early days as "at the end of the road" on the east side of the Morongo Basin....but it had many "firsts" in this entire valley, and one of them was a motion picture theatre. In 1937 Bill felt it was time to bring some entertainment for the growing populace, so he arranged to show Hollywood movies in the school room on Utah Trail that he rented for five dollars a night. He hung a bed sheet on the wall and used portable 35mm projectors.

This was in the first high school, now the junior high on the west side of Utah Trail. That was a time when that one room served the entire enrollment - four high school grades. He charged twenty-five cents admission with little kids free. There are still residents who remember what a godsend it was to have first-run movies, a place for everyone to go, since the only other entertainment place was the Blue Diamond Bar on the south end of Adobe Road.

By 1938-39 admission prices were raised to ten cents for kids and forty cents for adults since Bill progressed to larger quarters. He leased twenty acres from Bill Smith on the old Smith Ranch and constructed a large building (which still stands) to be utilized as a theatre, roller skating rink, community dance center, gymnasium, and for vaudeville shows, carnivals, and political events. This was the first such large building on this desert and the only entertainment center. In the summer he projected movies to an outdoor patio from the same projection room he used for indoor shows by turning the machines around. A diesel-powered generator provided electricity.

We Underhills managed and ran the theatre and skating rink businesses as well as the ice cream fountain at Smith's Ranch. This was when all the Smith children were quite small, but they grew up and in later years had their own showings. The official opening of this roller rink-theatre was on April 25, 1940. Over one thousand persons came to the celebration, and from then on for several years young and old made the new Underhill rink their headquarters for amusement and fun. There was no such entertainment within sixty or more miles, either way from Twentynine Palms. That building Underhills sold to the Smiths in 1945 and relinquished the leased land to them upon erecting the new theatre at the Plaza, now a furniture warehouse.

After Bill was appointed chairman of a fire department committee from the local Chamber of Commerce in 1938, he started searching for a piece of fire-fighting equipment. The next April a philanthropic man of Altadena, William D. Davies, contributed a fifty gallon chemical outfit mounted on wheels. Bill went to get the equipment and started forming a volunteer fire department. The apparatus was stationed at THE DESERT TRAIL office on the hill overlooking the entire valley - a central location. Bill was honored by being appointed the first fire chief in Twentynine Palms. That first fire fighting equipment is now on display at the present fire house with a plaque of identification.

Establishment of the Twentynine Palms Air Academy in 1942 was a boon to this desert. The first refresher course for glider instructors took place January 5, 1942, and the first class of twelve second lieutenants in the Corps arrived January 19th and entered in Class No. 42-1. Ground school for the first class was held at Smoke Tree Boiler, now the Josh Lounge, which had a large dining and dancing room on the south end of the building. At start of the glider school there were no buildings and only one glider. The men slept in convertible houses near Twentynine Palms Highway.

Because the Air Academy was the first glider school and became the largest in the United States, changes were rapid. Columns in THE DESERT TRAIL were soon filled with news from the dry lake on our north. Businesses in our town benefited greatly at a time when we were in a slump due to the war. Servicemen came from all parts of the country, and they had families and visitors who came here.

The 1943 year at the post office reflected business growth when receipts of $12,511 were the largest of any year to that date. Twentynine Palms was recipient of its first government housing project on Gorgonio, immediately east of the present post office. Lowest bid on the thirty-four "war houses" was $68,745.

Local businesses, supported by the many employees of the Air Academy, deeply felt the exodus of these residents who left to seek employment elsewhere. Training of air corps glider pilots came to an end in April of 1944 when the government's contract with the private group terminated. This meant closing the community's leading industry which for the last two years had brought scores of workers here.

"Navy Taking Over 29 Palms Air Training Base; Congressman Sheppard Effected Facility Transfer from Army." This was the headline on July 7, 1944 and was startlingly welcomed by area citizens. Condor Field became the Twentynine Palms Naval Auxiliary Air Station on August 1, 1944. The same year also saw numerous young men who had grown up here going off to war. THE TRAIL started running a new column to keep locals informed, called "Scuttlebutt." I was appointed first USO chairman.

The relationship between the town and the naval personnel was very pleasant. The Adobe Hotel on a hilltop and picturesque for many years became a social club for naval officers. We began to see an unusual sight for the desert in hundreds of navy men in their "whites" or "blues" throughout town. On the southeast corner of Four Corners, shore patrol headquarters was established.

Immediately upon commissioning of the naval auxiliary air station, naval personnel prevailed upon us to provide entertainment in a theatre. Before we could obtain a building permit, we were obligated to secure priorities from the War Production Board in Washington, D.C. After numerous trips to San Diego to see top naval officials, our application was finally approved in November 1944. We were authorized to build a four thousand square foot cement block reinforced concrete building on the southwest corner of Adobe and Two-Mile Roads. This was the first "hardtop" showhouse in the Morongo Basin, and we had four hundred upholstered seats with some loges too.

Ground was broken in the summer of 1945. The two lots were purchased for one thousand dollars each and the building cost us twenty thousand dollars. The slanted floor, the curved ceiling of foot-square, spun glass, ornamental acoustical tile was a first hereabouts and made for a beautiful interior. As the colored flagstone front patio walks were laid, friends were invited to inscribe their name in the cement. A colorful neon sign, reading "Theatre" with "29 Palms" lettering over lighted palm trees could be seen for miles.

Grand opening night was November 10, 1945, and the packed house saw "Johnny Angel" starring George Raft. We made arrangements for the Twentynine Palms Little Theatre to have its plays, accommodated various large meetings, and sponsored various events on the stage, one being the Easter parade king and queen contests.

One day early in May 1946, I asked Bill to "Get Marie Worthington to sell tickets the next few nights" for it would be time for delivery of our first baby, Ann Marie Underhill. She was born May 9, 1946, and six years later, son Bill came at the same Redlands hospital. We joyfully reminisced of the times when my Bill took little Bill in the bassinet to the projection room while he ran the film; "Mommy" was selling tickets in the lobby, and Ann was selling popcorn and candy.

In 1952 we purchased ten acres on Gorgonio Drive, two blocks east of Adobe Road, and built the outdoor roller-skating rink. A short time later we built the Starlite Twin Drive-In Theatre on that property. By this time television reception was introduced to the area. We had to close the indoor theatre, but the drive-in continued to grow. Seven years ago we sold this ten acre entertainment center.

So many times people ask when and how I first met Bill. It was while I was working for a Pasadena area newspaper. I was right out of high school and was hired to learn to be a cub reporter, keep books and the subscription list up to date. It only paid five dollars a week.

Bill came in from the desert to visit my boss. He was a handsome, well-groomed man whom I admired from a distance. Sometimes he'd phone from the desert to talk to the boss. In three words I'd cheerfully greet him with "How are you?" (Later he told me that little bit of interest in him created a question in his mind as to "what does she care?") It took a few years for him to find out, but his mother always told me "He was waiting for you to grow up" for I was only eighteen then.

In 1938 Bill came to our office and as he went out the door, he casually said, "Why don't you and your girl friends come to the desert sometime?" I said I would, but I didn't say what year!

By 1939 a girl friend and I had established Pownall and Mason Publicity Agency and together we made frequent trips to Twentynine Palms. These increased as the weeks went on, and Bill's jaunts to Pasadena repeated more often. In between, the mails were kept busy with our exchange of letters every day.

He asked if I could come out and assist in producing the midwinter edition of THE TRAIL on December 13, 1940. I happily said "Yes!" His mother was living at the homestead, and that's where I stayed. When we finished the paper and running the skating rink and show that night, he hurried me up to the homestead where his mother had the big fireplace aglow with a warm, winter fire.

At five minutes to twelve midnight on December 13th, he invited me out to his kitchen. Bill lit one burner on the kitchen stove and asked, "How would you like to be Mrs. Bill Underhill?" Of course, the answer was "I'd love to!" His previous plan was to propose Friday the thirteenth.

He always said he "broke up" the firm of Pownall and Mason. Nancy Clements, a popular Pasadena harpist, played at our wedding in Pasadena on May 11, 1941. After a honeymoon in Santa Barbara, we came home and he carried me across the threshold of Broadview where we lived several years.

There was no adjustment for me from city life to the desert. It all seemed so natural and comfortable. I loved the desert, and we frequented many beautiful spots. I immediately became active with Bill in the newspaper, skating rink, and theatre, and we were congenial in our work. I frequently went to "film row" in Hollywood to book our movies and to buy supplies. For many years we happily worked side by side in the print shop on Adobe Road writing stories reflecting happenings of the community. Bill set reader type on the linotype, and I hand-pegged type for story heads and made up many of the pages of type. Sometimes we worked all night.

William James Underhill with his mother, Prudie, at a social reception on the lawn of the 29 Palms Inn in June 1985. Photo courtesy of Prudie Underhill.

Prudie and Bill's daughter, Ann Congdon and her
family: husband, Dr. Michael B. Congdon, and
daughters, Jessica and Anastasia. The Congdons
live in Washington, D.C.

My late husband Bill was among the far-sighted men who realized the West was destined to become the most important part of
the United States. He loved Twentynine Palms, its people, and
worked hard to be successful. He tenderly recalled many times we
four -- Ann, Bill, he, and I -- camped all night in the Monument
and took short trips together. Sunday school and church were part
of our lives, as were civic organizations.

While we owned THE TRAIL, we had two other newspaper
homes, the second being in 1945 in the now razed Spanish building
on the northeast corner of Twentynine Palms Highway and
Tamarisk. Our dearest memories of that place was bringing there
our first baby, Ann, after her birth. Business was demanding more
and more of our time night and day, and trips to the homestead
five miles out became a task, so we "lived on the job for awhile".

Bill soon had his heart set on our own quarters again, and we designed the slanting glass-fronted building on the east side of Adobe Road across from the civic building. New, fast presses were installed, and on January 15, 1949, we had open house in the middle of an unexpected snowstorm. When we sold the paper in 1951 to Mr. and Mrs. Buren Briggs, they soon constructed their own building a block away.

An exciting day for us was October 17, 1970, when we rode in the annual Pioneer Days parade as Grand Marshalls. For many years we opened our home to the annual "Oldtimers Reunion" which we initiated and anticipated with joy.

Both our children attended local schools from kindergarten through high school. Presently Ann is an architect in Washington, D.C. and her husband Dr. Michael B. Congdon is with the U.S. State Department. They have two daughters, Anastasia, sixteen, and Jessica, fourteen. After college in Arizona, son Bill is happy in construction work here and living at the old homestead.

I live with precious, happy memories of the last forty-five years. Since my devoted husband's passing in January of 1984 at the age of eighty-three, these memories become more dear. In closing I reprint from a notation he kept under the glass on his desk, and which friends agree reflects his beautiful inner self, because they remember his happy, smiling face despite the pain he suffered to the end:

"I go with optimistic view upon the road of life, because I know that in this way I'll weather so much strife; those who look on the brighter side, possess a heart that's gay, for it matters not how rough the road - they always find a way. It may be difficult at times to walk the sunny side, or plod along when showers prompt the heart to hide, but with a smile upon my face, the sun comes shining through; and so I go along with optimistic view."

ROSALIE "PINKIE" GARLOCK GATES

Rosalie Garlock or "Pinkie," as she was nicknamed, was born July 30, 1914, in Cheyenne, Wyoming. She came to Twentynine Palms in March 1942 for what had originally intended to be a short visit with friends, Kate and Jim Garvin. Instead, she decided to stay and take over the duties of cashier at the canteen at the Air Academy.

She was described in a DESERT TRAIL article in March 1943 as having "one of those cheerful smiles that makes the payment of your check in the canteen slightly less painful and whose friendliness and helpfulness is a highlight of the Academy."

Pinkie was an artist, model, and designer, her early training being obtained from the Chouinard Art Institute, Art Center, and the Otis Art Institute. In addition to being an illustrator for the Walt Disney Studios, she was the model for the "Blue Fairy" in the Disney Production of "Pinocchio." The statue of the kneeling figure playing the harp in front of the Hollywood Bowl was also fashioned after Pinkie. In the late 1930's she designed costumes for actor Robert Taylor and the Hollywood Bowl Ballet Company.

Prior to her arrival in Twentynine Palms, she had worked as a model at the Royal Hawaiian Hotel in Honolulu which featured her costumes and designs. It was while she was there that she became ill and learned that she had diabetes.

Pinkie and Mervin "Mo" Gates were married in the early 1960's. Their mutual love of rocks and gemstones was a hobby which won them many first place awards. Even after the death of her husband and loss of her eyesight, Pinkie never lost the wit and keen sense of humor that had been so characteristic of her during her entire life. Her premature death on January 23, 1982, was mourned by a host of friends who treasure her memory.

*   *   *   *   *

I came out to Twentynine Palms in the spring of 1942 for a two week visit and went down to Condor Field to look around. It was still open. You could just walk in and look around, because they were still building.

428

Pinkie Garlock fondly remembered her three years spent in the Twentynine Palms area while she worked at Condor Field from 1942 to 1945. Photo about 1943, courtesy of Gwyn Keys.

They said, "We need girls. What can you do?"

And I said, "Well, I've been a bank teller and can run a cash register, an adding machine, and a bookkeeping machine."

"Sold!"

I got it right then....two meals a day and eighty bucks a month. In those days that was good.

I lived at the Garvin's house up on Utah Trail. It was a little U-shaped tan stucco place with a patio in the center. It slept four and the kids from the Field lived in that and a pump house with a big tank.

We used to haul a trailer down to the water pump and leave it. The first one out in the morning hauled the trailer down, and the first one home filled up the two fifty gallon drums and hauled it back. I believe it was six cents for a load of water.

They called it Condor Field because of the bird's ability to soar. With a wingspan of about ten feet, they could soar for hours. Just like the ailerons on a plane, they'd catch an updraft, get altitude, and just soar. The condor represented perfect gliding.

I remember the glider pilots used to be on the flightline at 6:30 in the morning. We had to get up at 4 to open the canteen. The old canteen had seats for about thirty and those kids would come storming in there about 5 a.m. for breakfast.

One fellow drew a picture of a cat on the cash register that I never could get off. He drew it with a piece of blackboard chalk on that rough metal that NCR used then. And he said, "This is a picture of a happy cat." And that was all. He got up and went off and sat down. We also had a bowling alley and juke box. I had to make change for it.

I think training was six or eight weeks. There were usually three classes going through there. I mean they'd have a beginners, an intermediate, and the guys almost ready to graduate.

Jackie Coogan was a glider pilot. He was a peculiar character, but we had fun. I used to dance with him. He did a buck and wing shuffle down at the old Smith's Ranch. Then there was one tow pilot that everybody knew. That was Jim Backus.

Gwyn Ferry and I were special friends with Sam and Alma Bailey. They were fun. Sam was Provost Marshall at the base and was head of the guards. He was an ex-Pasadena cop, so they put him in charge of the G-2. I think he had six guards under him.

Some of the people I remember were the two Schaffers who were instructors. One of them was short and fat and spelled his name with 2 f's, and there was a tall very good looking one. Both wore army uniforms, but they were really civilians. I think they were instructors. We called them "One F and two F's", because they were both named Schaffer. I remember the Deardoffs. He was a mechanic at the base. I used to go around with his daughter, Dorothy. She was a waitress at the canteen.

There was Les Cross, Chet Knee, and Charlie Matherly. He was a little, short stubby guy who wore a mechanics hat all the time. He was the chief mechanic out in the early days. There was Larry Larsen. I worked for him a while at the base. Lincoln Stonecipher was a guard at the gate.

Then there was Bob Whyers who ran the base. Gwyn and I stayed at their house one summer to water the trees and the plants and to take care of Pat, their great big Airdale dog. It was a beautiful place about two miles west of Twentynine Palms. They had a nice lovely house and three guest houses. We lived in one of the guest houses.

I remember when General Patton and his tank corps trained out there at Desert Center, and they came over the pass through Pinto

Basin. They didn't come into Twentynine Palms with the tanks, but I remember them going by the back of Garvins's place and what a cloud of dust!

I was hanging out clothes on the line, and these guys came along in these tanks. I didn't see Patton, but the fellows were all down inside these tanks until they caught sight of the house, and they turned out around it, went over to the right and saw me out there hanging up clothes.

Pretty soon the lid popped up and one of them said, "There's a woman!" Then another lid came up, and they went by waving. And my clothes were so dirty, I had to take them all in.

I remember the day the glider school closed. We'd been hollering for glider rides and no civilians could ride in the planes. Most of them were students and not allowed to take passengers. So I had never been up in one. But on the last day, the Commanding Officer sent out an order....a notice over the P.A. system that anybody that wanted a glider ride could have it, if they'd get out there. I borrowed some coveralls and took off, and I got a ride.

I went up with Lieutenant Fretz. He's the one that owned the chocolate candy company - Johnsons Chocolates. Anyway, he was a good pilot....but a nut. We got up there about five hundred feet when they cut off the tow plane. The minute he cut off, he flipped over, and I didn't know the difference. I got all this dirt in my face off of the floor. That was fun, and we had a good time.

That flight lasted not more than about ten minutes, and we landed down at the dry lake. But you could glide a long time, and if you got enough draft, you could go for hours.

It was real exciting, but we had a few crashes. One was a tow plane coming back. The pilot was suppose to fly back over the field and drop the tow line. That was one of the jobs I had for a while which was to tear out with this little stripped-down Model A and retrieve the tow line with the hooks on it. Anyway, he forgot to release the tow line, and he came in for a landing. He caught it in the telephone wires and pulled down a whole bunch of wires. Of course, the plane flipped and he was killed.

I stayed at the Garvin's all through the gliders....about two years. There was an old beat-up Dodge up there, and I learned to drive on that. I just got in, released the brake, and went down the hill. By the time I got to the base, I was driving.

I never had a license for two years. I went to Jack Cones and told him, and he said, "Well, nobody's here to give you an exam or anything, so just be careful."

So I drove every day to work in that old Dodge, no license and all. There were a lot of people out there without driver's licenses. Then I moved down town into a small apartment. After I left Garvin's, I didn't have anything to drive.

Pinkie Garlock (on the left) was close friends with
Alma Bailey Towle (in the middle) and Gwyn
Ferry Keys (on the right) in this 1940's photo
courtesy of Gwyn Keys.

The town was jammed then. We used to fight for apartments
and rooms. You'd have your eye on one you wanted, but there was
somebody in it. So you'd wait until they were transferred away
from the base, or were going to leave. Then you moved in the
night before so that it was still occupied when they left. The
landlord never knew who lived there, as long as the rent was paid!
Many of the boys liked it so well out there, they came back after
the war and stayed.

Dean's Restaurant was a very good little coffee shop. My sister,
Winifred, and I were in there one night when a sailor came in and
sat down next to us at the counter. He had a snake wrapped
around his neck.

Well, we didn't care about eating next to that, and so we got into a row. We really had a time, and my sister ran out into the kitchen. She was scared to death of that fool thing. I was too mad to be scared. The cook came out of the kitchen with a great big knife, and the kid got up and left.

As he went out the front door, I threw one of those glass sugar dispensers and hit him on the head and about knocked him out. But nobody did anything. Everybody came back in, sat down, and started eating again. Oh, that was a dandy night....we had a ball.

I can remember when we were going to have a Condor Field picnic, and Gwyn was elected queen. We had planned to have a big parade, to end up down at the oasis, and to have this big barbecue.

Well, we went down and dug the holes for the barbecue and lined them with rocks. We had it all done the night before and were working on the meat early in the next morning when this cloudburst came. It washed out all the meat and fixings, and everything was lost, but one big tub full of beer. Sid Lippet drove a laundry truck and rescued the beer. All we had for the picnic was beer, but everybody was happy. The headline in the DESERT TRAIL said, "Annual Picnic was a Washout."

After the base closed, I worked for the Navy for awhile. I think it was about 1945, then I left. I remember some of the Navy men and some of the planes....the Corsairs. Gee, they were beautiful.

HARLEY ALVIN PORTER

Harley Alvin Porter was born on January 21, 1917, in Pasadena, California, the son of Mr. and Mrs. Chester Porter. The family moved to San Diego where Harley graduated from high school and from San Diego State College.

In 1942 he came to Twentynine Palms to work at the glider training base at Condor Field. He remained here through the base's transition to power planes until its closing in March 1945, and served as Chief Maintenance Inspector. While he was here he met and married Dorothy Eileen Strickler, daughter of pioneer homesteader, Art Strickler, on February 14, 1943.

From 1945 until 1947 Harley worked for the Rohr Aircraft Corporation in San Diego. During part of this time he was involved in flight testing the PPYF flying boat aircraft which could carry three hundred passengers. This mammoth aircraft had a wingspan of 146 feet and was used to fly to Europe to bring home some of the American troops at the end of World War II.

Harley and his wife Dorothy returned to Twentynine Palms in 1947 when he began working with Charlie Matherly at his garage in the Plaza. Later that year he accepted a job with the San Bernardino County Department of Roads as a heavy equipment operator. Since his retirement in January 1972, Harley continues to live here and to enjoy his many hobbies including electronics and amateur radio broadcast monitoring.

* * * * *

When the Japanese invaded Pearl Harbor on December 7th, '41, I was working as a civilian at the Ryans Air School down in San Diego. We were training cadets to fly the PT-22s.

On December 19th, I quit the Ryan school to take another job. The Army Air Corps wanted to train glider pilots for the forces, and they needed to find some good locations for their glider schools. There were about eight of us, and we went from Bishop to Baker, to Victorville, Needles, Twentynine Palms, Salton Sea, Hemet, and Santa Barbara.

We tested out all of these flight locations and decided upon Twentynine Palms because the best qualifications were here. We had a dry lake, and the mountains surrounding it had prevailing

434

winds which made for the best flying up and down the ridges. The quiet weather made beautiful flying out here on the dry lakes.

So the government decided that we'd use this Twentynine Palms location for training. At first we had a civilian glider which we'd take apart each evening, take it up to town, and park in the Twentynine Palms Garage up at the Plaza. It was just a small garage run by Tom Martin at that time.

Then in the morning, we'd take it down to the field and put it all together again, and fly it during the day time. We'd fly up and down the ridges around here, around the various lakes - Dead Man and Violette Lake - which was about four miles to the west of Condor Field.

A Switzer that came from New York was sold to the school to use as the first glider. We used it here for quite awhile until the Army Air Corps themselves got contracts to build the gliders in Elmira, New York. There they were built and shipped out here to Palm Springs. Then we'd pick them up there out of box cars, put them on trailers, and haul them to Twentynine Palms.

A lot of times on the way back, we'd go through the Devil's Garden, and the high winds would come up. One time on the way home we lost three or four gliders that tipped over and were destroyed. We had to put in for replacement gliders which arrived with the next shipment. Then we'd bring all the gliders back here, assemble them, check them out, get them all ready, test hop them, and get them ready to fly. We had four gliders at first.

The glider school began to take shape. We had a man named Harry Hopkins who was a banker and financier. He brought money to build the hangars and barracks. Bob Whyers was the superintendent and manager of the school, and Bob Schaeffer was in charge of all the equipment and took care of everything on the flight line. He had an assistant named Larry Larson that worked with him.

Charlie Matherly was in charge of the garage, maintenance, the building of tow cars, tow winches, the tow trucks, and all the ground equipment. He was a very smart fellow who would get ideas for everything in the way of equipment. He knew people in San Bernardino and all over Southern California where he could get things. He was a man that could procure just about anything you wanted, and he had the garage down at the Twentynine Palms Air Academy.

At the beginning, they just had one little building there. We didn't have a barracks. We just had five tents that the cadets lived in. Then they started the construction of the little hangar.

In February 1942 they laid its cornerstone. It was a small one at the time. On the left side of it to the west, they built the parachute loft and the control tower. A few of the office buildings were built out on the west side of the hangar. They hired workers from town, as well as from all around in San Bernardino and Redlands. These fellows came up and began to raise other buildings - the administration buildings, the hospital, mess hall, and barracks. Then they started planting trees and lawns.

The road came in from Twentynine Palms to the main gate. There was a large circular drive going around the administration building and hospital. The canteen was built over on the east side of the administration building. On the west side of the administration building were built two long barracks. Inside of them was beautiful furniture - bunks, cases, dressers, and things for the cadets.

On the far west side of the hangar there was a long paved apron where they landed. Out here on the blacktop they'd do take-offs so they wouldn't raise so much dust. Dust was really terrible when the field got dried out. The airplane would rev-up and the dust would fly all over the place.

To the north side of the tower was the parachute loft where each cadet who flew the primary flying session had a parachute. Every thirty days the parachutes had to be unfolded, aired out, repacked, and put all back together. This was the reason for the large, long, high tower.

The Maintenance Department at Condor Field inspecting a glider in 1942. From L to R: Guy Cole, Harley Porter (checking the wing foreground), Clyde Morrison, Ben Kalmis, and Dick Karmon. Photo courtesy of Harley Porter.

The tower had ropes and pulleys at the top which would come down to pick up the parachutes and raise them up. They'd have about forty parachutes hanging in there at a time to air and dry out.

To the north side of the tower was a long room which had tables in it. Here the parachutes were laid out and repacked. They were rolled up and put into cases, inspected, and put back together. From here they would take them to the south side to a room with large bins in it. Here each guy had his own parachute because they were numbered. He was responsible for it from the time that he came in until he left.

Paul Fletcher was our parachute man who did all the packing and inspection. He would take the parachutes, dismantle them, put them into the drying room, hoist them up, and dry them. Then he'd take them down and repack them. He had three assistants who would help him put these packings together.

In 1943 after the field had been going for about a year's time, they decided they needed a larger expansion to put airplanes, gliders, and equipment that came in. So they built a larger hangar...hangar #2. On the east side of it they had offices where people worked.

In the beginning we had the Army Air Corps in 1942, and all of the gliders had red and white stripes on their tails. Then at the last of '42, they decided to do away with the Army Air Corps and make it Army Air Forces. When they took over, all of the gliders had their tail stripes removed and had a star insignia put on the side of the fuselage and stars on the top of the wings. It was a white star with a bar and a blue outline on it. This was the Air Force's first stage. Then the second stage came out, and they took the blue outline away from the insignia leaving only the white star and blue bars. In the third stage they added just stars on the wingtips of all the gliders and one white star on the side of the fuselage. The bars had been deleted.

When the Army Air Forces took over they decided they had to have paperwork for everything. They had to have five or six copies of everything that was to be done. Soon the paperwork began to pile up, and we were doing eighty percent paperwork, ten percent work, and the other ten percent was just loafing around. Then the paperwork got worse and we were doing one hundred percent paperwork, no work, and climbing the walls.

Over a period of four years, we had about forty six hundred people on the base, and that was counting the cadets and everyone. We had a civilian personnel staff of around thirty five or forty which was supervision and secretarial.

Business began to get so large that they had to build business offices. They built a great many of them to the south of hangar

#1. There were about two or three girls to each department, and they were classed as secretaries. Everyone had a secretary to do their work and keep up with the paperwork. My wife, Dorothy was a secretary in one of those big offices.

Finally the paperwork got so tremendous out there that they didn't have any room for all of the paper. So they just piled it up in a big truck one day and took it out in the middle of the field and burned it. That was the end. So consequently a lot of records got lost.

Well, the first thing that we had to determine was how to get the gliders into the air. In the beginning we had automobiles towing with a long piece of cable. The glider would be at one end of the field and the vehicle at the other. A long cable would be stretched out in front of it and attached to the towing vehicle.

The tow truck was a specialized Mercury truck made by Ford which had a transmission that would go one speed - fifty to fifty-five miles per hour. It would start out from a slow speed and go to a high speed and the glider would go up quickly in a big arc, go up above the truck, release and would fly around taking the thermals. Sometimes they could be up three or four hours at a time.

Early pulley truck on the dry lake bed at Condor Field. These Mercury trucks had tremendous horsepower with 327 cubic inch engines. Charlie Matherly had twelve of them made up to launch the gliders. Man in the left foreground is leading the glider tow line. Photo taken in 1942 by and courtesy of Harley Porter.

When these new winches were in operation, they would tow a glider up and the winch cable would never stop until the parachute got to the ground. It would completely wind itself down to where they didn't have any whiplash. Then behind it was a tow truck that would hook onto this cable and pull it out and hook it to the glider. This operation was very fast. In fact, it would get down to four and five minutes per tow. But that operation only put one glider into the air at a time.

That got too expensive to operate like that, so Charlie Matherly got a few of his helpers together and developed the winch. The first ones were crude and had a big, narrow drum and a couple of rollers. The cable would go down through the rollers onto the winch. It was built out of an automobile chassis that had a Ford engine in it. This big heavy winch would pull the gliders off the ground into the air in just a few seconds time....probably about eight seconds. It would do a very good job of it.

Unfortunately these winches had so much trouble with whiplash and kinks. We had a very high use of tow winch lines. Sometimes one winch would use about four lines a day. That began to run up the expenses.

The winch would only pull up one glider at a time. It took so much time to haul the cable back from the winch to the towing point and get that all ready. They also had to have so many men on the ground which were flagmen. It required one at the winch and one at the middle, and one out at the tow plane which was so far away. Very often on a hot day, the winchman could not see from the winch down to the glider because of the heat waves on the lake. Consequently, we had to use quite a few flagmen.

We had a safe operation using these men. The operation of the winch was getting to the point where it cost as much as an airplane to fly. Soon these winches got better and better.

At the end of their development, the man sat in a cage on a seat for protection. He had control of the winch cable because it was out in front of him. An arm with a pulley on it guided the cable going back and forth, as the cable was wound from one side to the other in a very uniform motion. Thus we had very little line trouble with those winches.

Then they developed another system so they could run a couple of take-offs side by side. Someone got the idea of taking the tow trucks and putting this great big wheel with a couple of rollers on the back of it. Then they'd take one end of the cable and deadman stake it down in the middle of the field. The tow truck would get to the other end of it, and the cable would pass through this big wheel and go clear back to the glider which was about 750 feet away from the truck.

The truck only had to go forward one-half the distance from

the towpeg, and then in that distance it would catapult a glider from the ground to a point about fourteen hundred to fifteen hundred feet directly above him. In the process of going forward, the truck would go from zero to twenty-eight miles an hour.

At a certain point we had flags out on the runway where the truck was to stop. If we went beyond this point, the forward motion of the pulley would actually pull the glider down, if he didn't release. So the tow truck actually had to stop right where the flag was.

In that short distance they used less fuel, and its economy was beginning to show up in this system. It was much cheaper than using a winch, because that system uses full power from the take-off to the release point. But in this pulley system, only part of the mechanized pulling system goes from the beginning of the pull to the end of it which is only one half the distance.

Charlie Matherly was responsible for a lot of the development of these beautiful new winches. So was Larry Larson, Bill Thompson and a few of the other men. Fred Eade was the fellow that was in charge of all the towing equipment. In the beginning he even got on the equipment himself and did the winch work. In the end he was just supervision, but he was always on the job seeing that everything was done correctly.

Early winch with protective cage for operator. Fred Eade is the operator in this photo taken in 1943 by and courtesy of Harley Porter.

HARLEY A. PORTER

As development went on, they wanted to try and get more gliders in the air. The third system that was developed here and tested was the towing of gliders into the air by pulling them with an airplane. At first this proved to be very expensive because the airplane would only tow one glider at a time. Then they began to experiment with them until they got two gliders into the air at one pull.

The first airplane that was sent to us was a big monstrous plane called the L-1A. Now days it would have the same use as a helicopter because it was able to hover with so much power. It had a big engine that had tremendous pulling power. This one airplane would tow off three gliders at one time. It speeded up operations so we could get more flying time done each day.

These L-1As were called tugs and would be assembled at one end of the field with the three gliders hooked up behind them. Then another tow plane was up ahead of it about four hundred yards, and it had three gliders on it. Very soon we had about twelve gliders into the air all at one time in this method of airplane towing. That stepped up flying operations greatly.

Yet there still was the tremendous expense of the airplanes pulling them, but that was all taken care of by contract work where all the towing planes would have their procurement for gasoline allotment. This was during the war when we had a gas shortage.

It was even very hard for a civilian like myself to go anywhere. We were issued stamps and stickers to put on our windshields, and we had coupons for just so much gas. But somehow the government managed to get enough gasoline to fly these airplanes and the other equipment to do all this towing work.

BT-13 pulling a TG-6 glider into flight over Condor Field in 1943. Photo by and courtesy of Harley Porter.

In the beginning of the roll-out, one man had to hold on to one wingtip to keep the glider from falling over. He would run along until the glider got airborne to keep its wings up under its own power. Then he'd release it and let it go, which meant him taking only about twenty to twenty-five steps before the wingtips would hold themselves up.

When the wind was blowing, this man would just hold onto the wingtips, and the glider would move just a few feet before it was airborne enough to keep itself up. Yet they always had a wingman at the beginning of a flight, even with two gliders being towed together. Each wingtip was held up by a wingtip man.

During training, they would tow the gliders out in a batch in the morning to the middle of the field or down to the far end away from the hangars. Here was a shed called a flight shack. It had tables, chairs, and cupboards in it where the cadets could get the necessary flight jackets on and get everything procured ready for flying in these gliders.

Then they would get into the gliders, do their training for the full day, and then at the end in the evening, they'd come back and dispose of their parachutes, take their flight suits off, hang them in their cupboards, and a bus would pick them up and take them back to the barracks.

As the operations went on and things began to improve around here, they decided they needed a swimming pool for the recreation of the cadets and everybody. So right in the middle between the two barracks and behind the administration building, a large swimming pool was built. It was about 90' by 120' and 12' deep. It was sure good to have nice, cool water.

It got hotter than dickens in the summertime. The sun beat down on it, and it didn't have a cover over it. In fact, in the middle of the day, you wouldn't find very many people in it. But in the mornings and evenings, it was full all of the time.

A canteen was built to feed the workers and the rest of the outfit. It had a large round table with stools around it, a big kitchen in the back that would serve the finest meal you ever saw. They didn't spare anything at the canteen. Great big steaks were an inch and a half thick and about fifteen inches in diameter. That really was something and it was only sixty cents for a big steak dinner!

Nearly everyone that worked down at the base lived in town in Twentynine Palms. We'd come to work in the mornings and the first thing we'd do after we went through the gate would be to punch a time clock.

In the evenings and at night when the gliders were not flying, the gliders would all be put into a hangar, the lights turned on brightly, and the men would all go to work inspecting them. We had a crew of about six and one supervisor named Guy Cole.

"Charlie Matherly was in charge of the garage, maintenance, the building of tow cars, tow winches, the tow trucks, and all of ground equipment." Photo from author's collection.

Each glider would have a man go into it from the nose to the tail and all over the wings inspecting every little part to make sure it was okay. If work had to be done, we'd take it all apart and replace any worn or loose parts with a brand new piece. There wasn't anything repairable that was repaired. It was always replaced with something new.

At the time they were planning on using glider training for primary training in airplanes, they sent us a large number of gliders that were converted light planes. Their engines had been taken off and the noses had been added where the pilot would sit out in front like in a glass house. These gliders called TG-5s at the beginning were smaller winged airplanes in which we flew for quite a while and trained the cadets in them.

HARLEY A. PORTER

Flight Instructors and other personnel at the 29 Palms Air Academy, 1943: Wally Nugent, Larry Creighton, Charles Smith, Willey Kimball, Howard Morrison, Frank Wolcott, Laurence Edgar, Walter Ballard, Homer Hannaford, William Helling, William Landon, William Was, Bill Atwood, Robert Bowman, Jim Gilliam, Robert Argill, Clarke Ferry, Edward Haynes, Hubert Beckers, John Gibler, Harry Ringland, James Ryan, Ray Parker, Bill Putnam, Ed Laine, Warren Merboth, Ed Reeder, Andy Longbotham, John Robinson, Woody Brown, Paul Fletcher, Ron Sanford, Harvey Stevens, Harley Porter, Gordon Shaffer, Charles Kohl, Leo Miller, Newell Shafer. Photo taken at the Mission Inn, Riverside, courtesy of Harley Porter.

Finally they needed a little more development, so they came out with that same aircraft using a larger span wing called the TG-6. These gliders had such a bad wingload that after taking off into the air, they would only have about one circle or flight out and then have to come back in and land. They were only for a very short duration, but they served the purposes of flying and landing.

That's all the training that these cadets needed at the time. They weren't being trained like the earlier ones who were trained to fly soaring planes and gliders and to stay in the air for an hour or more. These fellows were trained just to go up, fly a little bit, and come right straight back down. Later on that training was to be used in the larger gliders which would just take off, fly to their destination, release, drop right down to the target and get rid of their loads right away.

At the beginning of the second stage, they sent us some airplanes called PT-17 Steermans, and in these the cadets would be

444

trained to fly primary airplanes. We had had glider training instructors that were with us from the beginning until primary airplane developments started. Then we had to get a whole new batch of instructors. The older instructors that were with us from the glider days had to develop into airplane pilots for flying instruction and high echelon work that they had to do above flying gliders.

From November 1943 until February 1945 we did nothing but primary airplane training. Then a whole batch of new airplanes were sent to us - the BT-13s. Primary cadets flew them, then they would be transferred into larger aircraft like the B-26 and other bombers.

Harley and his wife, Dorothy Strickler Porter at the Pioneer Days, 1986 Old-Timers' Reunion. Photo by the author.

BLANCHE LOOMIS ELLIS

Blanche Loomis was born in Los Angeles, the youngest of five sisters. After completing her education, she worked twelve years in J.W. Robinson and Company. There she helped establish their Wedding and Etiquette Bureau, assisting many of the area's foremost debutantes. Later other fine stores patterned their departments after this first successful bureau.

She decided to make a move when her sister, Grace Kingman, bought Las Casitas Motel, a flourishing business in Twentynine Palms at that time. So she and her small son, Gene, arrived in August 1946. Blanche felt that after guiding so many prominent families through the maize of social problems, managing a fourteen unit desert motel should be easy.

She found managing the motel did not occupy all of her time, so she soon began to work for Anna and Dave Poste who had the telephone system in town. Blanche became the town's operator, and soon added her own personal touch of providing extra service to the town's populace which endeared her to everyone.

Forty years later, Blanche and her husband of thirty-five years, Chet Ellis, are both retired and still enjoy the desert where they have lived since they met here. She still has her keen sense of humor which has been characteristic of her entire life and made her acquaintance a pleasure to all who have known her.

*   *   *   *   *

From the first moment I saw Las Casitas, I knew this was it for me. The tiny town and the big desert outside, I loved it all and was ready to go to work.

We had fourteen units, and I occupied one so I actually rented out thirteen. We had striped awnings all around, and we installed a big beautiful stone drinking fountain. It was probably the second drinking fountain in Twentynine Palms. The first one was at Bagley's. We had a little park adjoining Las Casitas and had swings for the children. Now, it's all erased. The desert will erase all human efforts in a short time.

During the summer the units weren't full. It was terribly hot,

446

and we did not have adequate air conditioning. So we would take our towels and put water all over them and wrap ourselves up in them at night. It was the only way one could sleep at night.

The only outside fun we had in those days was square dancing, baseball, and of course, horseback riding. But it was a happy life.

I didn't have a car....but I didn't seem to need one. I could just walk along the highway a minute, and my friends would pick me up. The road from the Plaza to Four Corners was actually our bridle path too. It was very narrowly paved road, and we counted the cars as our horses stepped out of their way. If a new car came in town, everybody would ask, "Who owns the new car in town?" That's how small it was. We knew everybody's car. The horses outnumbered the cars.

Four Corners was nicknamed Whiskey Gulch because they had a bar and we didn't have one up here at the Plaza..so we were called Snob Hill. It was silly, but it took a lot of years for us to grow up. Any time one of us talked about having to go down to Four Corners, someone else would say, "What do you want to go down there for?" Each area was a small town in itself.

A lot of people held grudges. They wanted the town road to go out of this area from the Plaza, and the Four Corners people wanted the road to go out to San Bernardino from the Four Corners, which it eventually did.

I tried to keep enough families permanently at Las Casitas the year round to pay the overhead, and then anything else was just "gravy", as the saying goes. It was a privilege to be out here because each family was so entirely different. They seemed to have a feeling of adventure in just living there.

For instance, the Smiths....Dr. Ed Smith and his mother, Martha Ann, were very sophisticated people from Montpelier, Vermont, and they acclimatized themselves in a hurry and became one of us. She always carried a big basket, as they must have in the East, to go shopping. She was very picturesque. They stayed at the motel about four years.

Las Casitas Manager, Blanche, on duty with son, Gene, and another helper about 1947. Photo courtesy of Blanche Ellis.

447

Margaret Lutz and her children came to Las Casitas also. I remember Betty was just a baby, and they had a maid who stayed right with them. Professor Lutz was teaching graduate school at Stanford. Margaret, Mary, and Betty stayed with us for about three years.

Then also, the Bill Stubbs family stayed at Las Casitas for a long time. When I needed to relax or get a good laugh, I would go up to #10 and converse with Jo. Those who knew her appreciated her unusual personality. They owned the Stubbs Men's Shop in the Plaza.

The Inces came into Las Casitas the year after I arrived. Here was this lovely Cadillac car driving in, and I thought, "Great, new people, big car, fishing poles, distinguished looking couple, that vacation look... They won't stay long....too bad, and she looks so cute."

Bill came in and said, "I'm thinking of locating around here. First, is there any place around to fish?"

Well, of course, I was trying to keep from laughing. I told him that we had a few trees down at Smith's Ranch...no water....no fish.

He thought it was very funny too, then said, "My wife is bothered with asthma, and I have a daughter who has asthma also. I think we'll stay the night, and look around a bit, anyhow."

Later on they decided to buy a house. This wasn't too long after they were here. Then he built the Ince Memorial Hospital. What a break for the town!

Ray Flickinger, the real estate broker, and his family were here. It would take a separate book to tell about that wonderful family. He owned a small interest in Las Casitas. So I called on him to take care of those unpredictables that accost a tenderfoot motel manager.

One warm summer evening I heard much laughter coming from the front area of Las Casitas. I was delighted to hear my guests were having fun, because I had just greeted Admiral Wood and his entourage who were to occupy #1 and #2 apartments for the week. The thermometer was standing at an even 100 degrees, so most cottages remained empty.

I strolled up there and was invited in to join the celebration. A nice captain handed me a drink which I meekly took, knowing it was not Pepsi-Cola and that this party looked as if it were gaining strength every minute. I saw corks flying to the ceiling leaving wet little happy marks on my new paint. Oh well!

The captain noticed that I was only playing with my drink, and he asked me if I wanted my drink sweetened. I surely did because it tasted very strong to me and a little sugar might take the sour taste away. He disappeared into the kitchen, but when he returned, my glass was filled to the brim again. Alas, I'd never heard the words, "sweeten" in that way. Never!

I embarrassingly drank it down quickly, said "good night," and fled out into the dark. The long straight sidewalk back to my cottage became very crooked, and when I finally reached my destination and thought I was safely home, I was wrong. I had entered the motel washroom next door instead.

I was so relieved to have reached somewhere and feeling all of a sudden so vigorous that I thought, "Why not do all this piled up washing." The laundry man would not be needed this week. Aha!

Sheets, pillow cases, and towels were crammed into that washing machine. I could never remember how many loads were done. I seemed to fly back and forth between sorting clothes, washing clothes, and hanging clothes on the lines (no dryers at that early date). The song, "Show Me the Way to Go Home", kept coming to mind, but I knew better than to burst into song.

Just at daylight when the last of that laundry was being hung out, Martha Ann Smith appeared with her own basket full of soiled clothes. She looked around with amazement, and said something to the effect of, "Blanche, you shouldn't work so hard. It looks as if you've been washing all night, dear." She then asked if I'd heard all the loud noise last night coming from that jolly crowd of Navy people! What could I say?

The next day after the impressive group vacated, I went up to clean out the apartments. In the kitchen were some expensive looking empty and not so empty bottles. And when I looked up at the ceiling, the dried up little marks left from the popping bottle tops seemed to wink back at me.

Manager Blanche Loomis Ellis at Las Casitas about 1947. Photo courtesy of Blanche Ellis.

Now I remembered about an invitation I was accepting that had the letters "B.Y.O.B." at the lower left corner. I did know what that meant. Why not take one of these beautiful half full bottles with me. My friends knew I didn't really imbibe, but they would know that I was a good sport and had brought my bottle along. I hated to spill out some of the other partly filled bottles, so I poured all of the contents into this one beautiful bottle.

Later when I did arrive at this party, I proudly explained about my bottle. My friends would not touch it, and of course, I didn't either, but it made me feel "in"! I decided to call it "Las Casitas Special" and from then on it accompanied me to many celebrations.

Once in awhile someone would dare a thirsty person to taste it as a last resort. It was finally marked by someone with a big Skull and Cross bones. When I married my beloved Chet, he made me pour it all down the sink, and that was the end of my Las Casitas Special!

While I was working at my little job at Las Casitas, across and to the north lived Judge and Anna Poste. He was the judge and also the Justice of the Peace. He'd had a unit of forty phones installed, and they hadn't been installed very long so he was very sleepy at night attending to his new enterprise. He would get terribly angry if anybody used the phone after ten o'clock.

One night I'd used it about two or three times, when it was about one o'clock in the morning. He called me back after I'd hung up, and said, "Blanche, I hope this doesn't go on and on, because it's disturbing my sleep. You'll have to do your conversing before twelve o'clock."

Now, it was a public utility, and I thought it should be in use twenty-four hours a day. So in talking to Anna Poste the next day, I said, "Why don't I come over and help you out. I can stay awake nights. It doesn't bother me at all."

So, it developed that I became their assistant. It was great fun, and by then they had, I think, fifty phones and one long distance line.

I ran the motel and worked for the Postes for about five years. These were right across the street from each other, and it couldn't have been more convenient. I could run the motel and have somebody take care of it when I was back and forth to the Postes. In case Judge or Anna were ill or otherwise involved, I'd just dodge in and take right over.

It was very easy to catch on, as I memorize very quickly. As far as I was concerned, when I'd see anyone around town, everybody had a number across his chest, I would think, "Well, hello four-o-two, or hello six-forty-two." So when somebody called from outside, I connected him in with his party, and really, I just plugged them in, not using the numbers at all.

Blanche worked for Dave and Anna Poste's telephone exchange. She not only was an operator who gave personal service, she also kept the books and did the billing. Much of her other responsibilities away from the switchboard were accomplished at Judge Poste's desk to the right of the telephone board. Photo courtesy of Blanche Ellis.

I would answer long distance calls by saying, "Twentynine Palms." Then if two people wanted to call out of town, and somebody rang in first, I'd call the other person back and say "Our long distance line is free now. You can use it." So right from the beginning I gave them personal service - family style.

I didn't know it was against the rules, and I still don't think it was. I got horribly bawled out by supervisors from other towns later, who said, "You're not supposed to give that kind of service." But I still think that there must be operators some place in small towns who do still give that good service. I surely hope so.

While at the telephone board on one busy morning, I received a long distance call stemming from somewhere in the East. An operator with a sort of sophisticated twang said her subscriber wanted to place a call to Kenney's Drug Store and so asked for the number.

I said, "Let me speak to your subscriber." I told him that the Drug Store didn't open until nine o'clock, but that I would gladly phone Ed Kenney at his home if it was any kind of an emergency.

Miss Twangy voice entered in again and said all I should do was ring the Drug Store and not to give out so much personal information. She said, "Give me your supervisor".

I said, "One moment please," and lowering my voice said, "This is the supervisor."

Miss Twangy, very properly I expect, told me I should put my operator on report for giving out unnecessary information.

I replied, "Thank you. I shall speak to her." I giggled thinking, "If she only knew!" My thoughts later were, "What a cruel world this could become if rules weren't bent in cases of emergency. How could it hurt?

Every time a new phone was connected in town, Gordon Smith performed all the necessary hocus pocus. He was our trouble shooter and saved the life of our telephone system countless times. People also came in and paid their bills to me, so I had to keep track of the money, give them change back, and stamp their bills paid. I also had to trace all the fights about "I didn't make that call to Arizona" or some other place. "Take it off my bill!" was the command.

Judge Dave Poste, a pioneer of 1923, at switchboard of his telephone exchange. He was also the justice of the Twentynine Palms Judicial District from January 1935 until his retirement in 1951. Photo courtesy of Blanche Ellis.

BLANCHE LOOMIS ELLIS

Well, all kinds of outlandish things happened from earthquakes to thunderstorms. One time a thunderstorm was very terrible. I was practically frightened to death, as it hit the telephone board. By then I had a two position board, and it knocked out one position completely, blue smoke, and no lights. Nothing would work. So I had to hand crank each and every number. It certainly built up my muscle.

One side of the board was completely out, and I was figuring out what to do. Now I heard someplace about putting newspaper around your head and that would insulate you. I was afraid I'd be electrocuted, so I wrapped my head all around in newspaper and put the earphones on the outside of it.

About that time a repairman came in from Whitewater Telephone and Telegraph Company, and he said, "My Lord, what has happened to you?"

I said, "Oh, I'm so frightened. I'm insulated. I won't be hit by lightening this way."

And he said, "Get all that contraption off. That's the worst thing you can do." Then he said, "If I only could have a picture of you wrapped completely in newspaper with your face sticking out yelling 'number please, number please,' and keeping things going the way you are."

I had an operator who had come in and helped me for awhile, but she didn't have time to learn. It was such a speedy thing, so I had Judge Poste put wheels on my chair, and I just moved back and forth and worked both positions. It was much easier for everybody, including myself.

When anybody would leave town for a few days and come back, the first thing they would do was call up and say, "Hey Blanche, what happened while I was gone?"

And I'd tell them and fill them in....what safely could be told, of course. This was current events one would say. I thought these were the duties a telephone operator should do, and so really I would. I'd say, "Now let's see what happened Thursday and Friday?" And I kept a running account of it.

Once we had an earthquake and a few people called in to ask what happened. So I told them. At the time of the earthquake, it was a shocking thing to me. When it happened it made all of the lights come on for just a minute. It was quite a glaring situation. Then it went absolutely blank...not a sign of a light on the board, and then all of a sudden it bloomed like a Christmas tree. That's because everyone was so alarmed, and then ran to the telephone to see what had happened, causing all lights to come on at once.

They said, "Oh, are you all right? I just wondered if my telephone was still working. Where did the earthquake hit?"

In order to keep hysteria from all the voices I said, "Gee, I just

453

barely felt it. Was it bad where you were?" And at the same time my own chair was still rocking back and forth, and I thought I'd really had it.

Then a woman called in, "I'm afraid to be by myself. Could you talk to me?"

I said, "I can't possibly talk to you, but I'll leave your phone open so you can hear my conversations with other people."

So after a long while she said in a whimpering voice, "Thank you. I'll hang up now."

This was illegal too, but I'm sure that if I had it to do over again under the same circumstances, I would do it. Everybody had togetherness. I felt natural with it. Sometimes I would get up to go home after some crazy awful thing had happened, and I'd have to walk stooped over all the way to Las Casitas. I could hardly straighten up after sitting tense for so many hours at the board.

One thing about which I was puzzled for a long time was finally solved. Quite often a few lights here and there would twinkle on and off on my board, but when I'd plug in saying, "Number, please," the phone would go blank.

This time upon hearing my voice, a caller answered, "Oh, I was just dusting and cleaning my phone. It only takes me a couple seconds!

Well, this was one less worry for me! Puzzle solved. To this day when cleaning my own phone, I make sure that the receiver is kept well down on its cradle.

As time went on, I found that I'd become the main focal point for fire reports. A subscriber would phone in saying he could see a lot of smoke "to the south". Pat and Val Lafferty lived high up on Donnell Hill, so they became the volunteers to spot where and if there was a fire in that direction.

If the smoke was to my north, Clara Cones, Constable Cones' wife could easily be reached. From her little hill top, she could let me know if I should put in a call to the Forestry Department. This was our only fire protection at that time, and it was located in the same spot as the 29 Palms Fire Department now occupies. Ray Bolster and Billie Bolster seemed to be on deck there twenty-four hours a day.

The public knew what hours I was on, which was only right because the Judge was very gruff, and was a little more businesslike. He had other things to do, and Anna wasn't on the telephone too much.

The Judge's chambers were in the same area of the small house located on the corner of Homestead and Smoketree Avenues. When people came in to confer with him no matter for what issue or complaint, I was an obviously captivated witness only a few feet away from him and his "Hearings".

BLANCHE LOOMIS ELLIS

Judge Poste used to kid me about becoming embarrassed, because when he looked over and saw that my board was not lit up, still I was murmuring, "Number, please." I blush to remember some of the conversations.

One day I did get even with him when a woman complaining that her husband had bitten her, raised her skirts to a high level to show him. He made me look closely to verify that there were indeed teeth marks at that high spot. And believe me, there were many.

But mostly when man or wife came in to register a complaint,and the Judge was out, I was instructed to listen to them and then to suggest that they sleep on it. Then if they still wanted to prefer charges, the Judge would take over. A great percentage of the time that was the end of it. They had really wanted only to show their spunk. That they did. Also in that way it saved a lot of paper work for us. And they could brag that they had been to see the Judge about their problem.

Throughout my years as the telephone operator, I had a unique baby sitter for my son, Gene. My neighbor, Ralph Dunn, was the Recreation Director. How lucky for me!

On summer mornings, Ralph picked up Gene at Las Casitas, took him to the pool which is now Luckie Park, then brought him home for his lunch, returning him for the afternoon hours of swimming, and then home again in the evening. Could one ever beat having finer neighbors than Judy and Ralph? Ralph used to say, "Where could you find a cheaper baby sitter who charges you only five cents" - the admittance price for the swimming pool at the time.

We had a small jail about one half block east on Homestead Road, and on occasion, someone had to be held over until Constable Jack Cones could take them into San Bernardino or until we had the trial here. The few trials we did carry out here were held in the old DAV Hall. The little building still stands south of Luckie Park.

Only men were held here in our small jail. They had to sleep on a narrow cot with all proper facilities of course. And of course, they had to be fed. I took time off from the telephone board to walk over to Wiggins' Cafe in the Plaza and carry the tray to the jail door. I never felt squeamish about knocking and then unlocking the metal door.

First, I told them in kind of a quiet voice that there was no way that they could escape. If they were guilty or not, they would have a better chance not to ask for a jury trial, but should rather throw themselves on the mercy of the judge, because he was very fair. So actually we very seldom had a jury trial. When we did, we fought like cats and dogs trying to be conscientious about it.

People took sides. It was very hard not to in such a small town.

I think that one of the interesting parts of Anna and Dave Poste's telephone board was his being the judge also. It was really important to have the town straightened out and to fly right. This was the only law we had. We didn't have any attorneys. In this way most defendants had to get up and plead their own cases.

I recall one evening when the twelve of us jurors could not agree. We were escorted to Patolie's Restaurant by Jack Cones, and he told us not to divulge a word of the trial to anyone. We were sequestered - what an important word that became! It was 2 A.M. before we agreed to agree.

One Saturday we heard that beautiful Esther Williams was here visiting her brother, Dave, and sister-in-law Virginia, and that she must learn to ride horseback over the weekend. It developed that she was to be in a picture where she would be riding and that she'd never in all her vast education learned to ride a horse!

Someone dreamed up the great idea of having the hay wagon pulled along in front of her horse, so that it would be enthralled with eating the hay and not shy at its tenderfoot rider. I rode with others along in back of her to pick up the pieces....just in case.

She stayed put, developed saddle sores I'm sure, but by the end of this day, she rode straight in that saddle and looked like a dream of a western cowgirl. I was ashamed to remember back to when I, too, was learning to ride.

First, I tried being friendly to my mount. He wouldn't even look at me. Next, I went over the top and landed on the other side in a sitting position on the ground, and the horse hadn't even moved as yet.

After clutching the saddle horn and being led around the stables by a bored cowboy, I finally got up nerve enough to say I could walk my horse by myself. I did until I looked downed and saw a very small child talking to the stable man. To my embarrassment, I heard this little dear say, "I want my horse back." And to think this beautiful movie star never stopped smiling while she learned even to wave to the crowd and to stay in a slow canter on her very first day.

We had weekends when big events happened, and certainly the Chamber of Commerce did everything they could, but they weren't open all hours. So people would call up and say, "Blanche, we've looked every place. Are there any rooms vacant?"

Then I'd call around to all the different motels and quickly write down if they had any rooms, how many, and what kinds of beds. Then when anybody called, I'd say, "Sure. Listen. Go down to the Garden Spot, the El Rancho Dolores, or the 29 Palms Inn or others. They've got an opening." Of course, I'd make sure Las Casitas was full first.

Esther Williams was proclaimed Mayor of Twentynine Palms by Chamber of Commerce President, M.G. "Watty" Watkins at the special March
1948 ceremony held at the oasis in the shadow of
the palms. Photo from the author's collection.

Once a year we had Pioneer Days, and there were never enough
motels, and lots of our lovely people would say, "I have a back
room to rent" or "my kids aren't going to be home over this
weekend. If you want to rent my room, I'm going to have to
charge......" Then I'd even tell the inquiree how much it was going
to cost.

One cold night at Las Casitas during Pioneer Days when we
were "over-full", we were laughing hysterically, because we had to
take our drapes off of the windows and wrap up in them and sleep
on the floor. We were absolutely out of blankets, beds and even
anything that would cover anybody. But we slept nicely under the
drapes.

There seemed to be a glow over everything in those days, a
feeling of our being the very real pioneers, after all. The hard
work was a challenge.

I felt that I was completely in charge as hostess for the
weekend. Who else would be? What do people do in a small town?
How do out-of-towners know where to go? They'd call up and
ask, "Operator, where is the nicest place to eat in town?" And I
would give them a list of spots.

Or Twentynine Palmers would call me and say, "Blanche, is
Baskervilles' open tonight?" And I would call Baskervilles and find
out if they were open, and hold the party line open to deliver the
message. Sometimes I would even pass along the menu.

When I didn't know what was going on or what I could give in
the way of information, I'd say, "Let me take your number and call
you back." I always called them back. I never left anybody by

saying, "Pardon me. I can't do that." I never, to my knowledge, said the words, "I can't."

At all times I knew where I could reach the doctors! I think of the copious notes that I kept pinned up on my board of their whereabouts. I'm sure it was a comfort to all to know that I kept such close track of these men.

There were many lives saved through the Ince Hospital. It was a marvelous thing. Dr. Bill Ince would give of his time and his finesse anytime. For instance, Ralph Dunn would be down at the pool and about three different times, children ventured out and could possibly have died unless he had taken them up to the doctor quickly. In ringing the hospital, sometimes one had to wait awhile, so I arranged that I'd ring three times fast when Ralph needed action. I always had to do the ringing anyhow....And that meant that Dr. Ince and one of the nurses should wait on the curb because there was an emergency coming up from the swimming pool.

Later on, a pay phone was installed at the Plaza at Bagley's Market. Helen and Frank Bagley's story is a sentimental journey in itself, starting when they first arrived around 1927.

Children would pick up that receiver, and I would say, "Number please."

They'd say, "I want my mother."

Well of course, I knew all of the children. Meanwhile, I'd say, "Honey, your nickel please."

And their reply was, "I don't have a nickel."

I'd say, "You're not suppose to use the phone unless you have five cents."

Well, if they started to cry or say, "Mom will give it to you sometime," I'd connect them. All the little voices knew that I knew them. If they had a nickel, they'd give it to me, and if they didn't and weren't prepared, they just wanted their mothers. So I thought that was kind of a baby sitting thing, and it was perfectly all right.

One time the Judge was on the board and said, "Your nickel please," and a child said, "Blanche doesn't make us give her nickels."

So I thought I'd better adhere to the rules. I admonished them, but I never turned a child down. How could you? In a small town the children were out there hot and tired, and they'd call up. I usually knew where Mom was, because if anybody was leaving their phone, they'd say for instance, "Blanche, I'm going to the drugstore. If anybody phones, tell them I'll be back in fifteen minutes. I took all of those notes. It was very easy to do.

One time Lucille Metzger phoned person to person from the East to her husband, Colonel Sammy Metzger. I knew he wouldn't answer, because I knew where he was. This time the long distance operator had a heart and let her talk to me.

BLANCHE LOOMIS ELLIS

I told Lucille that Sammy had been over to the haystack fire at Ince's, but had gone home to get his fire helmet. She shrieked with joy that he'd at last had a chance to use it.

This operator practically choked with laughter. After she had disconnected Lucille, she rang me back and I could hear giggling in the background. She said, "What kind of a town do you have out there? Does your supervisor permit you to go on and on because I'm sure we've plugged into your conversations before. We think you're hilarious."

By then there were probably about five hundred phones. But it's like these new machines. The more you feed into them, the more efficient they become. So really I got more and more efficient. At the time I quit, I was still giving everybody the same service.

Everything happened at once. I got married so I was leaving the motel. Grace decided to sell, and that was great. The phone system was going to go into a dial phone system, because it was really overloading toward the last. By then there were seven hundred and ten phones when it went dial and still only three long distance lines. It seemed like whoever was watching over us in this small town realized that it was getting to a saturation point.

So I married Chet, whom I met over the phone, and it happened this way. One time we had a parade and Chet Ellis was parade master. He had three or four girl friends in town all at once, and he'd keep calling me to say, "Tell this girl I've gone down to see a man about some lumber." He was manager of Hastings Lumber Company at the time.

I'd say, "Well, sure Chet."

And then he'd say, "And if any other girl calls, tell her I'm down seeing about some more lumber and I'll get back to her."

I thought that anybody who was that popular having four girl friends in town, I'd kid him too. He was a nice bachelor, so we joshed back and forth.

One day he phoned and said, "When the bowling alley gets finished, why don't you take me bowling?" (Later called the Bowladium.)

I said, "Oh, I might just do that if I can find a time when your other girl friends aren't around."

So, we kidded back and forth on the phone which operators aren't suppose to do, but we did.

Then one time he said, "Blanche, there's a bowling alley up in Pioneer Town. Why don't we go up there? Why wait until this bowling alley is open?"

We did and had a lovely time. It's crazy how one can become very thoroughly acquainted on a first date. I found that he was a Methodist, and I was one too. I thought anybody who'd been raised a Methodist was a safe person. Isn't that funny? So we got to know each other very, very well and about three months later we were married.

We didn't let anybody know, because he was quite popular, and I was reasonably popular being the little widow. We knew that it would cause quite a chaos, and the telephone board would be full of calls all of the time. So we never let on to anybody that we were thinking of getting married.

We got married over the weekend at Quartzite, which was the closest place over the border. My sister, Grace and her husband, Victor were witnesses. We left Gene, who was nine years old, to announce to the town as soon as we left that we were getting married. Poor little guy. He didn't even know how to spell his new name, but he felt very important with a new Daddy.

He announced it, and people got busy in town and decided on a chivaree for us. It was a chivaree like nothing in this world. The crowd decorated up the house that we were going to live in outlandishly! It was not exactly a mess, but....... For one thing, they had tubs and tubs of canned goods with all the labels removed. We would open up what we thought was a can of peaches, and it would be roofing tar for instance. We had those crazy cans for about three years.

We'd shake them, and we'd tap them, and we were always wrong. The only thing we were really sure of was the canned toilet paper. Bill Ince had a canning machine, and he always canned toilet paper for his picnics and trips out. So we knew them because they were lightweight.

We bought the Shell Station at Four Corners soon after we got married. That was a good business, and we decided that it was so lucrative, we bought the Union Station across the street along with a great partner, Frenchy Pomainville.

A funny thing happened one Saturday night. Our Shell Station at Four Corners remained open very late that night because Chet was finishing switching tires for the Power Company. He was adamant about people switching their tires, as the roads were mostly hard pan around here, and he wanted them to stretch the life of their tires.

Late this night, John Allen, our night watchman, led two disreputable looking men into our office and asked to use the phone. I was alone, but luckily I could hear Chet out in the service garage banging on tires.

While John was using the phone, one man broke away and dashed out the door! John yelled to the other man facing me to, "Hold it right here," and he ran out the door into the night after his escapee! This left me looking at this mean-looking character all by myself! I believe I babbled something to him about waiting right there, that John would be right back.

He glared at me, and I reasoned with him that he could probably prove he'd done nothing wrong and then be set free. He did promise me that he would stay put. Then sadly, he must have had second thoughts, because he thanked me (imagine), opened the door, and was gone also!

I screamed for Chet, who by then had heard the noise inside, and wanted to know what was going on! When I sorted out the events, he too charged out into the dark, and the last I heard from him was the noise of his pounding feet going up Adobe Road.

I stood there doing exactly nothing, which is unusual for me. It did seem a long silent time until I heard the voices of John and Chet on their return up the driveway.

Chet was yelling at John something about "Another twenty feet and I'd have caught him!" John's words were not exactly printable.

Both John and Chet were shaking off dust when the predicament finally came to light. What had happened was this. When Chet was running past John, catching up and ready to grab man #1, John thought Chet was man #2, so he rightly tackled him in the pitch dark!

By the time they both got up out of the dust and John had gotten it across to Chet why he had knocked him down, man #1 and man #2 were long gone. Nothing remained of that dark chase but a pair of disgruntled heros and probably two speeding petty thieves, free to pursue their petty little crimes in peace once more. I could never think of a proper moral to this true story.

One time we asked John Allen what he'd rather be in town, and he said, "I'd like to be judge." And sure enough he was much later.

We finally had an ambulance. Jack Cones drove this first one. It was kind of a community ambulance, and somebody had to change the sheets, and somebody had to provide them. So evidently they took up a collection. We did have three sets of sheets. So I said I would change them after each time that it went in. They paid me a dollar every time I changed the ambulance. I said that the first time I found a left over arm or leg, I'd resign.

Among unusual things that occurred to us while running Ellis Shell Service was the day the ambulance was left in our hands. The owner had fallen upon hard times, and as we had been servicing it gratis, he said, "Here. It's yours." Just like that.

So there it sat - no liability license, no driver. Now I'm sure many other people had done great things for this town before us. Now it seemed that it was our turn to do something. There just had to be an ambulance service.

Chet used his men at the station for drivers, and he, with our son, Gene's and my help took over at night. I was elected to get all pertinent information from phone calls, such as location of the accident, was a doctor called, and how many were injured.

Gene kept his clothes ready to dive into no matter at what time the phone rang, and was fully ready to go by the time Pop turned the siren on. We used to remark about this, because he was never in this same frame of mind when his alarm rang in the morning and school was pending.

One of Gene's biggest worries was that his Dad, being so much taller than he, would tilt his end of the guerney up to such an extent that he would be the full recipient of a very sick or injured customer.

This was about 1948. Then when Gene got old enough to go away to the University, we felt we just had to do something. So one time we called a mass meeting down at the school, and my husband said, "We have to form a community ambulance. Something has to happen because we're going broke if this keeps up."

Sometimes when flash floods occurred, it didn't always have to rain here. It could rain up in Fortynine Palms Canyon. The word "flash floods" really means something, and in this case it did. When we had a bad flood, people were usually at the service station or the real estate office way out on this side of Fortynine Palms Canyon. And they would call to say, "The water flood is getting deeper and deeper."

And I'd say, "Now, when it gets bad enough, let me know and I'll let the fire department know." Then the fire department would go up and down Twentynine Palms Highway all through the business district with loudspeakers and sirens saying, "Everybody get your cars off the streets." In a short period of time the whole street would have to be cleared. There definitely could not be a car there or it would be washed away.

The water would take about twenty to twenty-five minutes from the time it started rumbling up in the mountains before it came down. And it seemed like the water would gather up back of a dam of rocks, then it would come over the rocks and start flooding down the canyon and dashing towards Four Corners.

So we'd have enough time to call the fire department to clear all of the cars. And lots of tourists would say, "Oh, what are you talking about? A flood out here in the desert?" They'd have many people who would not want to move their cars. And the fire department would tell them they'd tow them away, if they didn't move them.

The sun could be shining here and the clouds would all be up in that area of Fortynine Palms Canyon. So it was really hard to believe. Then of course, when the water flooded down it would be tremendous, and they would become believers as it swept down Twentynine Palms Highway waist deep and fast!

We would all hurry down to Kenney's Drug Store....when it was on the opposite east corner from where it it is now. It faced the oncoming floods, and Kenney's had lots of sacks full of sand. We would hold up the whole street while we piled those sacks against the doorway. Usually we could save it, but once it awhile it would inundate the entire drug store.

Another of our famous tricks was to stand around Kenney's Drug Store with the streets absolutely clear, dry, and fine, with the clouds only up in the Fortynine Palms Canyon area. We knew a flood was coming, and we'd stand and say, "Look! look!" to passer-bys.

And the tourists would ask, "What are you looking at?"

We'd say, "We're waiting for a flash flood. Stay here and you can watch it."

And they'd say, "This is ridiculous."

We'd tell them, "Stay right with us."

Soon you could hear the roar and see the first waves come down with rolls and rolls of tin cans, garbage, and debris of all kinds. This big tidal wave had a kind of dredging action, and then it would stream into Twentynine Palms and flood above curbs inside the stores. You'd have to step back from the sidewalk into the stores to get out of the mad flood. Then it would straighten out and become a big muddy stream.

A summer rainstorm usually meant a flood through the streets of 29 Palms. Ted Richardson's Photo Service is located at the former site of the first Kenney's drug store location. Photo courtesy of Elise Poste and Cheryl Erickson.

463

Flood waters across the Twentynine Palms Highway looking east of town. Photo courtesy of Elise Poste and Cheryl Erickson.

Our son used to ride the flood on tires. One time Mary Ann Beller did too when someone dared her. She got some tires and rode all the way down the middle of Twentynine Palms Highway sitting on tires. She was a good sport. Ada Hatch poled a raft right down 29 Palms Highway!

But it could be dangerous during a flood. For awhile it would be about shoulder high and then waist high. It could kill you to go across with the tumbling rocks and everything. Vi Carson's car was washed away, and she had to get out and swim to safety. Then it was dangerous because of the broken glass.

One time our son, Gene, and Chet's brother, Gayle, went down that "river" under water with their snorkels on. As they passed Four Corners where some workmen were trying to save a sign, they surfaced and said, "Boo!"

The flood could stay for about three or four hours, and then dry up. Then all of the damage had been done. It would take the road company three or four days to clear it. After the flood control channel was put in, it was a strange thing not to have big floods down at Four Corners. Then when the bridge was built on Adobe Road, we used to put big signs, "Do not fish off the bridge," and people thought that was funny. But it wasn't half as much fun as it used to be.

One fine day my sister, Grace, and I found a good-sized rattlesnake snuggled against the drinking fountain in our children's park. We decided this would never do, so we "offed with its head" with a hoe. As we hoped never to have to do a thing like this again, we dared ourselves to cook and eat it, saving the skeleton bone structure to run a thread through it and wear it for beads. We had seen Ada Hatch's display, and her's looked great on her.

After gingerly removing the insides, we put it in the frying pan to cook. All of a sudden to our horror, it stiffened and moved about. Then we shakily decided that the muscles were contracting, so it was okay to go on.

We did eat it, or should I say, took bites of it. It smelled like fish, but tasted like chicken.....a sick chicken! We put the bones to dry up on the roof, then proceeded to climb up there to peek at it daily.

It must have been a week of looking, when one day, it was gone! Later we noticed a big black buzzard sailing around, and while we couldn't choke a confession out of him, he had put an end to our big dream forever more!

Adelaide Arnold was one of our early timers. She lived east on Amboy Road on a picturesque rise. Her view for miles around seemed to come up, completely encircling her tiny homestead house. That small wood and rock home held the secret treasures that should compliment any museum.

I used to kid her about not being able to close her kitchen drawers, the sterling silver just seemed to hang out. First edition books lay on every available shelf and cupboard. Her two big old friendly dogs would give an unhappy grunt when pushed off the couch. I do wish I could remember their unique names, but many years have passed between then and now.

The saddest day that I can remember was the day someone saw black smoke from out east. The alert went up that it was Adelaide Arnold's homestead, and further news that she was in around town.

We found her and pleaded with her to wait with us for news to come back about this catastrophe. She said that she hadn't brought the dogs in with her this time, but that if they smelled smoke, they would jump out the nearest window. And as long as her two animal children were safe, she could live with the situation.

Unbelievably, those dogs did not jump out the window. They perished along with all the untold collections, her own irreplaceable manuscripts included. No more standing with her looking toward Sheephole Pass, or watching her as she gazed with dreaming eyes looking slowly in all directions, bringing together tales of a beautiful childhood....No more.

BLANCHE LOOMIS ELLIS

She lived for a short time up in the Hanson Tract, but her life faded from that day on. I gave her back the little mementos she had given me throughout the years, and I'm sure other dear friends did too. But her spark for reality just couldn't be relit. How helpless we are made in a situation like this.

We weren't all desert rats who came out here. Many of us were thinkers. But the desert way was new to me too, so everyone did it their own way. We did crazy things like closing off Adobe Road for a race between Johnny Bagley and Dave Williams. And the whole town had to detour. But we did this thinking it was fun. How many other small towns did similar things? Probably not too many, but this town had a sense of humor.

We have stayed here for so long that many of the old-timers have closed in together, not so much in distain, but because of what we thought of as sentimental is still here, but only with us. The mountains haven't changed and the sun still comes up. It's still the same terrain.

Whenever I feel lonely for the past, I look backward and think about when I first came to Twentynine Palms. My first night here was spent in Henry Daniels' Smoke Tree Villa. He and his wife looked like a romantic couple to me. But at that time, of course, everything looked romantic. I was kind of in shock then that I had really arrived way out here....long, long miles from Los Angeles.

After a nervous sleep, I got up and went out before sunup, wanting to hike over the desert rim to the north to see what I could see beyond. I hiked along humming, "The Bear Went Over The Mountain To See What She Could See". Well, when this little bear reached the top of that ridge, she would never ever be the same again. There stretched before my eyes miles and miles of flat desert that reached out and right to the bottom of the raggedy naked looking range of mountains.

That early morning forty years ago, I bought the whole vast area, feeling kind of shy about it, but my eyes had bought it. I still secretly feel its all mine after all these years. I've never been away from it for more than a few weeks' vacation. And I still can look over it right from my own dining room windows to the north, anytime I want.

I've never gotten over the feeling that this town is mine. To this day when I hear an emergency or tragedy, I want to reach out to get the proper authorities on the move quickly, to get in touch with the unfortunate ones out there, to assure them that help is coming, that a neighbor will be over to assist, and that I will stay on deck until the crisis is over. I have admiration for all of us who are still here through all such growing pains of this small desert town - the bad with the good. You might say, "We made it!"

SALLY OSMUN INCE

Sally Osmun was born in Hollywood, the daughter of Dixie and Leighton Osmun. Her father was a playwright, and when she was two years old, the family moved back East, while her father had several plays on Broadway. They moved to the little town of Essex on Lake Champlain where they lived for five years. Here, she remembers, the winters were so cold that the pipes in their home burst each winter, forcing the family to temporarily move to the Algonquin Hotel in New York City.

They returned to Hollywood in 1926; later they moved to La Jolla. After her father died in 1929, Sally and her mother moved back to Hollywood. Here she met William Thompson Ince who was completing his residency at Los Angeles County General Hospital. They were married in November 1937 and sailed for England where Bill did further work for a year at the College of Osteopathic Physicians and Surgeons under one of the foremost surgeons in London.

Afterwards, the Inces returned to the Hollywood area to live, and Bill opened his practice in an office on Wilshire Boulevard. Later they moved to Beverly Hills, but Sally was plagued with health problems. From a neighbor, June Clark Atkinson, they learned of Twentynine Palms and decided to come here in 1946 with the hope of improving her health.

They soon made plans to establish a hospital early the following year in January when architects' plans were drawn. On June 29, 1948, the Thomas H. Ince Memorial Hospital opened, named for Bill's father, an early motion picture pioneer in Hollywood. They continued to operate the hospital and serve the medical needs of the community until its purchase by the newly formed Hospital District in April 1962.

Bill and Sally were active members of the community. Both were charter members of the Saddle Club, while Bill was a member of Lions, and later president of Rotary Club. He was also an active member of the Sheriff's Search and Rescue Unit, with whom he led searches for lost persons in his World War II "Recon", a surplus weapons carrier. Sally was busy with her social activities and raising her three young children into adulthood. Bill continued his practice until ill health forced his retirement and premature death on October 6, 1972.

Since then Sally has continued to take an active part in the community. She is an active member of the Twentynine Palms

SALLY OSMUN INCE

Artists Guild, and in 1986 was chosen Co-Grand Marshall with her friend, Judy Dunn for the Pioneer Days celebration. Sally is an avid sports fan, whether it be watching games at home on tv or when the weather is good, out playing golf on our local course. Her quick wit and keen sense of humor have endeared her to a host of friends during the forty-one years she has been a member of our community.

* * * * *

We came out here the first time in October of 1946. We were sick and tired of Beverly Hills because the smog was creeping in even then, and the kids were all sick. I couldn't keep help because I had a ten room house and three children. Nobody really wanted to come and do anything, so they came and left with great regularity.

So one day I called Bill at his office down at the corner of La Brea and Wilshire. I said, "We've got to get out of here. We've simply got to move from Beverly Hills. The last cook just walked in and said, 'I'm going to cook you pancakes for breakfast, and I'm going to Oregon,' and I said, 'well, that's nice.'"

So we started looking around in the desert. The reason I even thought about the desert was because when I was in London in 1935 I got the flu. There's no colder place than London. I was very sick and the doctor came around every day and prescribed something or other. I kept sending my mother around to the local library to get me books by Zane Grey. I had never read Zane Grey before in my life, and all these books about people dying of thirst and the heat and the sand and the sun made me think, "Doesn't that sound marvelous."

I decided that we had to move and so we started looking around the desert communities. We went to Palmdale, Lancaster, and to Apple Valley. And every weekend we'd take off someplace and no place seemed to be the place.

All of a sudden I remembered that when I went to Beverly Hills High I knew June Clark Atkinson who had parents who live in a funny little place out in the desert with a funny name that I'd never heard before. I called June who only lived two streets from us and said, "Hey! Where is it that your parents live?"

She said, "Twentynine Palms."

And I said, "We're thinking about moving. We'd like to be in the desert."

She said, "We'll be right over. We'll bring all the DESERT TRAILs. They need a doctor, and you've got to move out there."

468

So they came over with all of these old copies of the DESERT TRAIL to show us what a swell town Twentynine Palms was. June had said, "The first thing you have to do is stop at my mother and father's at Stardune." (That's Sherm and Amo Clark.) "You have to stay at Las Casitas Motel, and then you go and see Ray Flickinger about real estate."

We came out, and you can imagine the ride - no freeways, and gosh knows how long it took us.

We stopped at Stardune. The place was charming and so were the Clarks. Then we went on to Las Casitas which is on Two Mile Road just west of the Plaza. It was owned by Grace Kingman and managed by her sister, Blanche. We got a cabin. It was cold and very windy.

Then we went around to see a real estate man - Ray Flickinger. He was later Justice of the Peace. He was sitting in his office with his feet on the desk. The first thing he said was, "They're sure catching hell downtown."

I said, "What are you talking about?"

He said, "Well, when it blows out here, it's raining like crazy in Los Angeles."

And I thought, "Which is worse?"

So we told him what we wanted. We wanted a four bedroom, two story house with three bathrooms.

He just looked at us, as if we'd come out of nowhere, and he said, "If you will come tomorrow morning about eleven o'clock, I will take you and show you what I have. In the meantime, I'll think about it."

So we went back to Las Casitas, and the wind was still blowing. About ten o'clock that night Grace came down, and she had some towels over her arm. They had an oil heater, and I'd never seen one before. The thing was making all kind of noise, but it turned out some heat and that was fine, because we needed it.

The next day Mr. Flickinger took us out to look at property. The two story, four bedroom, three bathroom house was non-existent. He took us out in the desert and showed us the old dairy. At that time it belonged to the Healeys.

I said, "Mr. Flickinger, how do the children get to school?"

And he said, "Oh, they just walk across the desert to the nearest corner and catch the bus."

I said, "What about snakes?"

"Oh," he said, "Mrs. Ince, after you're out here a little while, you don't pay any attention to snakes."

I thought, "Well, maybe you don't, but I do."

I didn't think that place was just right, so we looked at a few more places that were also not just right. So we said that we had to get back to Beverly Hills, but would be back again.

In the meantime we had gone back to see the Clarks, and they had this little hogan. It was one bedroom, a kitchen, and a living room. It was a cute little adobe, and we decided that we would come back. We really did like Twentynine Palms, the scenery, and all.

The next morning Bill woke me up early and said, "If we're going to look at this place, let's look at it." He was wandering around saying, "Where are all the trees? Where are some streams?"

I said, "You've got to be kidding. There are no streams."

We went up through the Monument and came back and around, and then we went home. We said we would come out, bring our children, and stay two weeks. We would rent the little house up in Stardune. We had a perfect out, because Susie, the oldest, had asthma. She was six. Stephanie was three, and she had bronchitis. Sandy was one and a half, and he had the same kind of skin problem I had.

We said we'll go out, stay two weeks on the desert, and if we didn't like it, and we can always say the kids are allergic to something, and we wouldn't hurt anybody's feelings.

After two weeks out here in October, the only thing that really made me nervous was one day I went out in the driveway and there was a tarantula. It was absolutely enormous. Bill had big combat boots on, and he stepped on it. That was the end of the tarantula, but I thought, "Oh, Lord. If we're gonna have things like this and snakes, then I'm not sure that I want to come to the desert."

I told Amo Clark about this great big hairy creature.

"Oh," she said, "dear, they walk in October and November, and you don't pay any attention to them. They just walk."

When people found there was a doctor in town, they kept calling the Clarks saying, "We understand there's a doctor staying there, and we have a person that's sick, and we need medical attention. Do you suppose that the doctor that's staying with you would come and make a house call?"

So Amo would send the maid down who would say, "Dr. Ince, somebody wants to see you, and they live in such and such a place."

He said, "I have no idea where that is."

"Well, do you know where so and so lives?"

"No."

So then Amo would always say to the maid, "Now you just go and take care of Doctor Ince. I'll cook the breakfast, and you lead him to where these people need a house call."

So this went on for two weeks.....in the middle of the night....any old time.

There was one doctor here, but I can't remember his name. He closed up every night at six o'clock and went home. He would not come out on weekends. He wouldn't make house calls.

SALLY OSMUN INCE

After two weeks, we could hardly wait to get back to Beverly Hills and have a house cooling party and move. We moved out the second of December 1946 and lived at Stardune for three months.

I had to bring my dishwasher with me because my hands were broken out all over. We kept it on the front porch because there was no place inside for it. The door had to stay open at all times, because the hose from the dishwasher went through the front door, across the hall into the bathroom, and got connected to the hot water heater. And if you haven't ever had to put on gloves, a hat and coat to load your dishwasher, you haven't lived!

I would go out every night with my gloves and everything, and it was absolutely gorgeous. It was clear and sparkly. We could see a few lights at Four Corners. You could count them in those days.

There was an adobe house on a knoll just east of Adobe Road near the Plaza. I kept looking at it, and there wasn't anything around it at all. There were no roads. There was nothing.

Finally I said, "Flick. What about that adobe over there? It fascinates me."

He said, "No. You wouldn't want it. It only has one bedroom, and the adobe is crumbling in places."

By this time we had the three kids in a room that was about the size of an alcove. You had to climb over one bed to get to the other to make it.

But the people were nice. Everybody was nice. I met more people standing in line at Bagley's. If you stood in line there you got introduced to everybody else in line by Mildred Michels who introduced me to everyone.

And Amo Clark said, "You have to meet Major and Helen Huber because they have twin daughters just Stephanie's age."

At that point I thought, "By the time I meet Major Huber, he'll be a colonel." Well, I didn't realize that that was his first name. When we came out here the base was completely closed. It had been a glider school and then it had been Navy.

One night we were playing poker. The men used to have what they called Marching and Chowder. It was Ted Hayes, Ray Flickinger, Frank Horner and others....about seven. The men would meet at one house and play poker, and the ladies met at another house. That night we went over to the Huber's. Mary Hayes was there, Frances Horner, Bessie Flickinger, and Blanche.

I said, "You know something, I want to see the Wikoff house." The Wikoffs owned it, but it had been John and Virginia Stevens' house. "I want Flick to show it to me. I want to see it now."

And Bessie Flickinger with her cute southern accent said, "Oh, honey, you are who oughta' have that house. That's got the biggest livin' room in town, and you can have a lot of parties and we'll all come to them."

It was about ten o'clock at night with the wind blowing and a full moon.

I said, "Flick has a key, doesn't he?"

And Bessie said, "Oh, yes."

Frances Horner said the same thing. "You really should have that house. It's a super house."

So I said, "Let's call Flick and get the key and I'll go see the house," because I like to do things pronto.

But Bessie said, "Honey, I don't think I'd call Flick out of a poker game. I think I'd wait 'til the game's over. Then when he comes up here, we'll get the key, and we'll all go see the house."

I said, "Ok."

When the guys came in to get their wives, I looked at Flick and said, "Have you got the key to the Stevens house?"

He said, "Yeah, it's over at the office."

I said, "Fine. I want to see it."

"What?"

I said, "I want to see it and I want to see it right now."

Bill looked at me as if I was crazy.

And I said, "We're going to see that house right now with flashlights."

So we got flashlights, and Blanche came with us, and I think the Hayeses. The Huber's couldn't because they had the three kids that they had to stay and ride herd on. We had a baby sitter up at Stardune.

So we walked in this house at about midnight on this cold January night. With flashlights we looked at the ceiling, the big window, at the fireplace, and we said, "Fine. We'll take it." We didn't even bother with the bedroom.

It was just a cement slab and all adobe. Flick said, "The reason you don't want it is during the first big rain, all the adobe is going to come off. And you're going to have to take a wheelbarrow and go down the hill and get your house back. It needs stuccoing. You're going to have to stucco."

We said, "Fine. We're not worried about that." In those days there was no rain. It was just sunny and clear and sparkly all the time. It was absolutely beautiful.

We moved in on March 1, 1947, Susan's seventh birthday. We gave her a bicycle and said, "Go ride it in the desert and don't bother us. We're busy moving."

We have lived here every since, and it's grown like topsy. I guess it was in 1950 that we built on the two extra bedrooms. We decided that the two girls and the boy should each have a bedroom.

Then in 1952 I burned down the very small kitchen that we had. The fire department didn't talk to me for a long time, and neither did Bill Hatch, because he had the insurance. But the kitchen burned up, and that's how we got a dining room and a nice new kitchen. We absolutely adored this house.

Then we had the big haystack fire which was spontaneous combustion. Seventeen tons of hay went up in smoke behind our house. I guess the Fire Department wasn't very happy with me again. I'm sure every time a fire broke out they asked, "Where's Sally?"

Ralph Dunn was running for school board and it was election day. Everyone in town came to the fire and I asked them if they had voted. And if they said, "No," I sent them down to vote and then comeback and watch the fire.

And Maj (Huber) brought his skiploader and moved the hay around. They were building the base, and the guys from there sent up their big water truck because we didn't have any water pressure. We finally got the fire out and no one was hurt.

The four horses weren't hurt and nothing burned down except the haystack. Bill and I had Tennessee Walkers and Stephanie had a Palomino pony and Susan had a Palomino mare.

I guess we had the pony first before Stephanie was old enough to ride. Susan used to go to the Little Church of the Desert Sunday School. She would stick her Bible under her arm and get on her pony bareback and ride to Sunday School.

She would tie her pony to the flag pole, and all the kids would come out to pet it. Well, they didn't like what the pony left under the flag pole, so they said she was very welcome to come to Sunday School, but she would have to find another method of transportation.

In the old days you could look down at Four Corners and count the lights. You could go up into the Monument and look back towards town and see who was home and who was not.

There was a woman who had the taxi and the Western Union here in town, and they got tired of taking the taxi and driving way out to John Hilton's to deliver a telegram. They lived on way out off of Bagdad Road.

And so they would call me and asked me if I would look through my telescope and see if the Hiltons are home. If their car is there, they would drive out and deliver the telegram, otherwise they'd wait. I'd go look out and then call them back or maybe they would hang on so I could say yes or no, because I could always see their car. They didn't have a garage.

We used to leave messages at Bagleys'. They had a black board where you'd leave notices. If I wanted to see Barbara Hilton, since they didn't have a phone, I'd leave a message, "Barbara Hilton, please call Sal." She would come up to the market and see the message and either call or stop by. Then when she went downtown, everybody would stop and ask her if she had talked to me because they had seen the message up at Bagley's.

Bill opened an office, and the office was right behind the Paint Pot in that little duplex. It's still there. After he opened, we started making plans for the hospital.

Getting the plans okayed was something else too. Bill had a hard time getting San Francisco and Sacramento to understand the difference between a ninety-nine bed hospital and a five bed one.

They wrote back and asked, "Where is your 8'x 10' room to clean the garbage cans?"

And Bill wrote back, "We do not need an 8'x 10' room to clean the garbage cans, because we don't have any garbage cans. We have a garbage disposal. We only have five beds, and there's not that much garbage."

Well that didn't go over big, so finally we went to San Francisco. Bill spent about three hours talking to this guy and had it all straightened out. Finally the guy said, "Okay. Go ahead."

That's when we started the hospital. We actually broke ground for it on November 19, 1947. Walt Berg built it, Les Cross worked on it, Dave Williams did the plumbing, and Jack Fouch did all the electrical stuff. He had Palms Electric at that time, and for an opening present he gave us a little kerosene lamp in case the power went off.

The Thomas H. Ince Memorial Hospital was dedicated on November 19, 1947, named for Bill Ince's father, an early film producer in Hollywood. L to R: Sally Ince, Walt Berg, Mrs. Thomas Ince, Dr. Bill Ince. Photo courtesy of Sally Ince.

Welcome to the *Formal* *Opening*
of the

Thos. H. Ince Memorial Hospital

June 19-20, 1948   North Adobe Road   Twentynine Palms, California

When the Thomas H. Ince Memorial Hospital opened on the weekend of June 19th, 1948, THE DESERT TRAIL wrote, "This beautiful structure is a mark for all to set sights upon. It is an erection par excellence. In every respect the building rates a blue ribbon. The builders; Dr. and Mrs. William T. Ince and Mrs. Thomas H. Ince, can stand up and take a deep bow. They have done a great job. They have contributed to our community, not only its first hospital but also an ultra-modern one that consequently finds an unchallenged spot among the best of institutions in the country." Photo courtesy of Sally Ince.

The day before we were going to open for business, somebody remembered we had everything in the world except bedpans. There wasn't one in the place.

We opened on June 19, 1948, and had a corner stone. We put our local paper in there and all these other little things....some coins...and also a half pint of bourbon. Reverend Carle, an elderly retired minister, came stomping up to Bill. He said that it was sacrilegious, and that we should get the bourbon back out of the corner stone, because that was a terrible thing to put in the hospital.

Bill just looked at him, and said, "Reverend Carle, if you want a half pint of bourbon, you just go down to the drug store and buy it the way I did."

The hospital was named Thomas H. Ince Memorial after Bill's father. We opened it, and we had the most beautiful equipment, and the most beautiful rooms. They were all different colors, and we had wallpaper instead of just white or green. We had wallpaper on one side of each room, and we only had five beds.

We had the latest in x-ray equipment, and we had this beautiful terrazzo floor in surgery. The treatment rooms were on one side and the patient rooms on the other. There was also Bill's office, the waiting room, and the business office.

When we opened we had about four hundred people go through, and I walked my feet off. We showed them all the rooms and everything, and then we had this big party down at the Inn. Doctors came out from town, and all of Bill's buddies came out from Beverly Hills.

It was a beautiful night and we had this big party. A bunch of the outsiders decided it would be fun to go horseback riding. So they went trooping down to Flying W Stables. Healey had horses down here and so did Pat Graham.

Anyway, one of the doctor's wives fell off her horse and broke her collarbone. That was the official opening of the hospital. They were orthopedic people, anesthetists, and surgeons. None of them were in very good shape, because they didn't really come out here to work.

All of the wives went up to the hospital, and we were making hot coffee like crazy, while the husbands were setting this poor gal's collarbone. By this time I was exhausted.

I was just sitting there in the hospital lobby thinking this has got to end sometime, when a woman walked in. (This must have been one o'clock in the morning.) She said, "May I see the hospital?"

And I said, "Yes, but just don't go into surgery, because they're busy. You can come back through here and go down that corridor and look in the x-ray rooms, treatment rooms, and the offices."

She said, "Okay." And so she made the little turn and came back and said, "Thank you very much."

And I said, " You're very welcome," and she disappeared. I do not know who she was. I haven't the foggiest notion, but she was the last person through. That was the opening of the hospital.

We saved lots of lives. Our biggest thing was Pat Buttram when he got blown up, and that's a whole story.

The Flying A Studio which was Gene Autry's was up in Pioneertown, and of course, Pat Buttram was Gene Autry's right hand comic. He had a fake cannon that was suppose to blow out a bunch of black smoke. Well the thing backfired, and he got cut open so that when he was breathing you could see his lungs. He was absolutely split wide open.

They got him into a jeep and down to Yucca Valley. There was no telephone in Pioneertown. This was about 5 o'clock in the afternoon and the base still hadn't opened, so it must have been before 1952.

Blanche was on the phone. She was the operator at the time. She called me and asked, "Where's Bill?"

And I said, "I guess he's at the hospital."

She said, "No, he isn't. He must be on his way home. They had a big accident in Pioneertown and they've got the people in jeeps and they're down in Yucca Valley. They need the ambulance and they need a doctor. Let me connect you with the man I'm talking to."

The man was hysterical, and I said, "Now wait a minute. Do you want the doctor to come to where you are or do you want an ambulance to have the people brought to the hospital? You've got to tell me."

He said, "This is Gene Autry. I'm sending my plane for a Doctor Ince. My plane is going to land out at the old air strip at the base, and we need the ambulance."

When Bill got home, we jumped into his car and went ninety miles an hour down Adobe Road. The plane was coming in, and we just slid up beside it on the stripping.

The plane stopped and the car stopped. I even remember the name of the pilot of the plane.....Herb Green. He had a man with him, and they got out and got Bill and his bag, and they took him down to Yucca Valley in three minutes.

In the meantime, he'd called Johnny Johnson, who owned Johnson's Mortuary and drove the ambulance. Johnny got the call to get to Yucca Valley fast, so he grabbed a friend to help load the gurney. The friend was a local electrician, Jack Fouch.

The plane was there, and Bill was looking at all these people. One had shrapnel in his tummy, somebody else had something, and here was Pat Buttram who was really hurt. Pat wanted a friend of his who was a preacher to go with him, and he didn't dare close his eyes, because he was sure if he did, he'd die. Bill didn't dare give him too much of anything, but he gave him a shot of morphine for the pain.

They got him to the hospital, and when they took his boot off, it was full of blood. His leg had been hit too. Nobody noticed that at first because of the chest injury. Bill just put him on the operating table, gave Jack Fouch a sterile towel and said, "Roll your hands in and press down, because I'm going to sew him up, and I'm not going to give him any anesthetic."

Bill put him in a Trendelenburg position....head down, feet up on the operating table. Bill just sewed him up like you would a baseball.

They needed some more blood, and they wanted a doctor to come in. By then of course, it was dark. So Bill got on the phone

Pat Buttram, Bill Ince, and Gene Autry. Photo courtesy of Sally Ince.

and got Blanche. She called four places in town. They called somebody at Four Corners, somebody at Jimmy Williams Supper Club which is now the Josh Cafe, and they called two other places.

There was a ball game going on down at the park, and they got a message down to them. Everybody with a car was to go down and ring that air field. We didn't have any law enforcement except Jack Cones. We had reserves, and they just directed the cars to circle the field. They had a loudspeaker and told everyone not to turn on their lights until they were told to, and then everyone was to do it at the same time.

Herb Green said that field was as well lit as any field he had ever landed on. He just came in, and Johnny Johnson pulled up the ambulance, and they got Doctor Immerman, the Flying A's doctor, and the blood plasma.

By this time I had come home and I was watching from up here. Here was the ambulance with the red lights and siren and about one hundred cars behind it coming up Adobe Road. It looked like a Chinese dragon.

Pat was eighty-eight days in the hospital and made an uneventful recovery. But if the hospital had been any farther away, he would never have made it. He had a good strong constitution, and he was a young man at that time. The others he sewed up and sent them home after a couple of days.

Stanley Immerman said we couldn't have done it better if they'd been at Queen of Angles or Good Samaritan. He was very complimentary about what Bill had done for all these people.

When we first came out here we had meetings about eight nights a week. Everyone belonged to everything. We were members of the Chamber of Commerce, the Saddle Club, and PTA. Bill was a Lion and then he was a Rotarian. I was in Junior Women. We had to make our own fun. That's why we always had such swell parties. Anything was an excuse for a party. We had potlucks, costume parties, and picnics.

The Saddle Club was another big group of people. We went riding almost every weekend. If it was summer we had cornfeeds out at the old dairy on Utah Trail, and if it was winter we'd get so bundled up that we could hardly get on our horses. But if it was a moonlit night, we'd ride.

We joined the Saddle Club in the end of '46 or right in the beginning of '47. The Wrubels were here. Pat Graham was the first president, and he had taken over the stables behind Smith's Ranch from the Healys. I remember that the Healy father's funeral was the day that we broke ground at the hospital. That's why we were all there in western clothes, because the Saddle Club rode to the cemetery.

We used to have moonlight rides and corn rides. We'd go down to the old dairy which then belonged to Healys and have corn and beer and melted butter. People would bring their guitars and those that didn't want to ride would go on the hay wagon. Everyone else rode.

We rode up to Split Rock in the Monument on an overnight. It was quite a ride. The worst part was getting up the next morning and getting back on the horse and riding down. I was so stiff in every single muscle.

One time we had the horses all trailered down to Desert Hot Springs and rode in the parade down there. We rode at Circus Days in Palm Springs. We rode from Twentynine Palms to Quail Springs. There were about thirty in the group and sometimes more.

The stable started at the one behind Smith's Ranch. The Healys had it, then Pat Graham had it and then Gene Dorsey came in and that's when Allie Wrubel built the Flying W on Joe Davis Road. We rode the square dance on horseback at full gallop, and that was fun. We had breakfast rides, and supper rides. We had a president, secretary and treasurer.

Some of the people that were in the club included: Helen and Charlie Matherly, Helen and Maj Huber, Ev and Irv Enger. Blanche Ellis, and all the Healys, Pat and Vivian Graham, Les and Dorothy Crosse, Carlin and Johnny Johnson, and a lot of the teachers. It was fun, but it eventually ran its course, as people left or died.

I never kept a diary or journals so the years come and go and it's very hard to peg what happened in what year. I often wish I had.

But I do remember on New Year's Eve 1948 was when the horse sat on my leg. We were going to do the square dance on horseback, and we were all milling around and getting ready at the Flying W Restaurant. Everyone was pouring out of it, and we were all going to a big party at the Wrubels.

The Saddle Club was a very popular social organization in the late forties and early fifties. Above: members enjoy corn-on-the-cob on a night ride, August 23, 1948. Below: Bill Underhill, Prudie Underhill with Bill and Sally Ince at a Saddle Club function on the Kunasz' patio in 1947. Photos courtesy of Sally Ince.

Somebody I hadn't seen for a long time came up to say hello, and as I went to shake hands, I put my hand past this skittish little mare's eyes. Then she started to rear.

I could hear Gene Dorsey saying, "Sally, let go of the reins! Let go of the reins!" I was just glued to them.

So the horse and I both went over backward right on the cement porch of the Flying W. My leg was here, the curb was here, and the horse was sitting on it. Well the horse got up and went away, and I didn't.

Everybody wanted to do something for me. They wanted to move me or poke at me. Some man came out of the restaurant and said, "I'm a dentist. I'll see what's wrong."

I said, "You're at the wrong end. It's my leg. It's not my face. I don't want to be touched. I don't want to be moved. I know my leg is broken, but I'm perfectly all right and not in a lot of pain. Just get Bill."

Bill was making a house call over at Eddie Adams, who was a photographer. He had awful asthma and Bill was giving Eddie a shot.

Larry Swope went over to Eddie Adams' on Sullivan Road and said, "Doc, you better get down to the Flying W fast. Sal's been hurt and she's hurt bad. The horse reared and she fell on her head and shoulder."

This was about seven or eight o'clock at night, and Sid Lippen, who had the Shell Station said he never saw a car go around the corner on two wheels squeaking as Bill did when he hit Four Corners.

When he got there, all these people are standing around. I'm just propped up on one elbow smoking a cigarette being perfectly happy as long as people weren't poking at me.

He called the ambulance and Johnny came roaring down Code Three. He thought that was more fun than a barrel of monkeys. He got me into the ambulance, and of course the shortest way to the hospital from the Flying W was up Two Mile Road.

But I said, "Johnny, let's go around by Four Corners and hit the siren. Hit the red lights."

Nobody was going to stop us, because there was no law enforcement people in town. Of course, this was strictly against the law unless you're on an emergency run, and a broken leg does not constitute an emergency.

So we got to the hospital, Bill took x-rays and set my leg. All I could think of was, "I'm going to miss a party."

And I said, "Hey, after all this is finished, can we go back down to Wrubel's and to the New Year's Eve party?"

Bill said, "I don't know why not."

Of course, Johnny always stood around to help, because Bill

didn't have any help except nurses to get people on and off gurneys and on and off x-ray tables and so forth.

So I said, "Ok, Johnny, we'll go to the party, and we'll go by Four Corners."

We got to the party and everybody autographed my cast. Pretty soon I began to get tired, and said, "Johnny, I think it's about time I went home."

So I said, "By Four Corners again." This was the third time that night.

About three years ago I found out that Grace and Mike Carmichael were out here for the first time that night and at the Josh Cafe. They were thinking about moving to the desert.

And she told me, "You know, the funniest thing happened the first night we were out here. It was New Year's Eve 1948, and all we heard was sirens, and we decided this town must be full of crime. We weren't sure we going to move out here at all."

I said, "Grace, that was me going back and forth with a broken leg."

New Year's Eve was just nine days before the big snow. During that I couldn't get out and play because I was on crutches. Nobody did anything. No business was kept, although they did come and scrape our driveway so Bill could get to the hospital. But there were very few vehicles that could get around at that time.

Johnny Bagley had the big Standard Oil truck. He'd get out and see that people who lived way out and were absolutely snowbound had oil. He delivered fuel oil as well as gasoline.

Adobe Road and the highway was open, but none of the side streets. There were five thousand rolls of film ready to be developed. There was no film left in town.

Bill would get me up in the middle of the night on crutches to go and look at the snow. "Isn't that exciting!" he said.

"Bill, I spent five years in upper New York state. I have seen snow."

"Yes, but you haven't seen it in Twentynine Palms. So get up and get your crutches, and look at it."

Jack Meek was a picturesque character. He used to sit on the miners' bench out in front of Bagley's store. He'd get all dressed up in his bandanna and his western stuff. He always had gold nuggets in his pockets, and he loved to talk to the tourists.

He'd stop them on their way into the market and show them the gold nuggets and tell them all about mining. They were fascinated. The thing that really tickled him the most was to have some of the natives come along and say, "Hi, Jack. How are you?" That just made his day, because he was a famous character.

One time he didn't feel very well, so he brought his sleeping bag up to our house. We had an old couch on the porch at that time, and he lived there for about two weeks because it made him feel better. By the time that we would get up in the morning, he would be long gone. Then he would come back every night and sleep on our porch so he could be close to his doctor.

One time when he did get sick down there in his trailer behind Smith's Ranch - he had a heart attack - and could not get out of his trailer. He just fired a shot and that drew people. They brought him to the hospital where he stayed quite awhile. I don't think he died then but later.

Here's something funny that happened. The kids took piano lessons. One day I went down to the drugstore and had Stephanie with me. The minute I'd go in there, the kids would head for the comic book section and read all the free comic books that I wouldn't let them have at home.

Finally I was through shopping, and I said, "Stephanie, come on. Your piano lesson is in five minutes, and we've got to get up to Miss Lewis'."

There were two lady tourists standing on the sidewalk, and one looked at the other and said, "Imagine having piano lessons in a little town like this."

I guess they thought we lived on nuts and berries and lived in tepees...

One time Susan brought a friend home from Goucher College in Towson, Maryland. Of course back in Maryland, most people didn't think there was anything west of the Appalachians, much less west of the Mississippi.

She met this girl's plane in Palm Springs and on the way up the hill, Susan got one of her diabolical ideas. She just turned left at Pioneertown Road, went up, parked in front of the Red Dog Saloon, opened the door, and yelled, "Hey Mom. We're home!"

This poor girl nearly fainted. There was nothing up there. Even the Golden Stallion had burned down by that time. But when she got here, she thought it really wasn't quite so bad.

The phone system was marvelous because it was like having your own answering service....except it was much better.

When we went out to dinner, we'd tell Anna Poste, "We're going to the Dunn's, and if anything important happens...."

She'd diagnose people over the phone and find out how really sick they were. If she didn't think they were sick enough to warrant Bill leaving a dinner party, she'd say she didn't know where he was. She probably told them to take two aspirin and call back in the morning. I don't know what she told them.

Everybody knew where everybody else was, and they'd try all over town if there was a long distance call. Colonel Metzger used to get lots of long distance phone calls because he was retired Air Force intelligence.

So he'd get a long distance call and Blanche would say, "Colonel Metzger just went by in his jeep. I think he went to the market. Do you want me to try the market?"

The Wrubels moved out here quite early and bought the Campbell house. Then they built the Flying W for Gene Dorsey, because by that time Pat Graham had gone and Gene had the stables.

Allie Wrubel also had the Flying W Restaurant, but other people ran it. We'd all empty the restaurant and go and ride square dance on horseback. People would come out to watch us. We did it at a full gallop. We didn't just walk around. It was really fun.

Johnny Johnson would bring somebody in by ambulance to the hospital, and then he would lurk around to see if they were going to be his customer. He'd walk in the hospital in the morning, and Bill's secretary would just open the little door and say, "Nothing today."

Then he would come over and ask me, "How's so and so getting along?"

One time we were off on a holiday. An elderly man who cleaned up the Josh Cafe after hours got home about four o'clock. He had a very old stationwagon and lived at the end of Adobe Road.

When he got home, he realized that the car was sounding funny, so he left the motor running. Something in the back end didn't sound right, so he got out and got down on his hands and knees to see if he could see what was wrong. The brakes slipped, and it ran over his head.

Evidently somebody was there to call the ambulance. Dr. Luther Shaw was manning the hospital in our absence, and called County Hospital and told them he wasn't equipped to really take care of this. He got this guy all set to go down to County, and Johnny had a run down to San Bernardino.

By the time he got down about four o'clock in the morning, it was a madhouse. The emergency room at County on Saturday night was full of all kinds of accidents, and you just had to wait your turn. So Johnny was very calmly standing beside this guerney that he'd gotten out of the ambulance.

Finally this intern who had really had it came up with a whole fistful of papers in his hand.

"Okay, okay. It's your turn. What happened to your patient?" he said.

"This guy ran over his own head."

"That does it." The intern threw all his papers into the air and just walked out.

Bill and I went down to the County Fair in Pomona one year and there was one booth that was selling doormats that would put anything on it that you wanted. We bought a black rubber one that said "Drop Dead" and gave it to him on his birthday, the 25th of February.

Bill's birthday was the 26th, so Carlin and I gave a big birthday party for both of them one year, and that was when we gave Johnny the mat. I thought _he_ was going to drop dead, because he was laughing so hard. And that was the year that he gave Bill a big manila envelope full of travel folders with a poem that said if Bill left town, he'd have more business.

Bill was always saving lives of the people that Johnny brought in to the hospital. And Johnny would come back the next day to see if he could collect them for his place of business. Bill's secretary would see Johnny coming and slide open the window in the hospital and say, "Nothing today, Johnny."

Johnny was about six feet tall and was strong. He used to help Bill move patients on and off the guerney because Bill only had nurses to help him. So one time Johnny brought in someone with a gunshot wound in the head. Bill was shaving the patient's head so that he could sew him up; Johnny was running around picking up all of the hair off the floor.

"I'm going to need that Bill. If I have to bury him, I'm going to have to put all that hair back on again."

And Bill looked at him and said, "He's going to live, Johnny. He's not yours."

"Well, he might not," as he continued stooping to pick up some more hair.

When the Marine Corps came we thought it was just swell. We knew all the first contingent of officers and people that came out. Colonel Scantling was one of the first. And the Oldfields, and Colonel Brink, and Colonel Ray Pilcher. For quite a time it was run from Pendleton, and we didn't have a general.

The first general we had was General Thomas McFarland. He must have been here about 1955, because when we bought the cannon, the first time we fired it was an eleven gun salute for General McFarland on May 25, 1957. And that was when he was leaving Twentynine Palms.

We loved the base because it was new blood in town and some great people. They had parties out there, and they had parades.

General Victory assumed command after General McFarland, and Bill attended his retirement parade. It was held during one of the biggest sandstorms we'd ever had. Caps were blowing away along with some of the flags.

Bill came home and sent General Victory a telegram that said, "Old generals never die. They just blow away."

Bill was one of the instigators of Search and Rescue.....one of the founders actually. One time they called up and said, "There's a flash flood. It's hit Fortynine Palms Canyon. We're going to clear the highway. Will you please come down in your Recon?" So down he went.

Blanche Ellis and I were up at my house ironing. It was much more fun to iron with company, so people would bring their ironing boards and iron. All of a sudden we thought, "What in the world are we doing up here when there's going to be some excitement downtown?"

There wasn't a cloud in the sky. We drove down Adobe Road to the highway where we were stopped by a search and rescue man. He said we couldn't come across here, even though it was a perfectly dry street. Blanche stuck her head out of the window and said, "I live over there," which was a lie. So he let us across and we circled around to the bank, parked, and walked over to the drugstore.

By this time there was a whole group of people standing out in front of the bank. Some had chairs and were sitting. And there was another group in front of the drugstore.

Everyone was sort of standing around and a tourist came up. He looked at me and said, "What are you waiting for?"

I said, "We're waiting for the flood."

"Sidewalk fishing" in front of Kenney's Drug Store during flood conditions after a summer rainstorm. Photo courtesy of Sally Ince.

He gave me a funny look and said, "What flood?"

"The one that's coming. It's on its way."

So sure enough, around the corner between the Roundup Room and El Rancho Dolores soon came this great sheet of water. Nobody could get through except with trucks.

Blanche and I were standing by the drugstore with go-aheads on. Mary Ann Beller was floating down the street in an inner tube, and so were a bunch of kids. There was no way we could get across the street, because we knew if we stepped out in our go-aheads, the go-aheads would go. It was also very dangerous because there were broken bottles and snakes and things.

Finally Bob Dunn came along in his father's truck, and we said, "Hey, do you have taxi service 'cause we can't get across the street to get back to our car?"

He took us over, we came home, and started ironing again. It never did rain here. It just rained in Fortynine Palms Canyon.

One of the really nice things I remember about my first impressions of Twentynine Palms was that there wasn't any caste system. It was just swell. No one cared a bit what you did. Two of the best dancers in town were the trash man and the cesspool digger and they were the ones we all wanted to dance with at the square dances.

So on trash day I would go down and talk with Jess Hayworth and sort of remind him that there was a square dance on Saturday. Well, he would say, "Sally, will you dance with me?" And that was exactly what I wanted him to say. And A.D. Conners, the cesspool digger was also one of the best dancers. You were in, if they asked you to dance.

Watty Watkins Real Estate Office during the week of snowstorms in January 1949 that blanketed the 29 Palms area. Photo by Sally Ince.

SALLY OSMUN INCE

A.D. Conners was a man that was probably about 6'5". He had a black beard long before everybody had black beards, so it was sort of noticeable. He always wore an engineer's cap of ticking. He was very formidable looking, but he was the nicest man.

The milkmen were the heads of the saddle club, both of them had been president, so when they came to deliver the milk we'd talk about horseback riding. It was just swell. No one cared a bit what you did. Everyone met at the same parties and everyone did the same things and it was fun.

Well A.D., the cesspool digger, would tie one on every once in a while, and his wife would lock him out of the house. Then he would go and stay at Las Casitas.

Of course, everybody knew where everybody was. The Postes were manning the telephone, and they knew that Blanche was at the Huber's. She had put a note on the door that said, "Occupy number 10 and register in the morning. Signed the Manager."

A.D. called up from the pay phone at Bagley's and asked her if she had a place for him to stay.

She said, "Sure A.D. You go in and just stay in cabin 10, and I'll see you in the morning."

He said, "Blanche, that's swell."

So we went ahead playing our poker game, and pretty soon the phone rang again. This time I think he was in Blanche's office.

"Blanche, this is A.D. again. I had a little trouble over here."

"What's the matter," she asked.

"Well, there were some people in cabin 10, but they ain't there no more."

Evidently some tourists had come in. Can you imagine having somebody just open your door and throw you out....especially when he looked like A.D. did? He'd scare the devil out of you.

Blanche never did find out who the people were, and I'm sure they didn't come back.

I've certainly enjoyed my years in Twentynine Palms. We moved out here the second of December in '46 and the first time we went back to town....to Beverly Hills was in March in '47. And soon after we had dinner with some of our buddies at the Beverly Hills Club. I was sitting next to a friend and he said, "You're all better now. When are you coming back?"

I said, "Back where?"

"Back here. You're certainly not going to live in that place!

And I said, "You couldn't drag me back here." He thought we were absolutely crazy. "I don't want to leave the desert. It just grows on you."

I've been here ever since and haven't changed my mind!

Sally Ince at a Pioneer Days gathering at the Bill
Underhill's, October 1977. Photo by the author.

DR. EDWARD LINCOLN SMITH

Edward Lincoln Smith was born in Montpelier, Vermont, the son of Martha Ann and William Sidney Smith. He attended Lommis Preparatory School in Conneticut, then attended Yale from which he graduated in 1934. Four years later he graduated from Harvard Medical School and interned at Rhode Island Hospital and Chapin Hospital in Providence, Rhode Island.

In 1940 he joined the Navy Medical Corps and served with the Marines at Quantico, Parris Island, and at New River (later Camp Lejeune). Here he met Lt. Colonel Lewis "Chesty" Puller and became a member of his First Marine Division when they headed for the South Pacific. His account of the Battle of Guadalcanal, called "Marine, You Die!" was published in the September 1943 issue of HARPER'S MAGAZINE. Dr. Smith's own heroic medical service to our fighting troops was later revealed when General Puller's biography was published.

After evacuation to New Zealand, Dr. Smith served in an Oakland hospital, and later was medical officer for the V-12 School in Flagstaff. Here he was introduced to the desert. Several later assignments finally resulted in his being in Okinawa when the war was terminated in 1945.

Terminal leave from the Navy brought him to California to visit friends. During a chance stopping in Redlands, he learned of the need in Twentynine Palms for a physician. From December 4th, 1946, to his retirement on June 1st, 1979, he served Twentynine Palms day and night, caring for all that sought his care and healing expertise. His profound devotion and dedication to this community has endeared him to thousands of patients and friends that he made during his thirty-three year residence.

Dr. Edward Lincoln Smith now lives in northern California with his wife, the former Elizabeth Sherman Goss, herself a member of one of this community's pioneer families.

*   *   *   *   *

I came out to California in 1946 with my mother. We drove an old Buick to the west coast where we visited World War II friends that I'd known in Flagstaff. While I was in Redlands, I visited Dr. Beaver in the Beaver Clinic. He had no place there at the time, but he suggested that I come out to Twentynine Palms where there was a great need for a family doctor.

While I had no intention at that time of staying in California, I decided that I would show my appreciation to him for his courtesies by driving out here the following day which was a Sunday. When we came out here, I fell in love with the community at first sight and decided that I would not return to the east coast, but would get my license in California and practice in Twentynine Palms.

I called on Frank Bagley and Phil Zimmers, and they were very delighted that I was seriously considering practice here. They recommended that I go see Dr. Luckie in Pasadena, and the following week I did. He apparently approved of me and sent word to them that it would be all right for me to practice here.

While I was making my first visit to Twentynine Palms, we stopped at the Plaza. Bill Hatch and Wad Watkins had a realtor's office next door to the Stubbs' shoe store, and they were so eager to have a doctor, that Wad remarked that he would pitch a tent across the street, if I would just take his office. So they vacated that office.

We then went over to Las Casitas and made arrangements to occupy a unit of that motel two weeks later. We stayed at Las Casitas for one year, I think. Then we moved into a Zimmer's house on Adobe Road that had a little picket fence around it. I lived there for a year, and after that we moved over to Palo Verde and bought Wad Watkins' house.

I wanted adventure, and probably, that's why I liked the challenge of Twentynine Palms. It was like going to a foreign country. I was on my own. There was no hospital here. There was no bank. We had maybe a couple of dozen telephones and a few paved roads. It was really pioneering, as far as a doctor was concerned.

We had to either have home deliveries or take pregnant women to Palm Springs which was the nearest hospital. They had no real hospital, but it was a kind of a barracks down there. I remember many times taking patients by ambulance with Jack Cones, Wad Watkins, or Johnny Bagley who'd drive.

We'd take off down the highway, and when we'd get to Garnet, there was no overpass. In fact, there was no real highway or anything. When you'd come into Garnet, you'd come down a long slope and almost invariably there was a long freight train. It was always stopped across the road. But they would see us coming down the hill, get the signal, and as we drove up, the train would part. And like crossing the Red Sea, we'd go through and on to the hospital. Those trips were always very exciting.

EDWARD LINCOLN SMITH

When I arrived here to start my practice, of course, I had to clean the office. I remember standing outside washing the windows when Sara Schenck came by. I think she seemed surprised to see a doctor out there washing windows. I never felt that was below me. I enjoyed doing it.

I had very little money when I came here, and I had no receptionist. In fact nobody had any money. My mother said, "We'll get a card table, and I'll work as your receptionist." Johnny and Marguerite Lyons had a tiny store over in Smoke Tree near the intersection of Larrea and Two Mile Road, and I went over there and bought my first furniture.

You couldn't buy a baby scale at that time, because it was just at the end of the war and things weren't being made yet. So when I would have a home delivery and have a baby to weigh, I would always take them down to Bagley's and weigh them on the vegetable scales. This became a great occasion for the community. Everybody would get to see the baby, and we'd have a kind of a celebration.

Helen Bagley was always very nice about it. She said, "Of course we could weigh our babies." And that's the way it was. We'd walk down four or five buildings from my office, and everybody would watch us go and watch us come back.

Dr. Ed Smith and his mother, Martha Ann Smith, made a visit with the Hatch family during the holidays, Christmas 1948. Photo by Bill Hatch, author's collection.

EDWARD LINCOLN SMITH

During those first years from 1947 until the Marine Base came here, most of my deliveries were home deliveries. They were scattered all over the valley from the mountains above Morongo out to Dead Man's Lake. My sister, Helen, who's a nurse, helped me with some of these home deliveries and really taught me an awful lot that I didn't learn at Harvard - how to take care of newborn babies, how to dress them, how to bathe them, how to put diapers on them - procedures that Harvard could care less about, but were very important.

One thing about the home deliveries was that I would prepare for them by sterilizing my instruments, my gown, and sheets in the pressure cooker. Then I would wrap these things and put them in a big basket. I'd always have it ready, if any emergency occurred. Then after the delivery was over, I'd bring them all home. Of course, they were blood stained, and we'd wash them out in the washing machine, and hang them out on the clothes line. Anybody going past the house would see all these things, and that was a signal to the whole town that a new baby had been born.

I believe, the Michels boy, whose parents were Barbara and George Michels, was the first one that I delivered. But my first obstetrical patient was Vivian Anthony.

When I first got here, I think penicillin was just coming into commercial use for practicing physicians. I remember we didn't have disposable syringes at that time. Whenever I would go to a home, I would always find the stove, heat water, and boil a syringe and needle, and give the shot, because we didn't have apparatus for keeping syringes sterile. I knew everybody in town and knew where they kept the key to their house, under this rock or that one, or up in the rafters. I knew where more keys were to private homes and where their stoves were and how their kitchens worked.

I remember a delivery I made to a family called Stites....Gabe Stites and her name was Charlotte. He was a disabled veteran, and therefore had no money, so he lived on a veteran's pension, I suppose. I didn't know where they lived until the day came for the delivery.

I remember he came to our house on Adobe Road. It was morning around seven o'clock and a real hot day. It must have been in August. He came in an old rattle trap of a truck, and we went down the hill towards Smith Ranch, turned off, and went to Iva and Jim Hill's house. I think he simply wanted to tell them that Charlotte was in labor.

I remember Iva waving goodbye to us, then we headed off down Adobe Road. Then I think we must have gone to Indian Trail, maybe over to Mesquite Springs Road and then out north again. The base, of course, wasn't there at this time. We went across Dead Man's Lake, and I remember mirages which must have been the first ones I had ever seen. We went farther and farther toward the hills.

We finally came to his homestead way, way out there. They had no running water, no electricity, no telephones. They had two little boys who were real cute kids and maybe four and five. They were playing outdoors like kids do today.

So I got there and Charlotte was a very good patient. She was very composed and a typical pioneer type young woman. She was in her twenties I suppose. Gabe was older. It was a very tidy but very sparsely furnished place. There was only an iron bedstead and a few pieces of furniture.

Well, she wasn't very far along in labor when I got there, and I knew when I left the house that I would remain there until things were over. It might be a few hours or a few days, and here I was way out there. I had lots of time to spare, so I played with the little boys. They took me outside and showed me the turtles and lizards, which was fairly new to me. I remember one thing that they showed me that I've never seen since, and that was a sidewinder up in a tree.

I thought, what am I doing out here at Dead Man's Lake watching a rattlesnake, sitting by myself without a phone...without any help? Yet I was perfectly happy. It was a challenge. I was on my own, and whatever I've learned, I'm going to put to good use.

So time went on. I gave Gabe the ether can and the ether mask. There was no other way. I was careful that there weren't any stoves or anything that could explode or catch fire. So he poured and I proceeded to perform my task. Fortunately she had a baby girl, which is what she wanted, and I tidied things up.

I remember it was morning by the time I was ready to leave. The little boys accompanied me out through the gate to the truck. They kept looking in my bag, as they were just so certain that I had brought the baby in the bag. They wanted to look inside to see if I had any more.

When my sister was here, she would accompany me, otherwise I had very little help. One person who did help me was Lida Donnell. When Onie Jones had her babies over on Homestead Road, which is not far from the Postes who had the telephone service, Lida did come and help me. She stayed all day, and I think we had babies on successive years at that home. She helped me then.

I know that I had a number of the old-timers who were frequent patients and unable to pay. Those days we didn't have Medicaid. Charity was part of the way of life, and they were proud people. Not infrequently, I would come to my office and find a dressed rabbit, jams and jellies, or some fresh vegetables there. That was their way of paying me, which was great!

When I had my office at the Plaza in the very early days in the

'40s, Linda Bagley and Barbara Dunn were little girls. One day they came walking into my office and were crying. They had with them a doll whose head was broken. They naturally felt that I, being the doctor, would be able to correct the problem, so they brought the doll into me. I don't recall now what I did, but I patched up the doll so that at least it looked like I'd done something. And they walked out very happy that their doll had been restored.

We had no veterinarian here for quite awhile until the Crowls came. I had many calls from people who thought I should know something about the treatment of animals, but I didn't. It's a special field. Adelaide Arnold's dog, Toby, was wandering around the Plaza one day, and it stepped on a broken bottle. He got a terrible gash in his foot. She brought him in, of course, trailing blood all over the place. My sister was there at the time and was quite well along in her pregnancy. But here was the dog and nothing to do but take care of it. So she got down and sat on the dog, and I got down and sewed him up.

Another time this French nurse who lived on Donnell Hill called me and said that she needed a house call. So I said, "Very well, I'll come by."

When I got there, she looked all right to me. She took me into the living room and said, "Well, it isn't me. It's my canary who's got asthma." I didn't know what to do for the canary, so I didn't make any charge for my call.

Another time somebody brought a dog to me that either was ill, or they didn't want it anymore. They brought it to my office in the Plaza and said would I be good enough to destroy the dog. I said, "Well, this isn't my usual trade, but you're a friend, so I'll do it for you."

So I got out a can of ether and put the dog to sleep. Naturally I knew I had to do something with it, so I got a shovel and buried it behind my office in a shallow grave. The next morning when I got to the office, there was the dog setting at my back door, a bit groggy. I found out later it's actually very difficult to destroy an animal. Generally you do it intravenously and with quite a large dose.

Jack Meek used to come and sit on the little stone seat outside of my office. I remember the little Hatch girls used to come and he would talk to them. He gave them each little gold nuggets for their necklaces.

In the early 1950's the Marine Corps Base began to develop, and then of course, as the Marines came, their wives followed them. They had no hospital at the base, and presently, we discovered we had a real problem. Babies began to come in large numbers. So they turned to us to deliver these babies. We were hard pressed to know how to handle this.

Bill Ince had the hospital, and I was willing to handle as much of the obstetrical work as I could. So my load became heavier and heavier until I was really and truly swamped. I'm afraid that it interfered with my medical practice to take care of the town's people which was the reason I'd come here.

But it seemed like an enormous opportunity for a young man to expand his practice and to get ahead financially. So I accepted these patients, and they came in droves. I had to expand my office staff, as I think I was delivering up to five babies a day, which was just incredible for anybody to do that. I think to do it under these conditions was also quite astonishing. Of course, Bill Ince had to expand his staff too, to take care of them.

Well naturally things began to get pretty tight at the hospital. If you have five babies one day and maybe four the next (which is what happened once to me), and you already have some left over from previous days, then presently you don't have enough room. We had these girls in the halls, and we hadn't enough bassinets. So we decided the logical thing was to put the babies in the bureau drawers, and this is the way it worked.

I remember one girl who stopped at the sentry at the entry gate. The Marine who was on duty there rose to the occasion, leaped into the car, delivered the baby, unlaced his shoe, took the lace and tied the cord, and sent her up to the hospital.

So things began to occur which indicated that we were really getting in over our heads at the hospital. Furthermore, the strain of all this was getting to be too much for me, because I could not leave this town for eleven months of the year. I couldn't even go to Joshua Tree, because I was responsible for every one of these women. I was delivering twenty to thirty a month so that I was confined day and night.

At the Ince Hospital: L to R: Dr. Ince, Susie Ince, Eva Enger, Mrs. Dunkin, Dr. Ed Smith, Dr. Kinsey. Photo courtesy of Sally Ince.

496

On a brisk morning, January 29th, 1961, the town of 29 Palms turned out in masse to help local miner, Karl Schapel, rebuild his house at his Golden Egg Mine that he had recently lost to a fire. L to R: Betty Fields, Karl Schapel, Brig. General Lewis Fields, Sally Ince, Bill Ince, John Hilton, Isabelle Kunasz, Blanche Ellis, Grace Kingman, Victor Kingman. Photo by Bill Hatch, courtesy of Sally Ince.

When the base did build its hospital and all of that obstetrical business was removed from our hospital, that probably saved my life. Nobody should keep up that pace. Home deliveries also disappeared. Soon after this, the hospital closed and remained closed for about a year.

Dr. Kinsey was still there with Dr. Ince, but it was too great a burden on them. So Bill decided to get rid of it and sell it to the community, which he did. Soon after, we were very, very fortunate in getting first Dr. Galletta, who came here from the Marine Base, and who was instrumental in getting Dr. Guzman. They were classmates together. When those two doctors joined us, there followed a period of greatest progress and greatest activity in the hospital. The hospital with the help of the three of us, improved the quality of care and the quantity of care tremendously.

But soon the hospital became obsolete in the eyes of the authorities. In order for us to continue, we would have had to make so many changes and incur such expensive changes that we couldn't afford it. Soon after that Dr. Galletta said that if we didn't get a new hospital, he would consider leaving town. So there

Dr. Edward Smith hands Ada Hatch a board during the rebuilding of Karl Schapel's house in January 1961. Photo by Bill Hatch, courtesy of Ada Hatch.

was a lot of pressure put on the board to start the ball rolling for the new one now in Joshua Tree.

Dr. Nicholson was here when I came in 1946. He had waited on this community for quite a few years, and he was an ill man himself. He had very, very severe asthma. He was not resentful when I came, in fact, he was nice to me and I tried to be nice to him. I understood what he meant to the community, and how loyal the people were to him. When he needed help, he called me. I made frequent house calls on him to treat him for his asthma or any other problem. On rare occasions he would make house calls.

Another doctor I liked very much was Dr. Phillip Reynolds who lived next door to Margaret Kennedy. He and Lillian came in the '50s. He was a retired obstetrician, so when I would take my vacation each year in August, he would cover for me and handle my obstetrical patients at the hospital. He was a very nice, pleasant person. We got along fine.

Dr. Edward Lincoln Smith and his wife, Betty Ann Sherman Smith, Pioneer Days 1977 Grand Marshalls. Photo by the author.

JANE WHITE KRUSHAT

Jane White was born in Los Angeles on March 3, 1927, and raised in Ontario, the daughter of Dr. Marcus Demosthenes White and his wife, Letty Esther Wimsett. Her father believed that children should be transferred around so they would be better adjusted to change, therefore Jane believes she attended every elementary school in Ontario at that time.

When World War II broke out, she started at Chaffey High School, then transferred to Woodrow Wilson High School in Long Beach where she graduated in 1945. She attended Chaffey Jr. College and Redlands College, where during her studies, she received a provisional teaching credential and came to Twentynine Palms to teach the second grade in 1947.

Two years later, she married Les Krushat, son of pioneers, Sarah and Art Krushat. She traveled with Les, during his successful career as an Air Force officer and pilot, and became the mother of their four children.

After Les' retirement, they returned to Twentynine Palms in 1980 to build their house and resume their lives in a community that they both always considered home. Jane continues to pursue her love of teaching by substituting in the Twentynine Palms schools from time to time, continuing a vocation that began here almost forty years ago.

*　　*　　*　　*　　*

While I was at Redlands College, my father's friend, C. Burton Thrall, who was Superintendent of Schools, told him about the teacher shortage. He told him they were taking students out of the education program and putting them into provisional credentials, so they could teach in the wintertime and work for their degree in the summer.

So I was interviewed by several supervisors, and they would each tell us about their district. My friend, Phyllis Beekman and I had been talking to Hazel Croy, who was the supervisor for the Morongo School District. She seemed so enthusiastic about Twentynine Palms.

I had heard of Twentynine Palms when I was a child, because we had friends out here. My parents were friends with Ray and

Bess Flickinger, and we had come out to visit for the first time when I was seven or eight. Then my father used to come out here and stay in the little cabins at the Inn when he needed a break from his practice. When he could get away, this is where he wanted to come.

One time during the war when he was away, he wrote to my mother and said, "When I get back to the United States, the first thing I want to do is go to Twentynine Palms and just sit." He really loved the desert.

So Phyllis and I decided that Twentynine Palms sounded interesting. Hazel told us to go out and meet the principal.

We drove out here which I thought was to the end of the world. You can't believe it. It was a dirt road......nothing. Yucca Valley had a general store. Joshua Tree was a hole in the wall. When we got to Twentynine Palms, we met with the principal, Joe White.

The school was located on Utah Trail and Two Mile Road, and we met Joe there. Most school boards convened and met their prospective teachers there, and they are then told whether they were hired or not. Instead, we had to go and meet privately each school board member where they were working, and then they would call Joe and tell him whether or not we would be hired.

The first member we went to see was Bill Stubbs, and he was at the Paint Pot. Then we saw Mabel Marlow at the post office, and finally Ada Van Ness at the dime store that was up from the post office. They were the three who interviewed us, and then we went back down to see Joe. He said, "You're hired if you want the job, but we don't have a place for you to teach. We don't know where you'll be!"

When we came out the last of August, we weren't even sure that we would have a building. Dr. Ince had purchased two quonset huts, put them on Adobe Road, built a bathroom outside them, and that's where we started teaching.

Carol Miller was in the front and my room was the next one. The first grades had the two other rooms. The kindergarten was the building on the Legion grounds, and Phyllis was in the chicken coop in back of the old school building. It was really an unusual circumstance to teach.

Bill and Mrs. Hockett were the janitors and that was right after Bill's accident. He was still in a brace. Ivy, his wife, was just lovely. I never realized how much help the custodians could be to a new teacher. They were absolutely lovely to me.

In my first class of second graders there were Mary Van Lahr, Tommy Nicolls, Donny Newland, Therman Carson, Sandy Hayes, Susan Stubbs, Hedy Jane Haggee, Dolores Perkins, and Punky Sullivan. Punky was an instructor later out here at the Recreation Center for awhile. There were also David Smith, Harry Smith (who they called "Tookee"), and Elwood Smith. I can't remember all of the others, but there were about thirty altogether.

I remember once that Elwood Smith was disturbing the class, and the method of discipline that we had been taught in Redlands was to take the child from the area that he was disturbing, put him out in the hall, and to deal with him when you had time. To get him out of the class was the philosophy of that time.

So I sat Elwood on a chair outside the quonset hut. I went to get him when I had everyone else settled and ready to work, but he wasn't there. I looked and there was this little figure trudging across the desert. I had Carol call a recess and watch my kids and her kids. I had to get into my car and chase my wandering student over the desert. That was the last time I ever placed a child out of my sight.

The children were really well-behaved. I never had any problems discipline-wise which maybe was or wasn't a good thing, because I thought all classes were like that until I taught elsewhere later on. I realized then what a well-behaved class I had had.

Jane White's second grade class, 1947-1948. Santa Claus, played by Elwood Smith's grandfather is visiting the class. Elwood Smith, standing next to Santa Claus, may recognize the familiar face and voice. Jane's classroom was part of a quonset hut still standing on Adobe Road. Photo courtesy of Jane White Krushat.

JANE WHITE KRUSHAT

Sharing class space in the same quonset hut was Helen Owens' first grade class (1947-1948). Her students would become Jane White's second graders in the fall of 1948. This was a smaller class. Ada Hatch may have been substitute teaching the December day this photo was taken, as little Liz Hatch, too young to be in the first grade, was visiting (sixth from the left). Her sister, Ada, who was in the class, is seated to her left. Janie Van Lahr is fourth from the right. Bradley Huber is second from the right. Photo by Bill Hatch, courtesy of Ada Hatch.

The classroom was half a quonset hut. The windows were way up, almost to the ceiling and very small. As a result, it was very poorly lit.

There was an oil burning stove at the front of the classroom which was my job to keep it lit and to keep the room heated. If the stove went out, I had to relight it. If the stove pipe fell off, I had the soot all over me. It was really primitive. We had to get the kids around the stove in the wintertime, because it was cold out here. So we moved the desks closer to the stove.

In the springtime, we had to spend a lot of time outdoors. Toward April and May we mostly took them outside to read. The only time we brought the kids inside was for board work and desk work, because the building was really quite inadequate for the summer heat.

The kids learned and were mostly good students. A few of them needed special help. Susie Stubbs and Sandy Hayes were very bright children, and in order to keep them busy, I had them straighten up all of my supplies that stood behind the blackboard. I think that Susie and Sandy must have spent the year behind the blackboard, because they were so very quick to learn.

The way we called kids into class was that Carol went around with a bell and rang it. She walked all the way around the quonset huts ringing this bell, and then she'd come back to her room. There was nothing automatic about it.

We didn't even have a duplicating system when I first taught out here. I printed all of the "seat" work on a Hectograph. You put what you wanted to copy on a piece of gelatin. You put your master down and then ran papers off it. You had to keep the pad wet to do it, and you had to do each paper separately.

It still was better than writing it out in longhand. The copies curled so you had to have something heavy to put on them. And that was the way we made most of our seatwork. It used to take forever. Sometimes we had five sheets a day per student, so I spent a great deal of time just running material off.

There wasn't a lot of prepared material to be had, and we were supposed to teach the "look-see" method of reading, which is memorizing words or the configuration of them. It was not phonics. I thought this was wrong, so I taught phonics. Every time a supervisor came around, I'd just shove the phonics charts under any desk. Luckily, they don't do the "look-see" method anymore, but that was the method of teaching then.

The first year I made $240 a month. The living conditions out here were very different. The first year Phyllis and I found this cute little cabin up on Utah Trail. It had one bedroom with bunk beds in the wall, and it was adobe. There were four houses along the row, and we were second to the last.

One morning Phyllis got up and was looking out the window with a startled look on her face, and we discovered we had some practicing nudists living next to us which really shook us up. So my sister, Joanne came out and got us out of our lease and moved us to Mrs. Hasting's front house. It was on Two Mile Road almost catercorner across from Luckie Park.

Although there wasn't a park there then, there was a baseball diamond. At night everybody went down there to watch different people in town play, because that was about all there was to do. Either that or go to the theatre, which was located on the corner of Adobe Road and Two Mile Road. But every time Les and I walked into the theatre, the kids all turned around and said, "Oh, there's Miss White and Lester!" It got so if we went anywhere, we had to duck!

Watty Watkins had set up this blind date with Lester for me. People had told me about Les Krushat, but I had never seen him. Harold Hockett and Carol Miller, who he later married, told me that I really ought to meet Les. So Watty set up this date, and Les came to call and pick me up. It was for a square dance, so I put on a pair of boots, jeans, and a cowboy shirt. Les was at the door dressed to the nines in a coat and tie, and I felt so terrible. I could hardly look at him, but I didn't go with anybody else. Two weeks later we ran down to Yuma and got married.

It was probably love at first sight, and he must have felt the same way, because he came one afternoon to school and said, "Come on. Let's get married." It was his birthday. He was twenty-two and I was twenty-one. I told him I couldn't go that day because I had to wash my hair! The next day I went with him to Yuma and got married. Then he went away to pilot training for a year.

No one knew officially that we were married. Later we had a big church wedding in the Episcopal Church in Ontario which had been my church. I think all of Twentynine Palms came to the wedding. We were so surprised, because I didn't realize Les' family knew everybody in town.

Dora Ridley taught the fourth and fifth grade during Jane White's first year of teaching (1947-1948) in 29 Palms. Photo from the author's collection.

JANE WHITE KRUSHAT

The people out here were very good to the teachers. They entertained them. They had parties for them. They took them into their homes. It was a wonderful way to start teaching, and this was a wonderful place to be a teacher.

There were eight teachers in the elementary school. I think that Joe White taught the seventh and eighth grade, as well as being principal. Dora Ridley taught the fourth and fifth grade in the other room of the old school building. Phyllis had the fourth grade in a "chicken coop" behind the main building.

In the quonset huts we had Carol Miller, who taught third grade. I was in the same building with my second grade. A Mrs. Helen Owens had the first grade, and in the middle of the school year we gained another teacher for a first and second grade.

The second year I taught we started with four new teachers. My sister, Jo Anne, was one new teacher. We also gained a new principal, Howard Harmon. There were two men teachers - Rod Johnson and Dick Harmon - no relation to Howard. Phyllis and Dora had left. They both were getting married. Rosy Harmon came out to teach kindergarten. She was Howard's sister. Twentynine Palms seemed to attract families.

The high school consisted of Ted Hayes, who not only was principal but also taught English. There were two other high school teachers my first year here. They were Mary Jane Allen and Priscilla Timberlake.

We would socially get together and have picnics in the Monument or parties in a home. It seemed like there was always something to do. Life was not boring here in Twentynine Palms.

Being asked back to teach wasn't automatic from year to year. They really scrutinized their teachers. We had some rules that we had to follow as teachers. We weren't allowed in Sam's Character Room, which was a bar downtown. We weren't allowed in Jay's, called "the Bucket of Blood," which was another bar further down in town on the corner of Sullivan Road below where Homestead Lumber is now.

We also weren't allowed in the Smoke Tree Lounge either. So we really weren't suppose to patronize any of the bars in town. That's unusual, but you won't find that for teachers these days. They would allow us to go up to Pioneer Town to the Red Dog Saloon.

In my second year's class I had Ada Hatch, Janie Van Lahr, Davie Williams, and Bradley Huber. There was also Buzzy Kunasz and Stevie Phelps. Stevie had cerebral palsy and walked with a brace. But these kids didn't give him a hard time. He wasn't even classified as an exceptional child. He just fit in with everyone else. They are the ones that I remember. When I left, Howard Harmon's wife, Glenda, took over my class.

JANE WHITE KRUSHAT

During her second year of teaching, Jane White married Les Krushat, youngest son of pioneer homesteaders, Sarah and Art Krushat and left 29 Palms with him as he underwent pilot training. This June 1948 photo was taken at Randolph AFB, Texas is courtesy of Jane White Krushat.

Even my second class was small. These kids were one of the top groups of children that I ever taught. They were all very quick. Only a few didn't grasp a concept the first time it was presented. That's why this group was so good. It was a wonderful place to teach school.

The school site was an isolated spot with very few buildings around it. I could stand outside the quonset huts on yard duty and wave to Bess Flickinger, whose house is located next to the current Adobe Deli.

Field trips for our students consisted of various places in the valley. Luckily for me, one of the social studies curriculum was the study of the dairy farm. Here in Twentynine Palms, we had a dairy. It was located on Utah Trail and run by the Healys. That was a big event for the children. It was a very small dairy, but my students seemed to enjoy the "field trip." Tom Healy used to deliver the school milk too. How we kept it cool, I can't remember. We certainly didn't have any refrigeration at school.

Another bus trip we used to take was in the spring. Toward the end of May, we would get to go to Luckie Park to the swimming pool. It was a treat for teachers and students alike. My students looked forward to this, and it certainly was a way to get the best behavior out of them. "If we aren't good students and finish all of our work, we won't go swimming," was almost a magical sentence.

On the bus my students use to start undressing, shoes, and such until the bus driver, Tom Martin, made the rule, "No undressing until we reach the dressing rooms!" That solved many problems such as lost clothing and "smelly feet."

Ralph Dunn was the recreation director at the pool. He was also life guard and sort of jack-of-all-trades. Thinking back, I must have had a great deal of courage to take thirty students swimming. With Ralph there, I always felt very secure.

We had two buses. Tom Martin and Harry Smith were the bus drivers. Since the children lived so far away from the school, we couldn't keep any of the children after school for extra help. We could if we made special arrangements, but it just wasn't practical.

Teaching science here on the desert was really an education for me. We had a science table where the children could bring in science specimens. This was any thing they found on the desert. I was thinking in the area of rocks, plants, and maybe a few bugs. Much to my surprise, I found a dead rattlesnake, live tarantulas, scorpions, and spiders in jars on the table.

Each child would tell wonderful stories about how they had found these specimens. "My dad found this tarantula in my closet." Believe me, I would walk very carefully around my house hoping I wouldn't have the same experience.

Once I was correcting papers near the science table, when I looked over to see the "dead" tarantula making his way out of the jar. Without a lid, I must have piled every book I could find on top of the jar and ran out to find the Hocketts. After that, I'd check each donation very carefully to be sure they weren't going to be crawling around my room.

The skating rink at Smith's Ranch was our multipurpose room. It was about the only place in town where all of the parents could be seated. I remember in my second year, my sister, Jo Anne had come out to teach with me. We put on a Christmas pageant there. We had all the "quonset hut" school involved in it. It was a big undertaking, but certainly worth the effort, for I remember how much my students enjoyed performing for their parents and friends.

Even with lack of proper facilities, materials, or books, it never crossed my mind that Twentynine Palms wasn't the best place on earth to start a teaching career. This start helped me not only to gain teaching experience, but it also taught me that the teacher and the students are the two necessary "tools" you need for an education, and you can improvise with all of the rest.

Les and Jane Krushat returned to 29 Palms to visit his parents and to attend the Pioneer Days celebration, October 1978. Two years later they returned permanently to build their home and enjoy their retirement after Les' years in the Air Force. Photo by the author taken at the Underhills' Old-Timers' Reunion.

MARTHA HATCH REICH

Martha Eunice Hatch was born on September 3, 1948, in a Pasadena hospital to Ada Watkins Hatch and William B. Hatch, Jr. After her birth the family returned to their home in Twentynine Palms, where Martha grew up attending local schools with her older sisters, Ada and Liz.

After she graduated from Twentynine Palms High School in 1967, she attended Scripps College in Claremont from which she graduated in June 1971. In September of that same year, she married Cary J. Reich, and they now live in Mission Viejo with their two children, Jennifer and Katie.

The Reichs make frequent trips to Twentynine Palms to attend family gatherings at Grandmother Hatch's home. During these visits, Martha shares with her husband and own children an understanding and appreciation of the desert in which she lived as a young girl.

* * * * *

I no longer reside in Twentynine Palms, but I never let too much time elapse between visits. As I write, a cool desert breeze enters one window and exits another across the room. It's the end of the Spring season and vegetation is starting to look dry. I smell pungent creosote bush right outside, and hear the faint rustling of leaves...how I love the quiet desert evening!

I grew up in Twentynine Palms, the youngest daughter of Ada and Bill Hatch. As a child, the desert was my playground. My two sisters, Ada and Liz, and I would often make desert forts in some of the larger bushes and went to great effort to make them "livable." Removable branches became the doors, and blocks of wood served as tables. We would often hide trinkets in old cigar boxes, then carefully mark the fort somehow so we could find it another day and reclaim our treasures.

One summer, a new well was dug at the adobe house next door. Mounds of thick, wet, oozing mud were created as the dirt was brought out of the ground. What a place to play! As the morning sun became hotter and hotter, we would hurry to our newly created play area and literally be up to our waist in cool mud. Later, much hosing off was necessary outdoors before we could go inside for lunch.

Another activity involving dirt and water was building each summer what Ada, Liz, and I called "the harbor." We dug a large hole in the ground with tin cans, coated the sides with adobe, filled it with water, and had hours of fun. We had boats in the harbor, created islands, and had many roads all around also paved with adobe.

I have fond memories of picnics in the Monument, especially during the hot months when it was so much cooler at the higher elevations. One spring, a Joshua Tree National Monument ranger, Mr. Vanderspeck, invited my father and me to go with him to a watering hole, far up in the Monument.

We left the house around three in the morning, drove in ranger vehicles quite a distance, then hiked in, arriving at the watering hole just as the sun arose. We were there for the purpose of counting the big horned sheep. Sure enough, as we patiently waited and watched, we began to see these beautiful animals. They came down slowly, and only their movement gave away their location....their coloring blended in perfectly with the terrain. That setting of early morning light, a quiet source of water, the desolation surrounding us, and the rhythmic movement of these beautiful sure-footed animals, is one that I cherish.

The house where we grew up on Utah Trail had a windmill with a water tank for storage. The month of October often had little wind, and therefore stored water was scarce. If we accidentally left a hose on overnight, we were really in the dog house, as the tank could be drained or almost emptied.

The tiny little room directly below the tank, accessible only by old rickety wooden stairs, was always rumored to be "haunted." We were convinced it was inhabited by a poltergeist (a ghost or spirit that makes a racket). It did seem to play tricks on us, hiding little items, and moving small things from one place to another. Of course pack rats have a reputation for being similarly mischievous!

Dr. Edward Lincoln Smith, my godfather, was also our doctor. Sometimes when we were sick, he would come to the house. It was wonderful to have such a good family friend for a doctor, and I just assumed that all doctors made house calls, and always would!

The wood burning stove in our dining room made that room the most frequented room in the house, especially on cold winter mornings. Of course, we always had an electric stove also, but the wood stove was so cozy and Dad made hot cereal every morning which fortified us for the walk down the road to school each morning. We walked to Twentynine Palms Elementary School. However when I was in kindergarten, I rode the bus to and from school.

The Hatch family's Christmas card, 1965 taken at their 30th Palm home on Utah Trail. L to R: Ada, Martha, Liz, Ada Sr., and Bill Hatch. Photo from the author's collection.

One day Mother told the driver, Mr. Smith, to let me out at the Plaza where Dad's office was, instead of at the house on Utah Trail, as she had to be out of town all day. Well, by the time school was over, the driver had forgotten, and he stopped to let me out at the end of the long driveway leading to the house. I knew I shouldn't get out there, but was too scared to say anything, so away I went while fear of being alone in the big house overcame me. Inside the back door to the house I stood, crying and too afraid to move.

Soon I heard Mr. Smith's voice calling me - he had driven on, remembered Mother's instructions, and then returned to fetch me. Happy to be with someone again, I walked hand-in-hand with Mr. Smith, back down that driveway and on to that bus once again!

512

Martha Hatch Reich and her family: husband, Cary, and daughters, Jennifer and Katie taken at the Hatch family's summer island home in Michigan, 1985. Photo courtesy of Martha Hatch Reich.

It seems like I spent a lot of time on buses later. As a freshman in high school, the only bus I could ride, to Utah Trail, was the football players bus. This might not have been so bad, except these were players in full uniform, who had just played an hour of football, and even open windows in the bus didn't take away that smell!

All through high school we took numerous long bus rides - to places in Los Angeles, to Girls' Athletic Association tournaments, and of course to varsity football games. The cheerleaders always had ample time, on the long rides to distant places, to build up enthusiasm and ensure good school spirit. Another long drive during this period of my life, was to Riverside to the nearest available orthodontist. On these frequent visits we car-pooled with five or six kids and always made a whole day of it with lunch out.....everyone just ordered soup however....sore mouths!

MARTHA HATCH REICH

My whole family looks forward to their visits to the desert of Twentynine Palms. In these times it's so important for children to learn about nature firsthand....to be able to entertain themselves without television and sophisticated toys. Our daughter, Katie, age five, sees the desert as a giant sand box and enjoys feeding the slow-moving desert tortoise at her grandmother's house.

Our daughter, Jennifer, has just completed a model of one of the California missions for her fourth grade class. We collected some adobe from an abandoned adobe wall thirty or so miles east of Twentynine Palms. She made over three hundred miniature adobe bricks for the model. It turned out nicely and was un-doubtedly the most authentic!

My husband, Cary, and I enjoy living near the cool California coastline, but our visits to the desert provide us the opportunity to relax and to rediscover the fascinating forgotten earth. We enjoy hiking where the majestic desolation of the desert becomes so interesting upon a close inspection of flora and fauna. We especially enjoy the nights when Cary's telescope brings the distant stars close, and we feel the cool dry evening air and appreciate the absence of harsh sounds.

The Ray Flickinger family were close friends of the Hatch family while Martha and her sisters were growing up in 29 Palms. Ray Sr., his wife, Bess, and children: Chan, Ray Jr., Phillip, Florence, and Betty Lou. Photo taken in the early 1950's by Bill Hatch, courtesy of Ada Hatch.

LUCILE AND HAROLD WEIGHT

Lucile Harris was born in Buffalo, Missouri, the daughter of William Sullivan Harris and Ada Rawlins Harris. When she was nine months old, her family moved to Sonoma County, California. After completing her formal education, she started gaining writing experience by working as a newspaper reporter, feature writer, and columnist for the OCEAN BEACH NEWS and other San Diego area newspapers.

In February 1937, Randall Henderson came over to Ocean Beach and offered Lucile a job to be the first staff member hired by his DESERT MAGAZINE when it started operation in El Centro, California that fall. She was soon working in a number of departments handling circulation, correspondence, and assisting in the critical review of contributions to the magazine. Later during World War II when Randall Henderson, the publisher, entered on active duty, Lucile would become acting editor.

During these early years with the DESERT MAGAZINE, she began corresponding with a young man from Pasadena who ordered publications and submitted entries in the magazine's photo contests, one of which he won. Lucile, who was one of the judges, was impressed with the knowledge he had about the desert and enjoyed hearing from him which was "only on business." This young writer and photographer was Harold Weight.

Harold Orlando Weight was born in Los Angeles, the son of Orlando Harold Weight and Genevieve Whipple Weight. His grandfather, a Civil War veteran, had come from Pennsylvania and settled in Pasadena in 1886. Harold's father was a railroad telegrapher, and the family moved frequently as a part of his job. He first visited Twentynine Palms on a trip with his parents in 1934. He returned again in 1937 and many times thereafter.

Harold had been involved in writing and related activities from childhood through his high school years. In the 1930's he wrote at night and worked as a printer in Eagle Rock during the day. He concentrated on fiction writing and sold articles to magazines. He also was involved in writing, co-producing. and directing plays, and writing reviews, columns, and feature articles which were published in Hollywood Film-O-Graph, a trade publication.

World War II interrupted his writing career, during which he served in the Army Air Corps, as an instructor in radar navigation.

It was during this time that he continued to write to Lucile at DESERT MAGAZINE. Randall Henderson, the publisher, asked Lucile to find out what plans Harold had after he had completed his military service.

After being tied down for four years, Harold had no immediate plans. He wanted to have some free time on the desert, and he wanted to write. He had written fiction before and soon found he made more sales after he shifted into non-fiction. His articles began to appear regularly in DESERT MAGAZINE in 1946, and soon after, he was hired as a full-time employee. In January 1947 he joined Lucile as an Associate Editor, and two months later they were married.

The young couple spent much time traveling together on field trips, gathering research material for their articles. Their specialty was lost mines and mining camp history. "We're interested in the real life that went on in those mining camps."

By the end of 1948, Harold decided to return to free-lance writing and resigned from his editor's position. They moved to San Diego and to Pasadena, while continuing to travel and to write, and eventually moved to Twentynine Palms in 1951. Harold's articles appeared in WESTWAYS, PACIFIC DISCOVERY, DESERT MAGAZINE, and other periodicals, while Lucile's articles were also appearing regularly.

In 1950 they had begun their own publication, CALICO PRINT, which contained "tales and trails of the Desert West." It started as a tabloid, then converted to a small slick paper magazine format, hopefully to allow more time for research and field work. By the end of 1953 when they ceased publication, their subscribers numbered more than four thousand. They continued to research, write, and publish small books on the history and lore of the desert under their CALICO PRESS label. They also published the first edition of Helen Bagley's SAND IN MY SHOE.

Harold also became assistant librarian at the County's Twentynine Palms branch library and served here for seventeen years. Meanwhile, Lucile wrote and edited for the DESERT TRAIL newspaper for twenty years, then continued until the present to write articles on a free-lance basis.

Both of the Weights have made valuable contributions to the collection, preservation, and interpretation of the history of this community. They were the instigators of the local history collection housed at the library. Their project of tape recorded interviews with early community pioneers began a collection that others have contributed to and now numbers more than one hundred. Harold personally copied, developed, and printed more than six hundred photographs to add to the collection's archives. Their efforts encouraged the donation of other photographs and memorabilia from early town families.

Today the Weights continue to research and to write. Harold is busy writing a history of Rawhide, Nevada, a mining community on which he has been intrigued and become an expert over the years. Lucile is continuing to gather material on area Indian groups, as well as to document our more recent history. Her articles continue to reintroduce community members to the rich heritage of our past. Their valuable research efforts have ensured that much of what otherwise would have been lost has been recorded for future generations and other historians.

*   *   *   *   *

Harold and Lucile Weight at a Cal Tech evening program. Photo by Floyd Clark, CalTech, courtesy of the Weights.

LUCILE AND HAROLD WEIGHT

In the late 1940's, when we decided that "someday" Twentynine Palms would be our permanent home, we bought ten acres that included a picturesque building site on an upper terrace behind the southern tip of the Bullion Mountains. We had carefully chosen that particular piece of Dick Davis' 160-acre homestead at the end of the Bullions, east of Mesquite Spring Dry Lake.

People along that sparsely settled stretch clear out to Dale Dry Lake were eagerly expecting power lines of the Rural Electrification Administration there and had signed up and paid a fee to the local association. We joined and paid, although we had visions of our lone pole standing in empty desert, with meter and non-usable power line attached, before we could build.

The "someday" came suddenly when the Weight family home in Pasadena was sold, and we had to move to somewhere else. We bought a home high in Pinto Cove, where we could at least look across and see our Bullion site. Then we started to move our household goods to Twentynine Palms in our Jeep ton pickup. Since the loads included thousands of books and a few tons of rockhound rocks, that turned into an endurance contest in which one Jeep clutch was sacrificed. That was the summer of 1951, and we still refer to it as our "moving summer."

All of that summer our possessions and living and business necessities were variously divided, while we were still trying to carry on all our varieties of work at both ends. Inevitably, the item we needed most proved to be one hundred forty miles away. In Pasadena, Harold developed, printed needed pictures, and wrote on promised articles, while I sorted and packed for the next load. We both worked on CALICO PRINT - both the production and the business ends. Then we would head for the desert again, often at midnight or later. Sometimes we stopped in San Gorgonio Pass for ten or fifteen minutes sleep, or at any open eating place for a snack. We consumed so much coffee, we were owl-eyed.

The worst obstacle on our route was Morongo Canyon. That was years before the expressway lifted the traffic out of the canyon bottom. The old highway was a narrow two-lane strip of paving which followed each curve and inlet, steep hill slopes on one side, and the wash bank on the other. At times we splashed through a little stream as the road crossed the wash. Boulders might have rolled down into the road.

With the pickup loaded to the top of its canvas back and the going slow, Harold usually had to drop the small four-cylinder engine into low half-way up the canyon. The road was too narrow to safely meet a fast car on a curve, especially where it had been undercut and eaten away. It was never safe to pass near one. At times at night we blew the horn as a warning when we could not see far ahead. Luckily, in those days we were met or passed by few cars between the highway, then US 99, and Twentynine Palms.

We still remember our first visitor to our new home. We had brought out books, bedding and clothing. It was a July day, temperatures were around 118; we had no refrigerator yet, and nothing to cool us. A hesitant knock brought us to the back door. Nellie Elting had padded slowly down from Twilight Drive, bringing a bottle of ice cubes. Could there be a more wonderful gift? She had come here in 1933 after a long career in show business. She was more than eighty years old when she had slowly walked down through the heat to welcome new neighbors.

Why did we choose Twentynine Palms? There was a deep mutual feeling that needed no words. Long before I knew Harold, he had visited this desert often, starting in 1934. I was first aware of this village and its people through reading THE DESERT TRAIL, a DESERT MAGAZINE exchange, and seeing some of the surrounding country through trips on behalf of the magazine.

El Centro, where DESERT was then located, was in in the heart of the Colorado Desert. When I first saw Lost Palms and Monsen canyons, and then in 1940, Queen and Lost Horse valleys, I was to have my first personal contact with the very different Mojave Desert.

My first visit in a Twentynine Palms home was at the adobe belonging to Gerald Charlton, who had finished it a few years before. It was the first house built on the land of the Twentynine Palms Inn Corporation. In Gerry's absence, Harry and Charline Jones were renting it. We were there to see a motion picture made by their son, Harlow, of a colorful trip through the Monument.

Harlow had come to Twentynine Palms in 1937. He opened a photo shop here and soon was taking photos for DESERT MAGAZINE, which had started the same year. At times he went out on photo stories with John Hilton, who then still lived with his family across from Valerie Jean's near Thermal.

Other times Harlow had Charlton or Frank Bagley as guide. He photographed in the Dale region extensively. When his parents followed him from Chicago in 1938, all three came down to DESERT MAGAZINE to get acquainted, and Harlow to consult on needed photo work. It was this contact that led to my first visit to just-developing Twentynine Palms.

One day in 1949, after a field trip in the Bullions, we spent the evening at the Postes' home, talked with them, and tape recorded many of their experiences in mining country - Dale, Death Valley, and Nevada. Theirs was not just a home. The southwest corner of the main room also served as the pioneer telephone exchange, with Anna and Dave as principal operators. And when Dave was Justice of the Peace, it was also the courtroom.

Dick Davis had introduced us, but we soon found we had

mutual friends and were familiar with all of the mining country where the Postes had lived. They had come out here with young son, Jimmy, in 1923 from San Bernardino, having taken a lease and bond on the pioneer Virginia Dale mine. Then they went to C.C. Julian's fantastic camp of Leadfield in upper Titus Canyon, Death Valley. There Dave built a schoolhouse in which Jimmy was a student. They mined in Gilbert, Nevada, soon after it was discovered by the Gilbert brothers, who were our friends.

A few more years and the Postes were back in the Dale country. They were living at their mill site when Dave was elected Justice of the Peace. The Twentynine Palms Judicial District was created in February 1930 with Sam Bailey appointed to serve as judge until the next election. Louis Jacobs was elected for four years.

Next, Dave was elected, assuming office January 1935. He served until January 1951. He had been re-elected to still another term in 1950 before he or the county officials realized that he was beyond the required retirement age.

Adelaide Arnold and Dave Poste were close friends of the Weights, and along with Dave's wife, Anna, would frequently accompany them on exploration trips out into the desert. Photo by and courtesy of Harold O. Weight.

Again, returning from a hot trip before moving here, we saw the shade of Smith's Ranch tall trees and turned in. There we found Thelma and two of the girls at the snack bar with just the cooling refreshments we needed. We could hardly believe the quality of the custom-type ice creams they made.

Next door was Fred Beebe in his tiny grocery store. We found later that, as at Bagleys', it could take a long time to shop at Beebe's, but it was time well spent. Fred, who came here in the late thirties, worked his heart out at his little store, going to Riverside for his own goods, cutting up his own meat, and keeping long hours, matching later convenience stores. He was a kind and gentle man, always ready to stop his work to help, to suggest, or just to talk. Crowded though it was, we found through the years that the miniature store was a favored place for homesteaders and prospectors, where we became acquainted with many.

Outside in the deep shadows of the great athels reaching almost to the buildings, we watched a medley of birds walking and splashing in the water seep under the trees. A rickety bob-tailed pickup drove in and backed up to the ice plant platform. Bill Smith appeared and helped to load the 100-pound block. He may have thought of earlier times when he would go to Banning and Riverside to get ice, hoping that half wouldn't be melted by the time he got home. Bill had come out here in 1923 and carved out an almost complete home-ranch complex.

From the start of DESERT MAGAZINE in El Centro in the fall of 1937, I had been on the staff, as head of some of the departments, as partner, and as associate editor. After Pearl Harbor, Randall Henderson, who had been a flyer in World War I, went back into the Army Air Corps and was eventually stationed in Africa. He left me with the full editorial responsibility for DESERT MAGAZINE.

In Africa he met his brother Clifford, who had been flying the Burma-India hump. In that warring land, their thoughts turned to our own desert, post-war. Together they mapped out a future complex in the Coachella Valley with DESERT MAGAZINE as an oasis in itself, surrounded by a beautiful residential area. After they both returned, the great cove at the foot of the Palms to Pines Highway was chosen, and Palm Desert was created.

In February 1940 Harold had entered a DESERT MAGAZINE photo contest. I was a judge and the first prize that he won was our first contact. During the next two years he wrote letters about desert problems and little known desert locations which caught Randall's attention. With our entry into World War II, Harold was inducted into the Army Air Corps and served for almost four years, most of the time as air and ground instructor in operation and maintenance of air-borne radar at Boca Raton Field, Florida.

During those four years, I received letters from him at various stations, principally to order desert books to be sent to his home in Pasadena.

With the war almost over, Randall asked me to write to him, feeling out his post-war plans without committing the magazine to offering him a definite job. Harold was interested but wanted time to write and to spend time on the desert before considering any job.

Randall knew that with the Palm Desert project under way, he would be spending much of his time working on plans, then overseeing construction of the new DESERT MAGAZINE building and the adjacent apartment complex for staff housing. He invited Harold to come down to El Centro as a second associate editor, which would relieve Randall of much of his magazine work.

Harold came in the fall of 1946, and in the spring of 1947 he and I were married in the Mission Inn, Riverside. At first we were able to get away together on field trips. That soon ended, as special promotion projects were set in motion and heavy holiday business kept me confined. We had moved up to the new Palm Desert building over the July 4, 1948 weekend, hoping that there the pressure might decrease.

But Harold was soon out in the field up to a week each month, making contacts, collecting material and taking photos for as many as three stories on a trip. I was operating our big book and gift shop and working with magazine distribution and subscriptions. When Harold got home, he had to process his photos and write most of his stories on his own time.

After six months at Palm Desert, Harold told Randall he wanted to return to free lance writing and resigned his editorial position. I agreed to stay through January 1949 to help clear up the mass of holiday orders and correspondence. Harold had agreed with Randall to continue to write for DESERT MAGAZINE with no deadlines involved. He also had begun to sell to WESTWAYS. With these two markets we felt we might be able to survive.

When we left DESERT MAGAZINE, we had no idea of publishing a magazine or of becoming involved in deadlines. A series of events, however, had put us in that position, and our first issue was November 1950. In our long range plans there was a book on Calico, whose newspaper of the 1880's was titled CALICO PRINT. Harold had already written on some phases of that colorful and rich camp.

At first our CALICO PRINT was a monthly tabloid format, which in 1952 became a bimonthly six by nine inch slick magazine, a change we vainly hoped would leave us with more time. We featured original accounts of historical high points in our desert and Southwest history together with first-hand stories of later history

LUCILE AND HAROLD WEIGHT

from tape recorded sessions with participants. At Twentynine Palms we were sole proprietors, two partners having dropped out of the "non-profit" business.

CALICO PRINT (appropriately) was printed in the 1895 gold camp of Randsburg by Paul and Bob Hubbard, who also published and printed THE RANDSBURG TIMES. Their plant was in the theatre building which dated back to the Yellow Aster boom. Before, we had driven from Pasadena to Randsburg with galley proofs and page dummies. Now the trip was far longer and rougher.

Going by the way of Old Woman Springs, then unpaved and on the original upper alignment, we endured about forty miles of punishing washboard, then on through Victorville, Atolia, Red Mountain, Johannesburg, and a few more miles around the hill to Randsburg, 157 miles away.

Delivering proofs and dummies, we checked in at the Cottage Hotel, also dating to boom days. At night we slept to the rhythm of the falling stamps of a gold mill just above us. At the hotel miners and would-be miners gathered. Whatever their walks in life, mining was the subject. In our trips to Randsburg, we met and tape recorded many surviving pioneers. One, up in his seventies, who had been millman on the Yellow Aster, still went down his shaft to mine every day.

Lucile Weight holding petrified wood on a rock trip near Gabbs, Nevada for DESERT MAGAZINE about 1950. Photo by Harold Weight, courtesy of the Weights.

LUCILE AND HAROLD WEIGHT

When the Hubbards built a new plant at Ridgecrest to accommodate the sophisticated and expanding printing needs of the Naval Ordnance Test Station, that meant twenty-six more miles of travel for us - an exhausting three hundred sixty mile round trip. And our series of deadlines was wearing us out. CALICO PRINT was totally a two-person operation: editing, advertising and business, circulation, preparation of photos, proof reading, page dummies, and most of the writing.

And after each number was printed, we loaded the five thousand copies in the truck and vibrated back to Twentynine Palms to become the circulation department. Not until the more than four thousand subscriber copies were individually wrapped, sorted, and hauled to the post office, and the newsstand packages mailed, could we relax, knowing then that it would soon start all over.

When we first started CALICO PRINT, Randall Henderson, thinking over his long years of effort on DESERT MAGAZINE, had warned us not to stay with it too long, if the pressure outweighed the satisfaction. He knew what he was talking about.

Our association with the Hubbards was that of close friends, and they continued printing our booklets. But we at last let reason close off CALICO PRINT at the end of 1953.

Harold and Lucile Weight on a field trip for a DESERT MAGAZINE story on the Arizona side of the Colorado River in the fall of 1951. Photo by Eva Wilson, courtesy of the Weights.

524

LUCILE AND HAROLD WEIGHT

Through the lives of Twentynine Palms pioneers, we had learned that many of them who had come here found themselves in occupations they had never imagined. Harold and I both had that experience. At Twentynine Palms after the suspension of CALICO PRINT, we simply were going to continue traveling, researching, writing, and occasionally publishing books and pamphlets in the field of Desert West history and life. And we hoped to have a little leisure and lessened pressure.

But within a short time, Harold was at the library, and soon after, I started what I thought was a fill-in job at THE DESERT TRAIL that has stretched almost to thirty years.

In the summer of 1956, Lida Donnell took an extended leave of absence from our county branch library. An additional branch library assistant was needed on a temporary basis until her return. Harold, feeling that it would be an interesting and valuable experience, took the civil service examination and qualified.

On Saturday August 4th, he was notified by telegram, (as we then had no phone), that he was to start two days later, Monday the sixth. That same Saturday's mail brought a postcard from Helen Toppin, acting librarian, asking Harold to come in that Saturday, as soon as possible, for a run-through of his duties.

At the library he found that Helen's annual vacation had been also postponed until the new assistant was hired. He was scheduled to start Monday, and Monday morning Helen was gone. So on his first day Harold found himself in sole charge, with probably one of the shortest apprenticeships on record. But thanks to the patience of friendly patrons, he said, and "hands-on" help from some who knew the library routines better than he did, he survived, even then enjoying the work and the contacts. When Lida resigned instead of returning, Harold continued at the library.

The county branch library was then located on Adobe Road about a block north of the highway, in what is now the 29 Palms Realty Building. It was Twentynine Palms' first intentional library, having been built solely for that purpose by Lida Donnell and leased to the county. It was clear even then, though, that soon the building would be too small for the increasing number of books and patrons. Our circulation already was larger than some branches in larger communities.

That was before television in Twentynine Palms and public entertainment was limited largely to the Underhill's motion picture theatre at the Plaza. It was routine, Harold said, for some patrons to load up with armsful or boxes full of westerns and mysteries for the weekends.

With circulation and numbers of library users steadily rising, the big new library was built at the Civic Center with funds from the 1956 County Building Bonds issue. Moving day was early in

May 1959.   Moving-in was very much a Twentynine Palms cooperative type operation. For some days the patrons had been hauling home extra books, to be returned at the new building. The County Library sent out a stake truck and driver, and the Toppin auto and the Weight pickup were pressed into service. J. Buren Briggs, publisher of THE DESERT TRAIL, turned up with his larger pickup, and other real friends of the library pitched in to aid the long series of loadings and unloadings.

The new library was everything expected. The stock of books was expanded rapidly. There was now room for tables and chairs for readers and students, a large magazine selection, and a separate children's area. Services were expanded and added, and library users and circulation increased. But for Harold there was a sense of loss. Another bit of that unique and indefinable atmosphere that was Twentynine Palms had vanished with Lida Donnell's little library.

One chilly morning in February 1957, when Harold stopped to pick up some letterheads and envelopes at the TRAIL office, Laura Briggs asked him if he though I would help her out in the office. The Marine husband of her assistant had been transferred. J. Buren and Laura Briggs, experienced newspaper people, had bought the TRAIL from Bill Underhill in January 1951, several months before we moved here. They published it for twenty years before selling and retiring.

I checked in on February 14, 1957, first reading proof, something I had done for many years, then editing or writing local news, and rewriting wordy handouts created by bureaucrats. Then came my first main story in May 1957 when everyone in town, it seemed to me, gathered on the lawn of 29 Palms Inn to honor Helen and Frank Bagley on the occasion of their 29th anniversary in Twentynine Palms. Scores of people had worked on the plan for weeks. There was drama, based on very personal pioneer history. There was music, vocal, and instrumental, including two songs written for the occasion by famed composer, Allie Wrubel, who lived here and in Hollywood, and whose songs are still heard on the air.

Publishing today is a world away from that of just fifteen years ago. The Briggs did all production right in their own building, except for photo engravings. Buren would package the photos and take them down to Johnnie Hastie's stage for a trip to an engraver.

One linotype in the back shop was for straight matter, while the other was set up for display advertising, usually operated by Jerry Van Alstine in my day. Al "Red" Roney could be heard banging and tapping on the type-filled forms. It took nearly all of their strength to hoist up the whole page forms. They were then locked in, the ink fountain checked, and we'd hear with a sigh of relief, the lumbering sound of the press in operation.

As time went on, an increasing number of my off-work hours were spent covering evening meetings. The town, at that level, was just developing. A water system had been a recognized need in the late 1930's, but as small subdivisions were developed, they were supplied by localized water companies. By the 1950's it was a hodgepodge. Now a community district had been formed and a large bond issue passed. But adjustments were causing problems - and hot board meetings were hard to follow, even with my later tape recorders.

And the schools. We had a Morongo elementary district, but belonged to the Victor Valley Union High School district. Unification was voted in just before I started reporting. The first Morongo Unified School board was elected -- and faced many problems at their meetings. The first meeting that I covered was that of the Park and Recreation Board at the now-vanished Scout Hut in Luckie Park, with Hazel Spell as secretary. The district was growing so fast with the influx of many young families that problems were complex.

Hospital care? That was the most costly and in some ways the most critical. Long debates took place. Finally Twentynine Palms voted to create its own district and Yucca Valley did likewise. At the same time the government stepped in and devised complex rules and more layers. We could have only one hospital for a specified number of people, and this area qualified for only one. Then there were more debates on location and type of building, but the Hi-Desert Hospital district finally was formed, and the "central" hospital built east of Joshua Tree.

In that period the upheaval in the Small Tract area resulted in the REA's Desert Electrification committee being transferred to Calectric, later taken over by Edison. Once emotions were so tense, we had deputy sheriffs standing by at the meeting. Harold drove me to most of these meetings, then returned to the library where he usually worked until nine at night. When the library closed, he would come to pick me up, napping in the car when some of the meetings lasted until midnight.

But whenever possible - including the many months during which the General Plan (Copper Mountain to Dale Dry Lake) and the related Zoning Plan were designed and adopted - he was at the meetings, taking news photos for my reports, all on an unpaid basis. At times when we got home, I was writing reports on these meetings until one and two o'clock in the morning. Despite the titles attached to my name, copy editor, editor, executive editor, the job was mainly this hard reporting in an effort to keep Twentynine Palms abreast of activities affecting our district.

Through my years at the DESERT TRAIL I learned more about

the people of this town than I could through any other means. And I think more understanding.

After Randall Henderson finally sold DESERT MAGAZINE, we were asked by the new owners in the late 1950's to do a special series of California travel articles correlated with the season. Along with my work on THE TRAIL, I wrote twentynine for that series, while Harold supplied the photos. With other owners in the 1970's, I was asked to do another series. I chose Indian uses of native plants as the subject.

I had been researching this field for years in early historical journals and ethnobotanical studies. Six of this series, with Harold's photos illustrating them, were published in 1977-78. I continued the series from time to time in THE DESERT TRAIL, especially in 1980-84. At least two in this field were published in the California Academy of Sciences' PACIFIC DISCOVERY magazine, one a twenty-page photographic study, "Trees in Our Desert," with thirty-six photos and the cover illustration by Harold, and one on Chia. Others were in NATURAL HISTORY, NATURE, and OUT WEST.

Harold had gone to work in the library in 1956, expecting to be there no longer than three months. He retired from the library in September 1973, presented with a resolution of the San Bernardino County Board of Supervisors, expressing regret at his retirement, and deep appreciation and thanks for "seventeen years of exceptional and outstanding service to the people of this area."

While working in the library and after his retirement, Harold continued to write both assigned and free lance articles, chiefly for DESERT and WESTWAYS, his last for DESERT in 1979. Altogether, DESERT published one hundred ten of his feature articles and WESTWAYS sixty, while the two used nine hundred of his photos for illustrations.

In other fields he wrote the foreword for Nina Paul Shumway's book, YOUR DESERT AND MINE, and supplied the photos for the jackets and illustrations and wrote the forewords for E. I. Edwards' two noted desert bibliographies, DESERT VOICES and LOST OASES ALONG THE CARRIZO.

Harold and I helped in the formation of the local history collection at the library. Having taped mining pioneers in Arizona, California, and Nevada for many years, we urged Cheryl Erickson to make such recording a key element in the collection with so many pioneers alive and active in the community. Cheryl and Ted Hayes made the first one. Cheryl and Harold worked together on a number of others. Harold also copied hundreds of historic photos, developed and enlarged them, and presented them to the library to form the basis of its Local History photographic collection.

LUCILE AND HAROLD WEIGHT

We met Fred Vaile through CALICO PRINT. We were in Pasadena and he subscribed to our magazine. When we were writing about the burros and trying to stop the slaughter of them, he started writing to us to tell us about his experiences and early days out in the deserts. In his first letter he said that he known springs where the big horns and burros drank together. He was in mining engineering then and out doing field work.

After we moved out to Twentynine Palms, he talked about being out at Dale. He had come out here in 1908. We had all of those years of correspondence from 1950. He and his wife, Louise, usually came out around Thanksgiving and then New Years when they could. They always stayed at the Inn. Fred introduced us to the Keys.

I started at the library in August 1956. During the seventeen years I was there, I worked with Helen Toppin, until she went down to San Bernardino to work in the library there. The county then had me as acting librarian. Phyllis Bailey worked with me for quite a while, and also Edna Benito.

Margaret Gray came in as a substitute at first. We had Lawrence Power, who was our first professional librarian. When he left, I had to take over for a few months until Cheryl Erickson came. Her husband, Rick, was stationed out at the Marine base. She was here less than a year, then they went back East. They eventually came back west and Rick went to USC to the library school. Margaret Gray was acting librarian until Cheryl returned.

Bagley's Store was the gathering place for miners. In the winter they had that big wood stove there - near where you now step up into the Market's wine department which was the office then. In the winter a lot of people gathered around there. In better weather we'd sit out on the bench and all of the mining news would come through there. It was really fascinating.

Most of the miners who came into the library to see me had read one of my stories and were looking for information on a lost mine or had some information of their own. A lot of times they just stopped in to talk.

It would take two books to tell about Adelaide Arnold. She talked to us about all of the different Indians that she knew and wrote about. SON OF THE FIRST PEOPLE is a classic. She used to live down below us. She always had her dog, General, on a leash. He was part Bedlington Terrier and Australian Sheep dog, Adelaide told us.

I started to work with him so he could run free and still respond. He usually obeyed, and we'd go everywhere. Once in a while he had a mind of his own when something would interest him. And I'd chase him.

We took Adelaide with us on trips to Indian country and fol-

dian trails with her, because that was her passion. She was
markable person, and I think one of the most beautiful
And some of the most remarkable things happened to her,
en you checked it, they really did. One time she was out
d took a picnic basket with her which she put down. They
d away and soon a coyote walked away with her basket.

Sometimes we would be coming back from a trip late at night
we would see her light on. We'd stop to see if she was all
ght. She would be sound asleep with the light shining down on
er and a book of poetry in her lap.

She could do translations from the Greek because her father
was a professor of Greek and also had a college up in Oregon.
They had moved to Hemet Valley because of Adelaide's health.
Her father became an officer in the Orange Growers' Association
over there, and I believe that is how she met her husband, Charles
Arnold.

She was a fine poet. Her poetry was published in some of the
best magazines like ATLANTIC MONTHLY and that caliber in
this country and also in England and Ireland. She wrote articles as
well as fiction. Some of her stories started out as conversations -
most with an Indian background - that's how her articles came to
be in our CALICO PRINT. We took them down on tape and just
reworked them a little bit. She had a style and rhythm that was
poetic.

The Sharps were friends of the Clarks from Cleveland. Dr.
Sharp's importance to the town, and hers too, was that they helped
to get our hospital district started. He could give them a lot of
professional and technical information. And of course, he had a
standing in the community that helped in getting it organized in
the beginning with all of the basic work. Marie continued when
they formed the Hospital Auxiliary. She was very close to Jean
Crowl, who was the president of the board when it was formed.
Jean and Dr. Walt Crowl, our veterinarian at that time, were involved with it from the beginning.

Today Twentynine Palms still has a beautiful setting and has a
great variation in the mountains because of their different geologi-
cal make-up. It gives a great variety of tones and colors under different circumstances of clouds and seasons. Every time we come
through the Morongo and Yucca Valley, I have the feeling of being
closed in.

Yet here in Twentynine Palms it spreads out with its beautiful
mountains. Of course, the more you know about the past, the more
you realize that it's still the people - from the Indians, the first
people, on down that has made this community what it is. Too
much development can ruin the values that originally made any
community so appealing.

SUSAN LUCKIE MOORE REILLY

Susan Caroline Luckie was born on June 22, 1916, in Pasadena, California, the eldest of two daughters born to Dr. James Buckner Luckie (1888 - 1965) and his first wife, Gracie MacPherson Berry Luckie.

Her father, due to his encouragement and support of World War I veterans whom he sent out to this desert area to recover their health, has been called the "Father of Twentynine Palms" by early town historians - Maude Russell, and Hazel Spell - and others, including homesteader and civic pioneer Frank Bagley, Susan was very close to her father and often accompanied him on trips to this young community when he came to check on and treat these ill veterans.

Susan's early education was received at schools in Pasadena and Laguna Beach, and then at Flintridge School for Girls where she graduated from high school. She received an AB degree in social sciences from Stanford University in 1938.

Soon after graduation, she attended secretarial school and entered the job market in Los Angeles. Within a year she married and moved to a succession of cities within the state, while her husband was transferred around by the armed services. Later he returned to college to receive a Ph.D. During the four years he studied at Stanford, Susan worked in the Microwave Laboratory at the University. After he received his degree, they moved to Fullerton where they lived ten years during which time she went to Cal State - Fullerton and took courses in wildlife, conservation, marine biology and outdoor science education for teachers. She also helped to organize the Youth Museum and Natural Science Center, which was designed to give young people a taste of nature, natural history, and science.

On July 4, 1965, dedication ceremonies were held in Twentynine Palms, officially naming Luckie Park for Susan's father whose generous gift of land over three decades earlier had been the park's beginning. Forty acres of land originally part of William and Elizabeth Campbell's homestead had been given to Dr. Luckie by them in gratitude for medical services that he had provided without charge to these early town residents. Unwilling to accept the gift, the doctor donated the land to the American Legion which in turn deeded part of it to the newly formed recreation district.

Luckie Park was named and dedicated to her father for his assistance and generosity to the veterans who settled Twentynine Palms.

Susan and her husband divorced in 1964, and she moved to Twentynine Palms the following year to accept a job as a seasonal ranger-naturalist at the Joshua Tree National Monument. She worked there until 1968.

In 1969 she started her conservation efforts to protect the desert area from environmentally damaging encroachment from outside influences. Her first battle was directed against the building of high power transmission lines the length of the valley, coming from Mojave Generating Station at Bullhead City to the Devers Substation north of Palm Springs. Her efforts led to a public outcry against the lines and a denial of this route in 1980. Later she spearheaded the movement against high density housing and its threat to our underground water supply.

On November 1, 1986 Susan married William C. Reilly, a longtime friend and neighbor. His premature death several months later sadden the Reillys' many friends.

Susan Luckie Reilly has devoted all of her efforts to protecting this desert area from projects which she feels could destroy the clean air, good water, the openness, and the uniqueness that most of us have come to enjoy and love about Twentynine Palms. She has been affectionately called our environmental "watchdog", a title she finds amusing. But all of us owe her and others who have worked with her, a debt of everlasting gratitude. Like her father, she has had a profound interest in the town and influence on its development and history.

*   *   *   *   *

The American Legion Post in Pasadena was anxious to find a place for ailing World War I veterans to go, and my dad was leading them in their effort. Dad went all around the desert looking at different places. I remember when he went to the Victorville area one time and took me along.

He was hunting for a place that would be the most suitable for veterans' health to be rehabilitated. He chose the Twentynine Palms area because it was fairly accessible to the big cities and it has a moderate elevation that is good for people with heart trouble or respiratory ailments. Above all, it had clean, dry air.

The Pasadena Legion Post formed a committee to encourage settlement out here. Dad and Joe Davis were great friends and had been looking together for places for the veterans. Unfortunately Joe met an early fate after settling out here. While going down to

Dr. James B. Luckie served as Tuberculosis Examiner with the U.S. Army Medical Department at Camp Kerney, San Diego, California from October 1917 to February 1919 and held the rank of First Lieutenant. Photo courtesy of Susan Luckie Reilly.

Banning or Beaumont, he was caught in a flash flood, contracted pneumonia and died.

But most of the people that Dad sent out here recovered and lived good full lives. Some, like Colonel Benioff, even went back and resumed their work down in the coastal area after living here for a time.

The well-being of the ailing veterans in Twentynine Palms was Dad's first priority for many years. Although he never lived here, he visited often. He spent much time in the cities attempting to secure financial aid for the veterans' out here. He spent the remaining free time that he had here in the desert treating and administering pharmaceuticals which he had secured as a donation and stored in the basement of the Elizabeth and William Campbell home. He never charged for these medical services to the veterans.

Originally most of what is now Luckie Park was part of Bill Campbell's 160 acre homestead, and Bill gave some of his acreage to Dad as a "thank you" for his services. He in turn donated it to the American Legion, which eventually turned it over to the Park and Recreation District for a park.

Dad and the Legionnaires had a fine plan to use this land for a health center for the veterans. There was to be a little central clinic with cottages around it for the veterans and their families, where they would be close by for needed medical attention. They started to raise money for this but due to the Depression hitting right then, the project could not be financed. So Luckie Park became a park instead of a health center.

Dad was a great nature lover, and from him I acquired my interest in nature, working for the National Park Service, and working to protect the environment. We came out here when I was a teenager. He used to put harmless insects in my hand so that I wouldn't be afraid of them. We used to walk together in the desert, and he taught me about different kinds of insects, plants, flowers, and little animals. He would tell me their names; so I knew quite a few of them before I ever moved out here.

In 1938 Dad realized a long-cherished dream when Walt Berg built for him a vacation home in the Indian Cove area on land given to him in lieu of medical fees by Forest and Jessie Sroufe. My dad came out and told Walter what kind of house he wanted built. Walter listened and drew up a little sketch. Then my dad went back to Pasadena to find an architect to draw up the plans.

He hired Kenneth Gordon, a well-known Pasadena architect, who drew up the plans almost exactly as the house is presently built. But when Dad came back with the plans, Walter had already completed the house. The front bay window looks out over the wide horizons that he loved so dearly. Above the native stone fireplace is inscribed his favorite quotation: "Here far from noise and folly, fraternal love presides," from Mozart's opera, The Magic Flute.

I think that Dad would have liked to live out here permanently, but he couldn't give up his medical practice in Pasadena. He was a very dedicated doctor who became great friends with his patients. He treated the mind, as well as the body, and listened sympathetically to those who wanted to talk.

One patient of his had a stroke and was badly paralyzed. Dad felt he could be rehabilitated, so he worked with him. He had a valuable stamp collection; so Dad persuaded him to sell it and to invest the money in a nursery business. Dad said that the type of exercise he would get running a nursery was the kind that could get him to working his muscles again and to become active.

So the patient followed Dad's advice, and he recovered completely. The nursery became very successful and my dad's yard in Pasadena was filled with gorgeous camilla bushes that he was given by this grateful man. He had made over his whole life, which was typical of the kind of thing my dad did.

Dad was the kind of old fashioned family doctor that really cared about people. He made emergency calls at any hour of the day or night. He never refused to care for someone in distress, even when he knew that person could not pay. Many of his bills were never collected. He treated everyone as a human being with no discrimination as to race, creed, or sex. He was also a wonderful diagnostician, which was his best gift. At the end, he often stayed at the bedside of a dying patient, imparting through a warm human hand-clasp, a supportive feeling of love and caring as a last contact with this world.

He died in 1965 shortly before I came out here to live. I always loved it when I had come out for vacation trips with him, and I hated to leave. I thought I'd love to live out here someday; so when I got a divorce, I decided to move out here and start a new life for myself.

I applied for a National Park Service ranger-naturalist job, and when I got it, I came out. I led nature walks in Indian Cove to the pot holes, and I also gave campfire programs and led walks in the Jumbo Rocks area. I worked for the Monument in 1965, '66, '67, and '68, and at irregular times after that. They had a big cutback and the seasonal staff was let go. Later when they received more money again, they asked me if I wanted to come back. By then I had gotten so deeply involved in conservation battles, that I didn't want to stop in the middle of them. So my life has become swallowed up in that activity ever since.

The power line fight started in 1969. The Southern California Edison Company called people throughout the Morongo Basin and told them that they wanted to come and establish the corner points on their property. They didn't tell them what it was for. Most people thought it was probably just to run a line up to someone's house across their property or something minor like that. But it was for a huge transmission line. They wanted to run it right through the back of my property, between me and the Monument.

I had noticed their helicopters, and I wondered why they kept flying back and forth along the Monument boundary. I called the Edison Company and told them, "I want you to come up and explain this to me before I will say yes to allow you on my property."

So they sent a man up, and I got it out of him that it was for a new transmission line. He brought a map showing that they were asking people on either side of me, so I started calling up the neighbors and telling them what was happening and organizing a fight against it.

Young Susan Luckie with her father, Dr. James B. Luckie, at their Pasadena home about 1922. Dr. Luckie was called "The Father of Twentynine Palms" by the late Frank Bagley, Bill Hatch, and other community leaders of the past for his dedication to the community in its earliest days. Photo courtesy of the Local History Collection, 29 Palms Branch Library.

The line was to go from the Mojave Generating Station at Bullhead City, across the Colorado River, down through Sheephole Pass and across the south side of the whole Morongo Basin, ending up at the Devers Substation near Interstate 10.

After we started raising cain about it on this side of the valley, Edison planned to move it over through the High Desert Tract Owners' property, and put it through there. They moved rapidly,

536

buying up property all along the planned route, much of which, I believe, they have never sold.

So we wrote to Washington to the Department of the Interior and the Bureau of Land Management, and told them that we didn't want them making a decision about a transmission line going through here without coming to look at the country around here.

The BLM also had received a proposal for a line to come through the northern part of Arizona at the same time. So they sent a crew out with expertise in biology, geology, population trends, power needs, and other fields dealing with the environment to study the two routes. They came and talked to us in Twentynine Palms. They set up a railroad car for their office in Las Vegas, where they put up a wall map with overlays for all of these different types of expertise represented by the committee members. As a result they came up with a seventy-three page study that recommended just what we wanted.

I believe that it was our efforts that caused them to come out and make this wonderful study. They came to the determination at the end of their report that the route shouldn't go through this area, but along one of the two existing routes. This was what we had been fighting for all of the time.

Then they held a hearing. Others tried to get BLM to hold it in Riverside, San Bernardino, or Los Angeles far away, so that it would be hard for us to go. But we kept pounding on them that we wanted this hearing in Twentynine Palms. They finally had it here in the High School auditorium on November 7, 1970. About twelve hundred people showed up to oppose the lines going through the Morongo Basin.

The Morongo Basin Conservation Association, with members from Morongo Valley through Wonder Valley, organized and led the fight against the transmission line. It was the most unified effort by the Morongo Basin towns that I have ever seen, with the possible exception of the building of Copper Mountain College - a different kind of effort.

Organizations and individuals were drawn into it all up and down the Basin. So many wonderful people circulated petitions, wrote letters, organized bus trips, and spoke at numerous hearings to the Public Utilities Commission, the Bureau of Land Management, and the California State Energy Commission that I cannot attempt to name them all for fear of forgetting someone who was important. They were all very important. Every letter was a vital contribution, because it showed that someone cared enough to take the time to write down his or her feelings on this important issue and see that they went to the people who were making the decision. The cumulative result of all these letters and actions was the voice of the people speaking - and it was heard and heeded.

Luckie Park was officially dedicated on July 4th, 1965. L to R: William J. Underhill, who spoke on Dr. Luckie and the history of the American Legion Post whose members helped found the community; Frank Bagley, pioneer Legionnaire, homesteader, and businessman, who represented the Twentynine Palms Hospital District; Mrs. Susan Luckie Moore, daughter of Dr. Luckie; John Bagley, Chairman of the Advisory Board, Twentynine Palms Recreation District; Dale Vaughn, Commander Troy L. Martin Post 334, American Legion; Chester E. Ellis, President, Chamber of Commerce; Reverend Leland Kuns, who made the official dedication of the park; and William Proctor, Recreation District Superintendent. Of Dr. Luckie, Frank Bagley said, "You are not only the true father of Twentynine Palms but your work here gave origin to a community spirit which the Marine personnel tell us they find in no other place in America, a friendly atmosphere which sets us apart. Is it any wonder that the move to call a small portion of the land you gave, and which is now controlled for the benefit of all by the Twentynine Palms Park and Recreation District, should be a spontaneous one and that name "LUCKIE PARK." Photo courtesy of Susan Luckie Reilly.

The first decisive step was taken by the BLM, when it studied the situation and issued the report, "The Impact of Power Transmission Lines and Their Effect on the Southwest Environment," in September 1970. This was followed by the hearing at the Twentynine Palms High School, where more than twelve hundred people showed up to protest the huge power lines running through the Morongo Basin and say that they should be located either south of the Joshua Tree National Monument or north of the Marine Base along the routes of existing lines in those areas.

After that, Edison withdrew its application for the line through the Morongo Basin. The people asked that the BLM adopt a policy of running new giant transmission lines along the routes of existing lines, rather than allowing a huge steel web to be established in all directions across the desert. The answer was that utility corridors would be designated in the California Desert Conservation Area Plan, which was about to be formulated.

After shepherding their interests through many meetings in a long planning process, the people of the Morongo Basin succeeded in keeping out any corridor for extra-high voltage transmission lines through the Basin from east to west. Only a "contingency" utility corridor was allowed, through the northwest portion of the Basin along the route of the water pipeline being planned from Hesperia to Yucca Valley, to be used when and if that pipeline were to materialize.

The Lucerne Valley oil-burning power plant (which wound up being proposed at a Johnson Valley site) was proposed by Southern California Edison Company in 1970. It was opposed by many Morongo Basin people because of its potential for polluting the Basin. It was denied in April 1983 by the California Energy Commission, because energy conservation and lowered energy demand growth, resulting from soaring utility rates due to the "energy crisis", had made it unneeded. However, a solar power plant was approved for Johnson Valley.

Edison later wanted to build a coal burning power plant in the desert and applied for several alternative sites. The sites considered were at Boron, Rice, Cadiz, Ivanpah, and a site at Ormond Beach, which was eliminated early in the struggle.

Morongo Basin people opposed the line from the Cadiz plant that was proposed to come through just like the former one from the Mojave coal plant. We brought out the BLM report from 1970 that said there shouldn't be a transmission line through here, because it would be cutting through a brand new environment where there weren't any huge lines, and there were existing line routes that should be followed north of the Monument and south of the Base.

We fought against the Cadiz plant, because we didn't want this area polluted. The Indians over on the Colorado River opposed the Rice plant, because they felt the pollution would come over and spoil their agriculture. Edwards Air Force Base, NASA, and China Lake Naval Weapons Center opposed the Boron site as a threat to their visibility. And so the only area that wasn't opposed was Ivanpah. That was lovely open desert, but nobody battled that site. I must have attended about thirty-five to forty-five hearings before it was over, in Riverside, Long Beach, Los Angeles, and even over at Big River where the Indians are.

The Energy Commission Final Decision on Cal Coal in December 1980 said that the Energy Commission Committee in charge of this proceeding ruled in the Summary and Hearing Order that, "based on the evidence, the Morongo Basin corridor was judged unacceptable unless good cause could be shown for the Committee to rule otherwise. During the remainder of the hearing process, no evidence was offered by any party in support of the Morongo Basin transmission line corridor, yet voluminous public comment against the corridor continued to inundate the Committee. Because of the significant negative impact of a line through the Morongo Basin and the availability of an acceptable alternative, the Morongo Basin corridor is found to be an unreasonable and unacceptable transmission line corridor."

The Cal Coal 1500 MW power plant was approved for the Ivanpah site, with conditional approval of Rice and Cadiz as potential power plant sites. However, Southern California Edison Company never has built either the solar plant approved for Johnson Valley or the coal burner approved for Ivanpah, due to lowered demand growth and increased use of renewable resources. There are people who don't know, even today, about the Energy Commission decision.

Later came the fight against high density development. It began with the Germania project which proposed to put in fifteen units to the acre. This was the really first high density development proposed out here, which was something new and different; something that most of the people did not want.

Up until then density was allowed only up to eight units per acre maximum. We had complained bitterly about the first Res 8 that appeared and fought the project south of Luckie Park. But it went through; and then there was another one on Mesquite Springs Road.

So when Germania came up with fifteen units to the acre, a group of us got together and collected many petition signatures to stop it. This was the first effort against high density housing above eight units per acre.

Our petition read: "We the undersigned residents and/or property owners in the Twentynine Palms planning area strongly request that the density for the community plan be limited to a maximum of eight units per acre whether affordable housing or not. This had been the density limit under the old plan, and we want it carried through the present and into the new plan. Where land is so plentiful, we believe it is detrimental to the appropriate development of Twentynine Palms to have density greater than eight units to the acre. We also request that only certain areas of the town be designated for high density projects now and in the new plan.

"Many projects are being readied to over-run the town before the plan is adopted. If developers are allowed to site high density anywhere they please before the new plan gives us any direction, this could destroy the town's ability to form a well-organized plan. Specifically we request that the eight units per acre limit be placed upon the Germania project now moving through the County approval process. Otherwise this will be a carte blanche for other developers to submit for approval projects with densities higher than eight units per acre. To date the eight unit limit has been observed. The Germania project is asking for fifteen units per acre."

A lot of people did not like the idea of high density, but we found our really good argument to oppose it was the fact that it was over the town's water table south of the Pinto Mountain fault. That gave us the argument of possible future ground water pollution from concentrated underground sewage disposal.

Supervisor John Joyner made his decision to deny the Germania and Rainboldt projects based on the fact that, "The chemical quality of the ground water south of the Pinto Mountain fault is the only local good quality source for the Twentynine Palms area. It is important to preserve the water quality in this area if needed to blend with poor quality water to meet future water needs and demands......."

I've noticed since this decision was made, that no new applications have been made for more than eight units per acre, as far as I know. I am very pleased with the decisions Supervisor Joyner has been making to limit high density. However, we may have to fight other efforts in the future.

I loved Twentynine Palms when it was a little town. I don't want it to be a big, bustling, over-crowded city. Careful control of its rapid growth should be able to keep it a pleasant place to live.

The beautiful blue skies and clean air of Twentynine Palms, being able to see the stars at night, and the feeling of open space and being able to look for miles and miles without obstructions are things that I treasure. I love being next to nature, as I am here at my home. That matters more to me than anything. I feel like one with nature living in the midst of it with our natural desert plants and animals. These are the things that I will continue to fight for as long as I'm able.

Many people have come to Twentynine Palms to live because of the healthful, clean air and the openness of the town. They came to escape from the clutter, traffic, and dirt of the city. Our population can grow, and it will; but it can still be spread out to keep an open feeling. Making this town like the places from which many of our people come would destroy its uniqueness, its beauty, and the values for which they came here. We must not let that happen.

Protecting the land and its natural resources - air and water, animal and plant life - seems to be something that is bred into us, or learned when we are young. Once this interest becomes a part of a personality, it continues to be a motivating force throughout a lifetime. In fact, an interest in nature, in general, grows and becomes more fascinating throughout a person's life. It serves to make us realize that many spheres of life exist apart from our human world. An interest in these things serves to put us humans into our proper niche, as not the supreme, all-powerful beings, but as a part of a truly wondrous world.

Susan Luckie Reilly on the occasion of being co-Grand Marshall of the 1983 Pioneer Days with Ada Hatch. Photo by the author.

OUR HERITAGE

Twentynine Palms has grown and undergone considerable change from the days when the cowboys, miners, and homesteaders first came. We have also matured, learning from our mistakes as well as our successes, and never forgetting that without the hard work and dedication of those who came before us, our community would not be what it is today.

To these pioneers we say express our grateful thanks. The knowledge of their lives is our history and our heritage which will carry us onward into the future.

Aerial view of downtown 29 Palms early 1950's looking west. Four Corners is in the foreground; Donnell Hill upper left corner. Photo courtesy of the 29 Palms Historical Society.

ABOUT THE AUTHOR

ART KIDWELL was born in Baltimore, Maryland on March 4, 1944, into a family whose ancestors had settled in Maryland prior to 1659.   Having grown up near historic Annapolis, he developed an early interest in history which continued through his college and graduate school days.

In 1976 he came to Twentynine Palms to work as a seasonal interpreter at Joshua Tree National Monument. He was assigned to live at Keys' Ranch and to give tours of that historic site. His extensive research into the Keys' family history led to the film CHALLENGE OF THE DESERT, which he produced, directed, and co-wrote in 1977, and the book, AMBUSH, published in 1979.

During his eleven years in this community, he participated in the Oral History Program for the 29 Palms Branch Library, conducting interviews with early area residents. IN THE SHADOW OF THE PALMS reflects his desire that the history of Twentynine Palms be shared.

In 1982 he was one of the nine founding members of the Twentynine Palms Historical Society which now has more than two hundred members. In 1986 he served as its president. For the past ten years he has worked as a film and television producer for the Department of Defense and other government agencies.

ABOUT THE ARTIST

SUSAN JEAN FRUGE was born in Long Beach, California, and visited Twentynine Palms for the first time on a trip with her mother in 1943. They liked the area so well that her mother purchased some land and built a house in 1950. Here her mother lived until her death in 1959.

After completing her education, Susan worked as an editor in botany and English at UCLA for five years. Then in 1959 she married August Fruge and moved to Berkeley, California where he was Director of the University of California Press. After his retirement, they returned to Twentynine Palms to spend part of each year until their permanent move here in 1980.

It was then that Susan discovered her artistic talent in oil painting and, more recently, in pen and ink drawings. Some of her sketches were selected by the 29 Palms Artists' Guild for use as note cards. Her beautiful renderings of historical scenes of Twentynine Palms' past are included in these volumes. This is the first time that her work has appeared as illustrations in a book.

Susan is active in the 29 Palms Artists' Guild, has served on its Board of Directors, and in 1986 was elected to the Board of Directors of the Joshua Tree Natural History Association.

ACKNOWLEDGMENTS

I wish to thank: August Fruge' for his helpful advice and recommendations on printing style which have been incorporated in Volume II; Susan Fruge' for her beautiful drawings; Holly Yingling for her patient proofreading of the text; and Kay Yingling for checking my typesetting, rechecking it again, then turning the computer disks into printed pages.

Cover: The 29 Palms Oasis, 1936.
Photo by Derald Martin.

Back Cover: The Old Adobe in the 1930's.
Photo by Harlow Jones.